Pre-school to School:
a behavioural study

BEHAVIOURAL DEVELOPMENT:
A SERIES OF MONOGRAPHS

Series Editor
RUDOLPH SCHAFFER
University of Strathclyde
Glasgow, Scotland

BEHAVIOURAL DEVELOPMENT:
A SERIES OF MONOGRAPHS
Series Editor: RUDOLPH SCHAFFER

Pre-school to School:
a behavioural study

N. RICHMAN
Department of Child Psychiatry,
The Hospital for Sick Children,
London

J. STEVENSON
Department of Human Biology,
University of Surrey,
Guildford

P.J. GRAHAM
Department of Child Psychiatry,
The Hospital for Sick Children,
London

1982

ACADEMIC PRESS
A Subsidiary of Harcourt Brace Jovanovich, Publishers
London   New York
Paris   San Diego   San Francisco   São Paulo
Sydney   Tokyo   Toronto

9031991
DLC

7-20-83 JH

ACADEMIC PRESS INC. (LONDON) LTD.
24/28 Oval Road
London NW1

United States Edition published by
ACADEMIC PRESS INC.
111 Fifth Avenue
New York, New York 10003

British Library Cataloguing in Publication Data

Richman, N.
  Pre-school to school : a behavioural study.
  —(Behavioural development)
  1. Child psychology
  I. Title   II. Stevenson, J.
  III. Graham, P.J.   IV. Series
  155.4   BF721

  ISBN 0-12-587940-7
  LCCN 82-45022

Typeset by Oxford Publishing Services
Printed in Great Britain by St Edmundsbury Press
Bury St Edmunds, Suffolk

Preface

This book describes the results of a survey of behaviour problems and developmental delays in a total population of three-year-old children. At the time of the survey a group of approximately 100 disturbed children was identified and matched with a similarly sized control group of non-disturbed three-year-olds. One year and four years later, when the children were aged four and eight years, they were investigated again. On each of these three occasions a wide range of social, familial and psychological factors was assessed. The physical and mental health of the parents and the quality of the marital relationship were also investigated.

There are, of course, already available a number of studies in which the development and intelligence of pre-school children have been intensively examined. The unique features of this study include our focus on behaviour, the range of background factors studied and the longitudinal component. We aimed to identify those factors which were related both to persistence and recovery from problems occurring in the pre-school period. Further, we hoped to examine those factors important in the development of problems in young school-age children who had previously not shown difficulties.

This book is intended to be of interest to developmental psychologists, teachers, health visitors, social workers, paediatricians and psychiatrists. Its contents contain material relevant to all these professional groups. It should enable professionals to heighten their awareness of the significance of behaviour problems and delayed development in young children and has significance for clinical work, prevention and research.

April 1982

N. Richman
J. Stevenson
P.J. Graham

Acknowledgements

The pilot phase of this study was supported by the Medical Research Council, the initial cross-sectional part of the study by the Department of Health and Social Security and the follow-up by the Social Sciences Research Council. Throughout the study we have enjoyed willing and active cooperation from teachers as well as staff of the Waltham Forest Education, Health and Social Services Department.

The persistent and conscientious interviewers who worked on the study were Maggie Driscoll, Mary Hamilton, Rowena Kemp, Ruth Murray, Kathy Schneider and Toni Strasburg. Statistical advice and assistance were provided by Harvey Goldstein, Judith Pearson, David Boniface and Andy Hathaway. Carole Ellis carried the major responsibility for the administration of the first phase of the study. Jill Beale and Julia Davis worked as secretaries on the project.

We are most grateful to Judy Dunn, Peter Moss and Michael Rutter, each of whom provided detailed and most helpful comments on an earlier draft of the manuscript.

Finally, we should like to thank the parents and children who participated, not only by giving us their time and answering questions, in the great majority of cases most willingly, but also by providing fresh ideas for our work from their own experience.

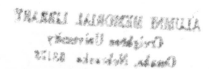

Contents

1 Introduction

Serious emotional and behavioural problems are common in school-aged children. Various surveys have found evidence for rates of significant difficulties of this type, ranging from 6 to 20% (Miller *et al.* 1974; Rutter *et al.*, 1970, Shepherd *et al.*, 1971). Knowledge is largely lacking in relation to the pre-school period, yet anecdotal reports suggest that the first five years of life are frequently as stressful as later years in the life of children and their families, and it would be surprising if behavioural and emotional reactions to stress were not also widely prevalent at this age.

An increased concern for the health and development of pre-school children has been reflected in recent Government reports such as the Report on Child Health Services Department of Health and Social Security (1976) and the Report on Special Educational Needs Department of Education and Science (1978). At the time we began our study pre-school provision was expanding, and there was a general hope and expectation that this expansion would continue. It seemed important to us that those who were involved in planning services for pre-school children should have available to them more comprehensive information regarding what many parents, nursery teachers, and play-group supervisors consider to be the most troublesome and worrying aspect of children in the early years — their emotional disturbances and behaviour problems. Much information exists on the importance of early cognitive development (e.g. Lewis, 1976), and on the degree to which early intervention can influence such cognitive performance in disadvantaged children (Little and Smith, 1971). But little similar work has been carried out in relation to early behavioural difficulties. Other than very small numbers of American studies (especially Macfarlane *et al.*, 1954), little information is available on how common behaviour and emotional difficulties really are, and how their course might be influenced.

Our first concern in this book is to describe a study we carried out in which we ascertained the prevalence of such problems in a total population of three-year-olds. But we were, of course, interested in doing more than counting the heads of disturbed young children. We wished to know to what degree the difficulties we identified were related, amongst other factors, to material deprivation, disturbance of family relationships, parental health, and the rate of development of the child in language and other abilities. We hoped that an investigation of such associated factors might illuminate the reasons why some children became disturbed and others not. In addition, we wanted to provide information which would be useful in planning health and social services for families and young children. The first part of this book, therefore, provides a description of our cross-sectional study of three-year-olds and their families.

We were also interested to examine further the link between disturbance in the pre-school child and the presence of similar difficulties later on in the child's life. Two of us (NR and PG) had participated in the Isle of Wight study (Rutter *et al.*, 1970), in which significant emotional and behaviour problems had been found to be very common in children aged ten and eleven years, occurring in about 6% of the population. Subsequently a further study (Rutter *et al.*, 1975) suggested that rates were twice as high in an Inner London Borough, and it seems reasonable to suppose that problems are no fewer in other large cities.

A number of issues were identified in these earlier epidemiological surveys which, we felt, could be clarified by following up a group of young children who had been studied earlier in their lives. When interviewing parents of children with problems, aged ten and eleven years, it was common to be told that the child had been difficult or "different" from birth, or that the child's behaviour had first undergone a significant change when he or she first went to nursery or infant school. It was impossible to validate such information in retrospect. Yet from the point of view of prevention it is obviously important to know how commonly disorders in school-age children do begin in the pre-school period. Previous studies had also revealed links between different types of problem which were difficult to explain adequately. For example, it was found in the Isle of Wight study cited above that there was a very strong association between retardation in reading and anti-social behaviour. The mechanism underlying this association remained unexplained. Did children who failed educationally resort to aggressive behaviour out of frustration? Did those with impulsive, anti-social behaviour find it difficult to concentrate on reading material? Or were there common factors underlying both types of problem? It seemed possible that a study which examined younger children before they were expected to be able to read, and then followed the children into school, would clarify this issue.

We therefore sought support to follow up the children we had studied in the pre-school period, firstly so that we could determine how long-lasting were the disorders we had identified, and secondly to attempt to investigate the early roots of disturbance found in school-age children. The second part of this book, from Chapter Six onwards, is devoted to a description of this part of our study, and the remainder of this chapter is intended to provide background only for the first part of our study, carried out when the children were three years old.

The child and the family

An important decision which faces the investigator in this field is the choice of the most appropriate unit for study. There are obvious reasons why it might be preferable to take as the basic unit the family rather than the individual child. Young children can surely not be considered except in the context of their families and current clinical practice is, if anything, moving even further than has hitherto been the case in the direction of a consideration of family rather than individual dysfunction or "pathology". Clinically, now more than ever, the problems of the individual child are seen as a reflection of family disturbance, and treatment methods increasingly involve family members other than the referred child and his or her mother (Glick and Kessler, 1980). Our reasons for rejecting the family as the basic unit, despite a clinical involvement in family therapy techniques, were twofold. Firstly, the variety of family structures depending on the numbers of children and adults present would make comparison of families drawn from a population sample extremely difficult. Secondly, as recent reviews of the methodology of the measurement of the family as a unit have made clear (Cromwell *et al.*, 1976; Tittler *et al.*, 1977), there are no widely accepted methods by which family units can be classified or identified as pathological. An alternative might be to attempt a classification of dyads and to conduct a survey of mother–child units. Again agreed methods are not available and it would in any case be alien to our clinical standpoint deliberately to exclude fathers and other family members from central consideration. Our decision, therefore, was to study individual children, or, to be more precise, disorders within children — for the labelling of a child as disturbed might connote a permanence to the problem which would do an injustice to the facts and risk stigmatization to the child. To talk of a child with a disorder clearly implies that the same child may be without a disorder in the not too distant future (Rutter, 1965). The special advantage of this approach is that it enables one to study family relationships independently of disorder within the child and thus to relate the two in a way which would not be possible if one only studied the child as a constituent of a dyad or whole family unit.

The measurement of some family factors such as social class, size of family and ordinal position presents a number of problems, but others, especially those involving the quality of family relationships are even less easily quantifiable. Fortunately, experience in the measurement of relationships using interview procedures and validated by direct observation (Rutter and Brown, 1966; Brown and Rutter, 1966) has shown that their assessment is feasible on a reasonably economic basis. There remains, however, the problem of ensuring that assessment of relationships is made independently of the child's behaviour and this also is not easy to achieve. A child whose behaviour is problematic is likely to be described in pejorative terms by his or her parents. The critical attitude the parent takes up can then easily be seen as a causative factor, whereas it could be an understandable result of a reflection of the exasperation produced by the child's disturbance or, more probably, a complex interaction between child and parent behaviour. The achievement of independence in the assessment of the quality of parent–child relationship is not easy, and in our study we were frequently made aware of the pitfalls in interpretation of data which a lack of independence in data collection could easily involve.

Approaches to the measurement of disturbance in the pre-school child

A central issue which needed consideration was how we should define and identify disorders within the children. Various alternatives presented themselves. A learning theory approach to child psychiatry (Ullman and Krasner, 1969) offers the attraction of methods readily lending themselves to quantitative analysis. This approach assumes that behavioural disturbance is best seen as a form of faulty learned response. Inappropriate learning has occurred because the child, possibly predisposed by unusual ease or difficulty in conditionability, has been exposed to particular experiences. These have resulted in the development of particular types of behaviour on the basis of operant or classical conditioning. While such a formulation can lead to effective treatment (McAuley and McAuley, 1977), it provides no easy answers to the identification of disturbance in particular children. The theory does not generate hypotheses regarding the circumstances in which a child might be regarded as a cause for concern.

By contrast, psychoanalytic theory, though distinctly less promising from the point of view of gathering quantitative information, does generate some rather precise ideas regarding the criteria which might be used to identify a child as disturbed or not. Anna Freud (1973) has articulated these particularly clearly. She points especially to the need to consider variation in personality development in a number of areas and to make judgements whether such variations and regressions in development are occurring as transient responses to stress or permanent distortions in personality growth.

Unfortunately, there exist no satisfactory methods derived from these concepts to enable one to identify children with disturbance in a reliable manner, and consequently the utility of the theory for the purposes of epidemiological research is currently very limited.

In this situation, and influenced by the psychiatric experience of two of us, we were encouraged to take a more descriptive clinical approach. This approach, which is not incompatible with learning theory or dynamic theories, has been characterized as "clinical-diagnostic" (Rutter *et al.*, 1970), and has now become reasonably well established as a framework for epidemiological research in child psychiatry. The concept of a "case" is applied to a child who has a disorder which causes significant social or psychological disability to himself or to others. The level of disability required for "significance" to be reached is agreed by the investigators on an arbitrary basis, but using criteria which are clinically relevant, i.e. they involve a threshold above which a child would become a matter for concern to an experienced professional in the field. Thresholds are tested by systematic studies of reliability and, where possible, a disorder having been identified, an attempt is made to classify its type also according to pre-arranged criteria. Identification is usually carried out by the use of questionnaires often supplemented by personal interview. However, high questionnaire scores are not taken on their own to imply the presence of psychological disability, for a child may be handicapped by behaviour which only produces a low score or alternatively he may be very little impaired but suffer from a number of minor problems resulting in a high score. The rarity or statistical abnormality of a child's questionnaire or interview score is therefore not, in itself, regarded as the main criterion for abnormality if this approach is used. It should be stressed that the use of the approach is likely to be strongly culture-bound. Social function and psychological distress can only be measured against a hypothetical norm or expectation which the investigator hopefully shares with his population. It is quite likely that, given a different society with an investigator drawn from that society, different thresholds for abnormality might be reached.

The selection of interview/questionnaire

At the time this study was begun in 1970, the availability of suitable instruments for the detection of behaviour disturbances in the pre-school period was very limited. In the event we decided to develop a new behaviour questionnaire for this purpose (Richman and Graham, 1971) and later in the book this is briefly described. However, since the beginning of the 1970s a small number of descriptions of other instruments have been published.

Behar and Stringfield (1974), for example, have modified the teacher behaviour questionnaire devised by Rutter (1967) for older children to make it
suitable for use with three to six-year-olds. They administered the questionnaire to nursery school teachers of 496 normal children and 102 children
thought to be disturbed for independent reasons. The validity of the questionnaire was established by demonstrating that there were significant differences in scores between the disturbed and non-disturbed groups. Kohn
and Rosman (1972) developed a similar though more extensive checklist for
use with pre-school children. There are now therefore a number of reasonably well-validated questionnaires and checklists for the identification of
behaviour problems in pre-school children (Walker, 1973). It should be
stressed that these instruments would be of very limited use for clinical
purposes with individual children, but their value for investigating large
groups of children seems established.

Types of disorder

The classification of behaviour disorders arising in the pre-school period
from a clinical point of view has not proved very satisfactory apart from the
delineation of one or two rare disorders such as childhood autism. Existing
classificatory schemes have either paid little special attention to the pre-
school period, or failed to provide evidence for the validity of the categories
suggested (Group for the Advancement of Psychiatry, 1966). Nevertheless,
factor analysis of the data obtained from use of various questionnaires
already described has provided rather consistent evidence for the existence
of different types of disorder. Thus Kohn and Rosman (1973), using their
symptom checklist on 1425 children aged three to seven years, identified two
factors related orthogonally to each other which they termed "interest –
participation" v. "apathy – withdrawal" and "co-operation – compliance" v.
"anger – defiance". O'Donnel and Tuinan (1979), using a revised Quay-
Peterson Behaviour Problem checklist with 196 children aged three to six
years, identified two similar factors, "conduct problems" and "personality
problems". The former involved aggressive behaviour and the latter anxiety, insecurity and inhibition. In this last study consideration was given to the
delineation of an additional factor, hyperactivity, but it was concluded that
this could not be adequately separated from the conduct problem factor.
Wolkind and Everitt (1974) used a slight modification of the Richman and
Graham behaviour questionnaire with the mothers of 131 three-year-olds
attending ordinary nursery school and the caretakers of 31 high-risk children
in the care of a local authority. They carried out cluster analysis and

identified two main clusters of symptoms. The first, which seems to correspond quite closely with the "personality problem" and "apathy – withdrawal" factors described by other workers already cited, consisted of sleeping and eating problems, together with fears and habits. The second, which seems similar to "conduct problems" and "anger – defiance", consisted of symptoms such as management problems, tantrums and bedwetting. Some evidence of the validity of this second factor could be deduced from the fact that 50% of the high-risk children scored highly on it, compared to only 13% of the nursery school group. Finally, Behar and Stringfield (1974) using the sample described above extracted three factors from their data – "hostile – aggressive", "anxious – fearful", and "hyperactive – distractable". It appears therefore that there is unanimity amongst those who have studied the subject that the problems with which pre-school children present can be divided into two main groups — the first characterized by aggressive behaviour and the second by timidity and fearfulness. There is disagreement as to whether an additional factor of hyperactivity can be meaningfully delineated, and opinion is about equally divided as to whether this is a worthwhile exercise. Clearly, however, various requirements for a useful classification of disorders in this age-group have not been met. In particular, apart from sex differences between these factors, no evidence exists to show they can be linked to specific aetiology or that they call for specific treatment. There is certainly a need for a more refined classificatory system for pre-school behaviour disorders.

Link between behaviour and other characteristics of the pre-school child

As well as studying associations between behaviour disturbance and various aspects of family background and relationships, we also wished to determine how closely behavioural problems were linked to other characteristics of the child — especially his language development and other aspects of his cognitive abilities. Fortunately, many standardized psychological tests exist for the assessment of these aspects of pre-school child development and our only problem here lay in selecting those which seemed most relevant to our interests and which could be carried out in a reasonably short period of time in the child's own home.

It was our aim therefore to examine not just the rates of behaviour and emotional problems, but also a wide range of factors both in the child and in the family, associated with them. In the next chapter we describe the characteristics of the borough in which we carried out our study, our methods of obtaining our sample and the social circumstances of the families selected for the first stage of our investigation. The chapter concludes with a description of the methods we used to assess behaviour disturbance and language delay.

2   The Setting for the Study

Waltham Forest is an outer London borough situated ten to fifteen miles north of the centre of London. It stretches about two miles from east to west and six miles from Essex in the north to Hackney and Newham in the south. Most of the area was built upon for the first time between 1840 and 1870 as the suburban railways were developed and travel to and from the centre of London became easy. Building of council estates and privately-owned houses in unoccupied land continued up to and including the between-wars period. Since that time much of the older building has been replaced by blocks of high-rise and low-rise council flats and a few council houses. Intermingling with these, especially in the north of the borough where there is more open space, are relatively newly-built privately-owned detached and semi-detached houses. Thus, the most northerly part of the Borough near Epping Forest, has most open space and the highest proportion of owner-occupied housing, while the southern part has the highest proportion of poor, older housing and the least open space. This part is densely intersected with main roads, especially those leading from Central London into Essex, and these carry a good deal of heavy traffic. These main roads also provide the main shopping centres available in the borough. Apart from the residential accommodation and shopping areas the borough also contains some light industry. There is, however, no heavy industry and many people travel out of the borough, especially into central London, to work. We do not have data on local authority health, education and social services during the period in question but our impression was that the level of these services at the time of our study was at least as high as in other similar areas of the country. It is also relevant to point out that the level of pre-school provision and services has increased in the Borough since our study was carried out.

The opportunity for the study

In 1969 the Medical Research Council Unit for the Study of Environmental Factors under the direction of Dr James Douglas, established the Waltham

Forest Family Register. The purpose of this Register was to provide total coverage of all the young children and their families in the borough so that instead of studying selected groups of children such as those attending general practitioners and welfare clinics, it would be possible to investigate a population representative of all children living in the borough. The Register consisted of a computerized record of all families with a child under five years. Health visitors, using a standardized form, provided information on all births to women resident in the borough. As well as information about births, health visitors also reported on moves into and out of the borough made by families with young children. We were able to show that the Register gave almost complete coverage of pre-school children (Richman and Tupling, 1974).

We decided to study children initially at three years of age. The fact that the children would, when studied, all be of the same age would rule out the need to make corrections for age — a procedure which is difficult to achieve especially with young children when development is proceeding rapidly and small age differences can have considerable effects. The age of three years seemed appropriate because we felt that this was about the youngest age at which it would be feasible to assess behaviour and language development systematically. It is also the age at which many pre-school children start nursery school or go on to some other pre-school facility and we would thus be in a position to study the children before the great majority of them were exposed to education outside the home.

Waltham Forest appeared particularly suitable for our study because its social class distribution is similar to the country as a whole. The conditions in which its inhabitants live are typical of the great majority of British people who live neither in very deprived inner city areas nor in villages or isolated homesteads. The immigrant population of Waltham Forest consisting mainly of people from the West Indies, India and Pakistan, forms a significant element, and again we felt that this made the borough a fairly typical one for London and many large cities — neither largely populated by immigrants nor without any immigrant representation at all, though in fact the proportion of immigrants was definitely higher than for the country as a whole.

The selection of the sample

There are roughly 4000 births a year in the borough. Using the computerized register a one in four random sample of children was obtained. Over a twelve-month period in 1969–70, each month one in four children was selected who was reaching his or her third birthday during that month. All children living in the borough, both those born while resident there and

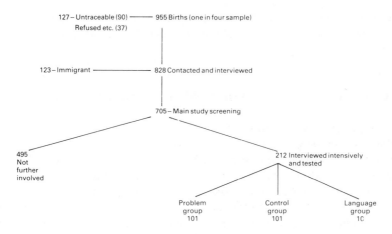

Figure 2.1. *Design of study*

those who had moved in after their birth, had an equal chance of being selected. Nine hundred and fifty five children were selected in this way. Of these, 90 (9·4%) could not be traced at the address given although they might still have been living in the borough: 32 (3·3%) refused, and five families could not be interviewed because of language difficulties. This loss of the more geographically mobile may have resulted in a slight sampling bias, with a consequent under-representation of problem families (Cox *et al.*, 1977). The remainder, 828 families (86·7%), were successfully contacted and interviewed. Of these families, 123 (14·8%) fell into the immigrant group defined by us as a family where the mother had lived in Great Britain or Eire for less than 20 years or whose first language was not English. The data presented in this book are those obtained from the remaining 705 families. Findings from the West Indian families have been presented elsewhere (Earls and Richman, 1980ab).

Screening interviews

The screening interviews in the families were in general carried out in the home with the mother, either alone (82%) or with the father (12%). In a small number of cases the father or other relative was interviewed. The interviewer gathered information on behaviour, first by the use of a behaviour check-list (BCL), and then by a semi-structured interview, the behaviour screening questionnaire (BSQ). In addition the interviewer assessed the child's health and development, housing, recent stresses, parental occupation and education. The child's language was also assessed directly at this interview. Height, weight and skinfold thickness (an index of overweight) were measured.

The social circumstances of the children and their families

The population we identified turned out to be relatively geographically stable. Seventy-seven per cent of the mothers and 88% of the fathers had actually been born in the borough of Waltham Forest or in some other part of Greater London. Only 11% had moved home within the year prior to interview and about three-quarters had been living in the same house for over two years. Many of the families had long standing roots in the borough with members of the extended family living close to them. Nearly all the children (95%) were living with both their natural parents and those who were not were usually living with their natural mother, either alone or together with other members of their family. On the other hand brief separations of the children from one or both parents had been quite common. Over a fifth of them had been in hospital at least once, and 16% had been separated from both parents for more than a week. Even by the age of three years one in ten had been separated from their mothers for at least a month.

Waltham Forest is not a borough of extremes of wealth or poverty. In "non-manual" families as defined by the Registrar General's Classification of Occupations (1971), most of the fathers worked as shop-keepers, managers in small firms or in clerical jobs. There were few fathers in professional occupations and, in those with manual jobs, few who had no trade or skill. Only a fifth of the fathers told us they were earning more than £40 a week, the majority earning between £20 and £40 a week, and, although some parents may have understated their income it did not seem to us that this was likely to have been a common occurrence. The interviews were carried out in 1972–3, and in 1972 the average weekly wage was £36·70. Twenty-seven per cent of the mothers were working in some form of paid employment. However, two-thirds of these worked less than 20 hours a week and 70% of them earned less than £10 a week — a relatively small sum even by the less inflated standards of 1972–3. Because of the relative absence of men in senior managerial or professional jobs, it is not surprising that rather few had received any form of further education. Indeed only 10% of the fathers and an even smaller proportion of mothers had received any full-time education after the age of 16 years.

By contrast with the rather narrow social differential in education and income, it struck us that differences in housing conditions were much more marked. The smart comfortable semi-detached houses near Epping Forest contrast strongly with some of the damp, deteriorating flats and houses in the south of the borough. There are many high rise buildings and a higher proportion than in the country as a whole (Bone, 1977), and 8·5% of the children lived in accommodation of this type on the fourth floor or above. However, 44% were living in owner-occupied houses with 28% in council-rented property and 18% renting unfurnished accommodation. The proportion of those in council property is very similar to those in Greater London, but slightly higher than for the country as a whole. Despite our impression of the inadequate nature of some of the housing, in objective terms there was little overcrowding and the domestic facilities available were considerably better than they would have been a generation ago. All the same, it is worth noting that 8% had no bath and about a quarter had no access to a garden. Just under a third of the children were living in flats the entrance to which was above ground level.

Overcrowding is strongly linked to family size, because in general family housing units are built with the two-or-three child family in mind. One of the reasons for lack of overcrowding therefore lies in the fact that in only 13% of our families were there four or more children — a figure slightly less than that for the country as a whole. There were also rather few only children (16%) so most of the children did indeed live in two- or three-child families.

Although one of the reasons for our taking three years as a starting point for our study was the fact that we thought very few of the children would have been exposed to a nursery school or other pre-school facility, in fact by this age 31% had attended a facility of some type. A proportion of these (about one in ten) had attended for a period but then stopped attendance mainly because of difficult behaviour, especially unwillingness of the child to be separated from the mother. A great majority of those who were attending were in some form of playgroup, either voluntarily organized or run by the Local Authority. About 3% were in other facilities such as a day nursery or a special group for children with developmental delay. Very few of the children (only 0·7%) were looked after regularly by child minders. These figures can be compared with those provided by Hughes *et al.* (1980) for the country as a whole. They are very similar. An additional number of the mothers (about 12%) wanted their children to go to a playgroup but were unable to organize this because of practical or financial difficulties of one sort or another. Nevertheless, the children were, as a rule, not socially isolated. All but 7% had played with another child over the previous week and over three-quarters had played with three or more different children over the same time period. Clearly mothers were making particular efforts for their children in order to overcome the disadvantages of living in flats without gardens.

Finally, it should be stressed that although quite a high proportion of the children had had brief hospital admissions, this was generally a very healthy population. Based on maternal reports and not individual medical examinations, it seemed that the most common problems to have occurred over the previous year were eczema (4·6%) and asthma (2·3%). About 4% of the children were said to have visual difficulties and 1% hearing problems. 1·6% had suffered some form of epilepsy or convulsive disorder (febrile or non-febrile fits) and 2·4% had had some other type of chronic health problem. A high proportion would, of course, have had antibiotics for minor infections, but the use of medication for management problems was not very common. Nine per cent of the children had had medication for sleep, 2·3% a sedative, and 3% some form of medicine to increase appetite. By contrast accidents in this age group are very common and a third of the children, even by the age of three years, had had an accident requiring medical attention.

This brief account of some of the social circumstances and physical health of the children provides a background to our main area of interest — the child's behavioural and language development. We now go on to describe the methods we used to assess the children in this respect.

Measures of behaviour and language

These were as follows:

(a) The behaviour screening questionnaire (BSQ) (see Appendix 1).

This is a semi-structured interview in which descriptions of twelve types of behaviour are obtained from the parent. The areas covered are sleeping, eating, bowel control, attention seeking and dependency, relationships with other children, activity, concentration, ease of control, tempers, mood, worries and fears. The findings of a pilot study which also established the reliability and validity of this interview (Richman and Graham, 1971) suggested that these areas of behaviour were most significant in the discrimination of young children attending psychiatric clinics from those in the general population.

During the interview, the informant (usually the mother) is asked for actual concrete descriptions of behaviour rather than for her attitude or opinions about the behaviour of the child. When the interviewer has obtained sufficient information to make a rating, the item is coded 0, 1, or 2 according to pre-established criteria. Thus a total score between 0–24 is obtained. The pilot study established that a score of 11 or more was the most effective cut-off point in identifying children with psychiatric disorder, but in this study, in order to miss as few disturbed children as possible, we decided to use a cut-off point of 10.

(b) *The behaviour check list (BCL)*
   (see Appendix 2)

This is a twelve-item check list derived from the behaviour screening questionnaire regarding the same items of the child's behaviour. Three statements are made about an area of behaviour and the parent is asked to mark which behaviour she thinks applies best to her child, e.g.

(1) Easy to get to bed and to sleep.
(2) Some difficulties in settling at bedtime.
(3) Often takes an hour to settle at bedtime.

The item scores are subsequently summed to provide a total score ranging from 0 to 24 and a score of 10 or more is taken to indicate that the child is at risk for emotional or behaviour problems. This check list was developed to be used as a simple screening device for identifying children that might need further assessment. It has been described in more detail elsewhere (Richman, 1977).

The BSQ involved obtaining more detailed information than the BCL which is merely a self-completion questionnaire. It should be explained that we used the BCL because we wished to determine how effective this rapidly administered cheap method not requiring trained interviewers or face-to-face contact with the interviewer would be in picking out disturbed children. The degree to which the BCL was effective as a screening instrument will be discussed in the next chapter.

(c) *Language development*

The interviewer assessed each child's language development using three simple tests. She asked the child to:

(1) Identify pictures corresponding to a named word, these being the first 20 items of the English picture vocabulary test (Brimer and Dunn, 1962).

(2) Name seven specified items on this test.

(3) She also talked to the child and listened to his spontaneous speech in order to assess his level of syntactic development on a five-point scale taken from the Reynell Development Language Scales (Reynell, 1969). These were:

(a) uses word combinations;

(b) has 20 or more words;

(c) uses sentences of four or more syllables;

(d) uses words other than nouns or verbs, e.g. adjectives;

(e) uses two of the following — pronouns, prepositions, questions other than by intonation.

A score of one was given for each correct point up to a maximum of five. Children who scored only 0 or 1 on the last two language assessment criteria were considered to have language delay.

Thus, to recapitulate, information was obtained on the health and development of 828 three-year-old children representative of the general population and their families, on two measures of behaviour and on language development.

Summary

In this chapter we have described the geographical setting for our study and the way in which the opportunity arose to examine a representative sample of three-year-old children. We have given a brief description of the social circumstances of the children and families living in the borough and have then gone on to describe the methods we have used to identify the numbers of children with behavioural disturbances and language delay living in the borough. We have described a simple behavioural check list which could be easily administered by health visitors as well as a more detailed semi-structured interview. In the next chapter we shall describe the rates of behaviour problems we identified in our 705 non-immigrant children and draw comparisons between disturbed and non-disturbed children based on information obtained in our screening interview. In the subsequent chapter we shall describe the results of a more detailed comparison made possible by an intensive interview carried out with parents of the disturbed children and a non-disturbed group matched for sex and social class.

3 Behaviour and Emotional Disturbance in the Main Sample

Overall rates

As indicated in the previous chapter each parent in the one in four sample of 705 children was visited by a trained interviewer who administered the behaviour check list and the behaviour screening questionnaire, as well as asking a number of other questions relating to health, development, housing, recent stresses, parental occupation and education.

Earlier work (Richman and Graham, 1971) using the behaviour screening questionnaire (BSQ) had suggested that children scoring over a cut-off point of eleven on this questionnaire could reasonably be regarded as showing a significant behaviour disturbance. In this study, in order to ensure that we missed as few disturbed children as possible, a cut-off point of ten was taken and 101 (14·3%) of the 705 non-immigrant children were identified as disturbed using this criterion. However, a high score on a questionnaire of this type is perhaps not the most valid measure of the degree of disturbance. Some children might achieve a high score because they showed a large number of rather minor problems and others, in whom dysfunction was only shown in one or two areas of behaviour, could be quite severely handicapped even though scoring no more than four or five points. In order to take account of this possibility each child was given a *clinical* rating of disturbance by one of us (N.R. or P.G), based on all the information available to us from the interview about the child's behaviour. This rating was made on a five point scale ranging from "no problem" to "dubious", "mild", "moderate", and "severe". Severity ratings were based on the frequency and duration of the problem behaviour as well as on the amount of suffering apparent within the child and affecting his relationships with adults and children, ability to play, and independence. A reliability exercise involving the judgement of disturbance in 25 problem and 25 non-problem children revealed that two of us (N.R. and P.G.) making independent judgements could agree well on the severity ratings ($r = 0.88$).

It was possible for us to calculate the overall prevalence of behaviour disturbance in the population using the clinical rating by noting the relationship between the BSQ score and this rating (Richman *et al.*, 1975). In fact all cases diagnosed as showing moderate or severe disturbance clinically scored over the cut-off point and no children scoring below ten points were rated clinically as showing disturbance of this severity. However, about 10% of children scoring below this cut-off point did show mild disturbance. The corrected prevalence of clinical disturbance in the population, taking into account false positives and false negatives, is shown in Table 3.1. It can be seen from this table that just over 7% of the children show moderate or severe disturbance and 15% mild problems.

Table 3.1. *Estimated prevalence of behaviour problems by clinical rating of severity and sex in the total population of 3-year-old non-immigrant children*

Clinical rating of severity	Boys	Girls	Total
No problem/dubious problem	76·0%	79·0%	77·6%
Mild problem	14·6%	15·4%	15·0%
Moderate problem	7·6%	4·9%	6·2%
Severe problem	1·7%	0·5%	1·1%

It is perhaps appropriate to digress at this point to consider how well the results using the behaviour check list (BCL) compared with the more intensive interview, the behaviour screening questionnaire (Richman, 1977). First, where the BSQ identified 100% of the children thought to be moderately or severely disturbed on clinical criteria, the BCL identified 82%. The BCL generally produced larger numbers of both false positive and false negative results. Using the BSQ, 6·8% of children in whom the clinical rating revealed an absence of significant problems were rated above the cut-off point for disturbance. This was true for 12% of the children using the BCL. 9·8% of clinically disturbed children scored below the cut-off point on the BSQ compared to 30·4% with the BCL. All in all, therefore, the BCL can be regarded as a useful cheap screening device for behaviour and emotional disorders although its use would result in missing a significant number of disorders, especially those of mild severity.

Clearly the decision whether a child has a problem, and if he has one, its level of severity is to some degree an arbitrary one. In order to indicate our own threshold for disturbance, we provide randomly selected illustrations of our ratings at this point.

(1) Michael T. Case No. 005.
(All names changed to ensure anonymity)

Michael is the youngest child and has three older grown-up brothers and sisters. His mother works and he is looked after by his sister. He goes to bed at 10 p.m., though his mother would prefer him to go much earlier. He gets into his parents' bed every other night. He is very active and is said to be hardly ever still. His concentration is short, but he can amuse himself. He can be disobedient, and have tempers but this happens rather rarely. He is not usually difficult and mixes pretty well. He seems to have no worries and there are no difficulties over separation.

Clinical rating — No problem. Behaviour screening questionnaire (BSQ) score = 5.*

(2) Sandra M. Case No. 012.

Sandra is the youngest of five, her brothers and sisters being considerably older than she is. She soils and wets herself, and is not a happy child. She cannot amuse herself and follows her mother around all the time. She is a very poor eater and faddy. She has some difficulties in settling at night and is generally restless with poor concentration. She can be left with others though only with some difficulty. When frustrated she goes on and on screaming until her mother gives in for the sake of peace. She will scream and shout in the street. She has tempers if thwarted two or three times a day and has quite a number of fears. She screams and shouts if her older brothers and sisters will not play with her and consequently she irritates them. She cannot play with other children because she has no idea of give and take. Her mother had to give up work because Sandra fretted for her and lost weight.

Clinical rating — Mild problem. BSQ score = 18.

(3) Moira C. Case No. 171.

She is the younger of two girls. Moira was said by her mother never to do what she was told, but to run around the room, never still, climbing on the table at mealtime etc. She has a smallish appetite and eats inappropriate

---

*BSQ score of 10 or more indicates deviance.

materials such as tissues. She takes about half an hour to get to bed and then sleeps through the night. She is a very active girl with poor concentration and is always playing with things that she shouldn't. She seems to annoy her mother deliberately. She is uncontrollable at times, for example when her mother takes her out shopping. She has infrequent tempers but is often grisly, whiney and moody, and her moods may last up to an hour. She fights with her sister a good deal and is generally boisterous and tends to get into fights with other children from whom she has to be separated. She wears both her parents out. She has no fears. She tends to dominate the other members of the family.

Clinical rating — Moderate problem. BSQ score = 14.

(4) Peter K. Case No. 131.

Peter is the older of two boys. He is very over-active and is said to "run around like a madman". He is reported to be very wild, and totally out of control, having a tantrum whenever he is frustrated. He torments his nine-month-old brother so that he cannot be left with him. He will not play with other children, but only fights with them. It is impossible to take him out. He follows his mother around all day. He has a poor appetite, is faddy, and he occasionally eats paint. It takes a very long time to settle him at night, and he often gets into his parents' bed. He shows facial grimacing at times. He can amuse himself but he is disinclined to do this. He cannot be left for long with others, and is irritable if he doesn't get his own way. He worries that his mother might die, and is also frightened of monsters and of noises at night. He has many other fears as well as nightmares. He frequently shouts and screams, and the neighbours and other children will not have anything to do with him.

Clinical rating — Marked problem. BSQ score = 19.

In our view children with mild disturbances can reasonably be regarded as an appropriate subject for concern and might be considered as requiring help from primary health care services. Children with moderate and severe disorders would certainly be regarded as requiring help from primary health care services and might be regarded as needing assistance from specialized professionals such as social workers, psychologists and psychiatrists.

It can be seen from Table 3.1 that there were very small differences between the sexes in the rates of mild disturbance. Boys showed moderate and'severe disturbance to a greater degree than girls but the differences are not statistically significant. Social class differences were also relatively unimportant. When the analysis of social class was carried out considering each occupational classes (I to V) separately, no significant differences were found. However, when all manual class were combined and compared with all non-manual there was a significant excess of children with problems in the manual group. Social class differences in rates of disorder were limited to girls.

In girls whose fathers were in non-manual occupations the rate of disturbance was 6·9%, whereas in girls with fathers in manual work the rate was 14·8%, a significant difference (see Table 3.2). There was less difference in rates in boys from the two different social class groupings. This finding suggests that girls are somewhat more sensitive to social adversity than are boys, even though boys tend to show higher rates of disturbance. Others, e.g. Rutter (1970) have found the reverse in older children. It may be that in this young age group vulnerability to social factors is overshadowed by a dominance of constitutional temperamental attributes in boys, but not in girls, or that the sexes differ in their maturational rate as far as sensitivity to adverse social factors is concerned and further evidence in support of this view will be provided later in the book.

The occupational class of the father is a rather crude indicator of social status and conditions. However, examination of the social circumstances of families from the two broad occupational groups made it clear that they did differ in other ways too. "Non-manual" families tended more commonly to live in more favoured parts of the borough. They were more often owner-occupiers, and less often in council or rented accommodation. The mothers of non-manual families were not more likely to be working but, if working, they were more likely to be in a non-manual job themselves. The education of "non-manual" fathers and mothers had more often extended beyond the age of sixteen years, and, of course, fathers in non-manual occupations had a higher level of income.

Table 3.2 *Percentage of children with behaviour problems (BSQ $\geq$ 10) at age 3 years by social class and housing type in the total non-immigrant sample (N = 705)*

Percentage of children scoring 10 or more on BSQ, i.e. with behaviour problems (numbers in brackets).			P^a
Manual	17% (77/454)	Non-manual	10·4% (23/221)	<0·05
Manual girls	14·8% (34/230)	Non-manual girls	6·9% (8/116)	<0·05
Manual boys	19·2% (43/224)	Non-manual boys	14·4% (15/104)	N.S.
Council accommodation	20·1% (47/234)	Owner occupied	12·5% (40/319)	<0·05
Tower block flats		Other forms of		
(4th floor and above)	26·7% (16/60)	housing	13·2% (85/645)	<0·01

^{a}Significance level of chi-square test with d.f. = 1.

Table 3.3. *Percentage of children with behaviour problems (BSQ ≥ 10) by sex within social class and housing type in the total non-immigrant sample (N = 705)*

		Percentage of children scoring 10 or more on BSQ i.e. with behaviour problems (numbers in brackets)		
Social class	Housing Type	Girls	Boys	P^a
Non-manual	Flats	0% (0/31)	28% (7/25)	<0·01
	Houses	9% (8/85)	11% (8/72)	N.S.
	P^b	N.S.	<0·05	
Manual	Flats	22% (22/99)	15% (13/86)	N.S.
	Houses	9% (12/132)	22% (30/137)	<0·01
	P^b	<0·01	N.S.	

[a]Significance level of chi-squared test comparing boys and girls within social class and housing type, d.f. = 1.
[b]Significance level of chi-square test comparing flat and house dwellers within social class and sex, d.f. = 1.

Type of housing was also related to the rate of behaviour disturbance, but in a complex manner. Thus in non-manual families boys but not girls were more likely to be disturbed if living in flats (28·0%) than in a house (11·1%). A reverse situation existed in manual families in which girls but not boys in flats (see Table 3.3) were more disturbed (22·0%) than those living in houses (9·2%). There was therefore a complex interaction between sex, social class and type of housing, which is difficult to interpret. The most clear-cut finding is that non-manual boys living in flats were more disturbed than flat-dwelling non-manual girls and the higher levels of physical activity shown by boys may be the important factor here. A further clear-cut finding (see Table 3.2) is that rates of disturbance were highest in those living in tower blocks (26·7%), when compared with the rates in council accommodation more generally (20·1%) and in all other forms of housing taken together (13·2%).

We feel that these findings regarding rates of disturbance in different types of housing deserve serious attention, but it is necessary to inject early on a few words of caution. Clearly parents who function poorly in a variety of ways may act as poor advocates for themselves and be housed selectively in less adequate accommodation. The disturbance in their children might be due to other aspects of this poor functioning and not be attributable directly to the quality of their housing. Nevertheless, the differences in rates of disturbance between children living in different types of housing are substantial and it was certainly our impression that favourable housing circumstances made it a great deal easier to cope with a difficult child.

A further indication of the importance of social factors more generally is provided by the relationship between childhood disturbance and family stress. A total stress score was calculated for each family by adding all the events which had occurred during the previous year of a seriously threatening nature, such as deaths, serious illnesses, births, work and money difficulties, housing problems and problems in personal relationships. Those scoring over ten points on the BSQ did not have a higher mean stress score than children scoring below this point, but there were a number of stresses which the problem group did experience significantly more often. Thus the families with a problem child were more likely to have experienced stress over physical or psychiatric illness, financial worries, difficulties over father's work and serious quarrels with neighbours or within the family.

Compared to children without behaviour problems, children scoring ten points or more on the BSQ appeared to have significantly more health problems and more contact with health services. As can be seen from Table 3.4, they had made more visits to the general practitioner in the previous year, and, although their visits to the local child welfare clinic were not significantly more frequent they were more likely to have attended because of a developmental or behavioural problem.

Problem children had not been admitted to hospital more frequently but they were reported to have had more frequent attendances at out-patients and more accidents requiring medical help.

We felt it would be of interest to attempt to relate measures of physical development to behavioural disturbance. In general the findings were negative. Birth weights as reported by mothers were lower in the problem group than in the rest of the population but not significantly so. Degree of over and under the correct weight was assessed by measuring skinfold thickness using skin calipers and the children were also weighed and measured. Some of these measurements were not available as a number of children were uncooperative. As far as available data were concerned, there did not appear to be a significant difference in weight, but the problem group had a mean skinfold thickness 2·6 mm less than the control group — a difference bordering on the statistically significant.

Differences between problem behaviour and other children with regard to their developmental status will be reported in the next chapter in which a more comprehensive comparison between disturbed and non-disturbed children in groups matched for sex and social class will be described. Here it is perhaps sufficient to mention briefly that the problem group had significantly lower scores on the Vineland Social Maturity Scale. They were reported by their parents (see Table 3.4) to have more speech problems, a higher proportion not yet using four syllable sentences or even single words.

Table 3.4. *Health and development in children with behaviour problems ($BSQ \geq 10$) in the total non-immigrant sample at 3 years ($N = 705$)*

Measure of health and development	Children with BSQ score of 10 or more Problem group Total		Children with BSQ score less than 10 Non-problem group Total		P^a
Percentage with visits to health centre with health problems	101	12·9%	603	8·1%	N.S.
Percentage making 6 or more visits to GP during previous year	101	27·7%	603	12·8%	<0·001
Percentage suffering accidents requiring medical care during previous year	101	58·4%	604	39·4%	<0.001
Percentage with birth weight less than 2500 g	99	12·0%	592	6·6%	N.S.
Mean body weight at 3 years in kg	95	14·3	562	14·6	N.S.
Mean skinfold thickness (mm)	64	5·22	461	5·48	<0·05
Mean Vineland Social Maturity Scale raw score	100	10·6	601	11·9	<0·001
Percentage using only single words	96	14·6%	583	5·1%	<0·01
Percentage not speaking in four syllable sentences	96	19·8%	583	10·3%	<0·02
Percentage with an articulation problem	93	37·6%	571	21·5%	<0·01

^{a}Significance level of chi-square, d.f. = 1, for percentages, or t-tests for means.

Of those who were speaking, more had articulation problems and were difficult to understand. On the language assessment carried out by the interviewer with the child, the children scoring ten or more points scored significantly lower on all three measures — pointing to seven items on the English Picture Vocabulary Test, naming twenty items on this Test, and achieving success on the five point syntax scale.

Table 3.5 presents information on the frequency with which separate items of behaviour occurred in this total population of three-year-old children. It can be seen that some items occurred rather rarely, e.g. only one in 40 children was thought to worry excessively, whereas others were much more common — over a third of the children wet their beds or were in nappies at least three times a week. As we have already emphasized, the

Table 3.5. *Percentage of 3-year-old children with specific items of problem behaviour from the* BSQ *definitely present by sex in the total non-immigrant sample (N = 705)*

| Specific items of problem behaviour | Percentage of children with item of problem behaviour definitely present | | | |
	Girls (N=363)	Boys (N=342)	Total (N=705)	P^a
Poor appetite	16·5	16·1	16·3	N.S.
Faddy eating	10·7	12·9	11·8	N.S.
Difficulty settling at night	9·9	14·3	12·1	N.S.
Waking at night (at least 3 times a week)	14·9	14·0	14·5	N.S.
Sleeping in parents' bed	11·3	11·1	11·2	N.S.
Overactive, restless	9·9	16·1	12·9	<0·02
Poor concentration	5·0	6·4	5·7	N.S.
Dependency	5·0	5·8	5·4	N.S.
Attention seeking	9·9	8·5	9·2	N.S.
Tempers	5·0	5·3	5·1	N.S.
Difficult to control	9·4	12·0	10·7	N.S.
Unhappy mood	4·1	3·5	3·8	N.S.
Worries	2·5	2·1	2·3	N.S.
Fears	9·7	8·8	9·2	N.S.
Relations with siblings	8·6	8·5	8·5	N.S.
Relations with peers	6·1	5·6	5·8	N.S.
Soiling (once a week or more)	8·0	17·8	12·8	<0·001
Recent onset soiling	0·8	3·8	2·3	<0·02
Night wetting (at least 3 nights a week)	30·6	44·7	37·4	<0·001
Recent onset night wetting	3·9	6·4	5·1	N.S.
Day wetting (once a week or more)	11·6	22·5	16·9	<0·001
Recent onset day wetting	1·4	3·8	2·6	N.S.

^{a}Significance level of chi-square test, d.f. = 1.

criteria we used to draw the line between problem and non-problem behaviour were arbitrary, and the pattern of frequency of individual items is necessarily determined by the criteria used in rating each item. Further, the presence of a particular item of behaviour in a child can clearly not be taken as evidence of disturbance. Many, perhaps most of the items, might be regarded as reflecting developmental immaturity rather than behavioural deviation, and we were able to examine this in our longitudinal follow-up. We think it worthwhile to present these data partly to facilitate comparisons with other studies of children of this age which might be carried out and partly because the data make it possible to examine sex differences — the same criteria being used to rate items of behaviour in boys and girls.

Sex difference in rates of behaviour

The main difference between boys and girls lay in the rates at which they acquired bowel and bladder control. Boys were more commonly still soiling themselves at least once a week and had more frequently relapsed in bowel control after a period of continence. Similarly, they wet themselves significantly more often by night and by day. Sex differences in bowel and bladder control of this type have been described by other workers (e.g. Oppel *et al.*, 1968).

The regularity with which such differences have been found suggest that physiological factors involving different rates of maturation must be involved. However, this may not be a sufficient explanation. There was a tendency for regular soiling and day and night wetting to be associated with a general behaviour problem. Thus 25·3% of children in the problem group were soiling once a week or more compared to only 12·8% in the total population. 47·5% of the problem group were wetting the bed three nights a week compared to 36·8% of the total group, 30·3% of the problem group were wetting themselves by day compared to 16·9% of the total population. This suggested to us that bowel and bladder incontinence could be seen even at this age as evidence in itself of behavioural disturbance. Other explanations are possible. For instance, incontinence could sometimes lead to the development of behaviour problems, mediated perhaps by frustration experienced by mothers whose children soil and wet for longer periods than they had expected: or there could be a common neurophysiological mechanism responsible for both behavioural disturbances and incontinence (Wender, 1971).

We examined the relationship between bowel and bladder control and the presence of adverse social factors. We found that neither boys nor girls from manual class families wet their beds significantly more often than those whose fathers were in non-manual occupations. Nor did the total stress scores or housing stress scores of those children who wet their beds differ significantly from those who did not, though there was a non-significant trend for them to be higher. It seemed, therefore, that social disadvantage at least at this age was unlikely to be important in the genesis of delay in gaining bowel and bladder control in either boys or girls. Boys are known to show more maturational delays in other functions such as speech development and it is now commonly assumed that there are physiological reasons for this sex difference. It seems likely therefore that the reasons for boys failing to achieve continence as early as girls are partly physiological, but they may also be partly related to the presence of behaviour disturbance. From our findings however it seems unlikely, as Douglas (1973), has suggested, that this relationship is mediated by social disadvantage or stress in the children's background.

As well as showing more bowel and bladder problems, three-year-old boys were also rated significantly more often than girls as overactive or restless. The greater activity of pre-school boys has been noted by many other workers and is reflected in the higher rates in boys of pathological overactivity or the "hyperkinetic syndrome" which occurs two or three times more commonly in males than females (Cantwell, 1976). In fact, the difference in rates of overactivity in this population was not dramatic (16·1% of boys and 9·9% of girls), although it was statistically significant. We discuss later the relationship between overactivity and restlessness and how we view this behaviour.

By contrast, girls were only slightly more fearful than boys, though others have found greater differences (Macfarlane *et al.*, 1954). Older girls have been shown to have more specific fears than boys (Lapouse and Monk, 1959), but it is quite uncertain whether this particular sex difference is constitutionally determined or related to different social learning experiences. It is certainly conceivable that, even as young as three years, girls are permitted or even encouraged to show fearful reactions to a greater degree than boys, and we shall have more to say on this point in discussing our follow-up data.

It should not be forgotten that in most areas of behaviour sex differences were not found. Thus management problems affecting eating and sleeping were shown with roughly equal frequency by boys and girls, and there were no differences in problems affecting social relationships either with adults or other children. Affective symptoms such as unhappy moods and worrying were not more common in girls as might have been predicted from studies of older children nor were they more clinging or attention seeking. On the basis of studies with older children (Rutter *et al.*, 1970), one might also have predicted that boys would be reported as more difficult to control, to have more temper tantrums and to show poorer concentration, but in fact this turned out not to be the case. Sex differences in behaviour in this population were therefore confined to bowel and bladder continence, with, in addition, isolated and not very dramatic sex differences in overactivity or restlessness.

Rates of language delay and general retardation

In addition to the information obtained on the rate of behaviour problems in the total population, our method of screening also allowed us to obtain estimates of the number of children with language delay and general retardation (Stevenson and Richman, 1976). The language screening procedure we described in the previous chapter gave 20 indigenous children at risk of having language delay.

These children were more thoroughly investigated using tests described in the following chapter, and by including a small number of children whom we studied more intensively because they did have language problems, but were only identified because they had fallen into the behaviour problem group, we were able to estimate the prevalence of language delay according to different criteria. Thus, using a definition of expressive language delay which involved an expressive language age 30 months or less (i.e. six months behind chronological age), we identified 22 children — a rate of 3·1%. Using a more stringent criterion — expressive language age less than or equal to two-thirds of the child's chronological age — we found a rate of "severe expressive language delay" of 2·3%. In both types of language delay, boys were roughly twice as commonly affected as girls, though, because of the small numbers, the differences were not statistically significant.

When one took the child's mental age into account and considered only those children whose language delay fell far below their mental age, as assessed by tests of their non-verbal abilities (that is those with specific language delay), the numbers involved were smaller. There were only four children (5·7 per thousand) with specific language delay who were not generally retarded.

Efficacy of language screening procedure

By using information obtained from assessing the large number of children described in the next chapter whose language and general development was tested even though they had not been thought to have language delay, it was possible to assess the efficacy of our language screening procedures. There were in fact no false positives, i.e. no children identified by the screening procedures as having expressive language delay were not so assessed by full psycho-developmental testing. There were, however, four additional children, all of whom had behaviour problems, who did have language ages of less than 30 months (language age six months or more below chronological age) who were not identified by the screening procedure (false negatives).

These four all had behaviour problems (three of moderate severity) and it had been difficult for them to be adequately screened. If, therefore, one undertook a screening programme for both language and behaviour problems, our information suggests that the number of children with significant language delay who would be missed would be negligible or non-existent.

Although our screening survey was not designed to identify all children with severe developmental delay, it is in fact likely that it did so. Only two children had non-verbal mental ages of less than 18 months (very roughly equivalent to an IQ of 50). These two also had severely delayed language, and there were therefore no children with specific severe non-verbal delay (i.e. without language delay). Including one additional child with Down's Syndrome who was also identified, this meant that there were three severely retarded children out of the 705 in the total indigenous population, giving a figure of 4·2 per 1000. Clearly because of the smallness of the numbers involved, this figure must be treated with caution, but it is nevertheless very much in line with that found in other surveys (Kushlick, 1968)

Social characteristics of children with language delay

In 8% of the families of children with language delay, the families were in manual occupations, a non-significant difference from the total sample. However, using information derived from interviews described in the following chapter, it was found that the families in which these children lived were especially likely to have suffered from a number of social stresses. 40·9% of the group had had three or more serious stresses compared to 23·8% in the total population. Over one-ninth had had serious financial stress, and over one-third had been in touch with the local social services department over the previous year. These findings parallel many other studies demonstrating an association between social disadvantage and language delay (e.g. Starte, 1975).

We found that the child with language delay tends to be the youngest or penultimate child in a large family of four or more children (Richman and Stevenson, 1977). Of those children identified as having language delay on the screening exercise, 45% came from families of four or more children, and this was significantly different from the 12·7% in the general population. In fact the prevalence of language delay in families with four or more children was 185 per thousand, nearly seven times more frequent than in the general population.

Links between language delay and behaviour problems

We have already discussed (and see Table 3.4) the tendency of children with
behaviour problems to show delay in articulation and delay in the development of expressive speech. There was also a high rate of behaviour problems
among children with language delay in our group. Thus, of the 22 children
with expressive language delay, 13 (59·1%) had behaviour problems compared to 14·3% in the general population. Of the four children with specific
expressive language delay not associated with general retardation, three had
behaviour problems. Here the numbers are too small to draw statistically
significant conclusions, but the link looks a close one. Thus there appear to
be close links between behaviour problems and language delay, and we shall
discuss the implications of this finding in more detail in Chapter 5.

Attendance at pre-school facilities

At the time that the study children reached four years of age, we also carried
out a survey of all children in the borough attending pre-school facilities
(nursery school, nursery class, day nursery and play group). By far the
largest proportion of children attending such facilities were attending play
groups (76%) and in general the children started around their third birthday,
attended a facility near their home, and stayed until they went to school. We
sampled 27 facilities — a one-in-three sample of the play groups and all of
the children attending other types of provision (Stevenson and Ellis, 1975),
and we identified those 226 out of the total 828 (immigrant as well as
non-immigrant in this case) who attended these facilities.
    By weighting the scores for the children in playgroups by three (in order to
take account of the fact that only one in three play groups was sampled), we
were able to compare the characteristics of children attending pre-school
facilities with those not attending in our total one-in-four sample. We found
that there were significant differences between the proportions of children
attending pre-school groups from different social classes. When compared
on the basis of single mothers, non-manual and manual social classes, highly
significant differences were found ($P < 0.001$), in that children of unmarried
mothers and non-manual social class background were over-represented in
the pre-school group. When children of unmarried mothers were excluded
the higher proportion of children from the non-manual class in pre-school
groups remained significant ($P < 0.05$), though the differences are not very
great — 28% of children in the total population come from non-manual
groups compared to 35% in those attending pre-school facilities.
    Children attending pre-school facilities were, however, very little diffe-

rent from the general population either in their likelihood of showing behaviour problems or in their level of language development. 13% of those attending facilities were estimated to show a significant problem as manifest by a score of ten or more on the BSQ, and 14% in the general population. On all the measures of language development, the children attending facilities were slightly better than those in the general population, and in one of them, expressive vocabulary, the differences reached a statistically significant level ($P > 0.05$) (Stevenson and Ellis, 1975). It should be pointed out that this part of the survey was carried out in 1972–3, since when there has been an expansion of pre-school provision in the borough. There may now be a greater degree of selectivity in the children attending the available facilities.

Summary

The findings on the 705 non-immigrant children in our population of three-year-olds have revealed that, using our criteria, roughly 7% had a moderate or severe behaviour problem and a further 15% had mild problems. Children showing these problems were also more likely to use health services to a greater degree, to have more accidents, and to show developmental delay to a greater degree than might have been expected. They had more social stress in their backgrounds, although social differences as measured by paternal occupational class were not very marked or clear-cut. Boys differed from girls mainly in the rates at which they acquired bowel and bladder control, and, although physiological factors may have been of importance in producing delay in control there was a definite relationship between such a delay and the presence of behaviour problems shown in other ways.

Rates of language delay were also assessed and found to be in the region of $2.3 – 3.1\%$ depending on the criteria used. There were only three children with severe general retardation identified in the population. The language screening procedure was highly sensitive and specific in picking out children with language delay. Children with such delay were more likely to come from large families, and their families were more likely to have suffered stress over the previous year. They were also very likely to show behaviour problems.

The study of pre-school facilities in the borough revealed that of those three-year-old children, who were attending such a facility most were likely to go to a play group (76%). The comparison of those children from our sample attending facilities compared with those not attending, revealed that attenders were more likely to come from the non-manual social class, and to be slightly superior in language ability, but to show roughly the same rates of behaviour problems.

In the next chapter we shall describe a more comprehensive comparison between disturbed and non-disturbed children that became possible as a result of a more intensive interview and psychological assessment carried out at a further stage of the study.

4 Comparison between Matched Problem and Control Groups

Introduction

In the previous chapter we described how we identified the 101 most disturbed children in our population of 705 by selecting those with scores of ten or more on the behaviour screening questionnaire. For each disturbed child the next child of the same sex and social class on the list was then chosen to act as a control for purposes of comparison. All those parents who agreed to be interviewed and provide further information were then revisited by another research worker. We carried out further interviews of these two groups when the children were four and eight years old. In this and subsequent chapters we only provide information on those 94 problem and 91 control children for whom data were obtained at all three phases of the study. The second interview in this phase of the study was generally carried out by a different interviewer from the first occasion and this was achieved in 84% of cases. In this second interview one or both parents (in about three-quarters of cases the mothers alone and in virtually all the rest both parents) provided answers to questions about family background and relationships, parental health — both mental and physical, social stresses operating on the family, and contact with friends, relatives and service agencies. As an addition to the second phase of investigation, a psychologist (J.S.) made a separate visit to administer a series of psychological tests. He also made systematic observations of the child's behaviour during his visit which was conducted in ignorance of whether the child was a case or a control.

Were the cases really disturbed?

The design of the study allowed us to check whether the cases were really more disturbed than their controls who all scored less than ten on the behaviour screening questionnaire (BSQ). The agreement between the behaviour check list and the BSQ has already been mentioned. This was one important check, but others were possible. First, as already stated, summaries of accounts of the child's behaviour obtained during the BSQ were independently rated on a five point scale — no disturbance, trivial, mild, moderate and severe disturbance. No control child was rated as having a moderate or severe disorder, whereas 49 problem children were so rated. However, nine of the control children were rated as having a mild problem. Only seven problem children were rated as having no or only a trivial disorder, compared with 82 control children (see Table 4.1).

Table 4.1. *Relationship between clinical rating of problem and score on the behaviour screening questionnaire (BSQ)*

BSQ score	Clinical rating No problem/dubious	Problem present	Total
Less than 10	82	9	91
10 or more	7	87	94
Total	89	96	185

A further check was possible from independent ratings described later in the chapter made by the psychologist who observed behaviour during the test session (see below for details). The problem children were significantly different at the 5% level in five out of the 14 ratings made, namely test orientation, speed of response, need for direction, need for tester praise and comprehension of test task. Differences in other ratings approached, but did not reach the 5% level. These various checks together with the differences in outcome described in later chapters therefore did provide good support for the notion that the children who were identified as problems on the basis of the BSQ really were the most disturbed.

Which items of behaviour best distinguished problem and control groups?

The behaviour problem group inevitably scored more highly than the control group on many of the ratings of the BSQ because this was how the groups were selected in the first place. All the same, it is interesting to compare the two groups, behavioural item by behavioural item, in order to ascertain which items contributed most to the difference.

In fact, as can be seen from Table 4.2, the problem children showed significantly more difficulties with feeding and sleeping. They were more active, concentrated less well, and were more clinging and less independent.

Table 4.2. *Percentage of children with specific items of problem behaviour from the BSQ definitely present for the behaviour problem and control groups at age 3 years*

Specific items of problem behaviour	Percentage of children with item of problem behaviour definitely present		
	Behaviour problem group (N = 94)	Control group (N = 91)	P^a
Poor appetite	44·7	14·3	<0·001
Faddy eating	30·9	14·3	<0·001
Difficulty settling at night	28·7	11·0	<0·01
Waking at night (at least 3 times a week)	28·7	11·0	<0·01
Sleeping in parents' bed	22·2	7·7	<0·05
Overactive, restless	56·4	8·8	<0·0001
Poor concentration	25·5	1·1	<0·0001
Dependency	17·0	2·2	<0·001
Attention seeking	40·4	2·2	<0·0001
Tempers	22·3	2·2	<0·001
Difficult to control	53·2	2·2	<0·0001
Unhappy mood	17·0	1·1	<0·0001
Worries	6·4	2·2	<0·05
Fears	21·3	6·7	<0·01
Relations with siblings	29·8	6·7	<0·0001
Relations with peers	24·5	1·1	<0·0001
Soiling (once a week or more)	23·6	15·4	N.S.
Recent onset soiling	8·5	2·2	N.S.
Night wetting (at least 3 nights a week)	48·9	33·3	N.S.
Recent onset night wetting	6·4	3·3	N.S.
Day wetting (once a week or more)	31·9	25·3	N.S.
Recent onset day wetting	3·2	4·4	N.S.
Thumb sucking	27·0	16·5	N.S.
Nail biting	12·9	9·9	N.S.

[a]Significance level of chi-square test, d.f. = 1.

They were more difficult and disobedient, flew into tempers more often, and were more often worried, miserable and fearful. They got on less well with their siblings and with other children. However, they did not wet themselves by day or night or soil themselves to a significantly greater degree although the differences in night wetting approached a significant level. They did not suck their thumbs or bite their nails more, and there were many specific fears such as fear of the dark and of strangers which they did not show to significant excess. This supports the view of those who have held that many isolated habits and specific fears are not good indicators of emotional disturbance. Over the total population, as we saw in Chapter 3, day and night wetting and soiling were linked to behaviour problems. These differences did not show up when the problem and control groups were contrasted. This could have resulted from the smaller numbers in each group, or from the matching for sex and social class. Broadly speaking, the items on the behaviour check list distinguishing problem from control groups were very similar to those on the BSQ, with wetting and soiling again standing apart as not distinguishing the groups (see Table 4.3).

A further characteristic which distinguished problem from control children was their predisposition to accidents. Seven of the control group, compared to 24 of the problem group, had sustained two or more accidents requiring medical attention.

Details of psychological testing and results obtained from this part of the study are described later in this chapter.

Family background

The parents of the two groups were no different in their ages or length of marriage. They were also similar in educational background, but this is not surprising as they were initially matched for social class. There was no significant difference between the two groups in the degree to which mothers went out to full or part-time work. Size of family did differ, however, with more children in the problem group coming from large families — thirteen of the problem group, compared to seven of the control group, came from families with four or more children. Single parent families were poorly represented in both groups, with only six out of the 185 families intensively investigated coming into this category. It was not therefore possible to investigate differences in this respect. It was possible, however, to examine ordinal position and there was no difference in the birth order of the children in the two groups.

The early upbringing of the parents also did not differ. Parents of children in the problem group had not been significantly more often separated from

Table 4.3. *Percentage of children in the behaviour problem and control groups at three years with specific items of problem behaviour from the behaviour check list definitely present*

Specific items of problem behaviour	Percentage of children with item of problem behaviour definitely present.		
	Behaviour problem group (N = 93)	Control group (N = 91)	P^a
Poor appetite	31·2	12·1	<0·001
Faddy eater	22·6	9·9	<0·05
Difficulty settling at night	19·4	12·1	<0·05
Waking at night	17·2	5·5	<0·01
Sleeping in parents' bed	17·2	3·3	<0·01
Overactive, restless	59·1	23·5	<0·001
Poor concentration	36·6	9·9	<0·001
Dependency	20·4	1·1	<0·0001
Attention seeking	30·4	5·5	<0·0001
Tempers	19·4	5·5	<0·01
Difficult to control	34·4	2·2	<0·0001
Unhappy mood	8·6	4·4	N.S.
Worries	12·9	1·1	<0·01
Fears	8·6	1·1	<0·05
Relations with siblings	1·1	1·1	N.S.
Relations with peers	5·4	1·1	N.S.
Night wetting	41·9	31·9	N.S.
Day wetting	16·1	18·9	N.S.
Soiling	14·0	9·9	N.S.

^{a}Significance level of chi-square test, d.f. = 1.

their parents in childhood and they did not report a significantly harsher upbringing. Further, the physical health of the parents in the two groups was similar — the great majority of the parents had no serious problems with their own physical health.

By contrast, differences were marked in relation to mother's mental health. The mothers were asked questions about a variety of psychological symptoms including depressive mood, anxiety, suicidal feeling, fears and worries, irritability, energy, appetite and weight loss.

They were also asked to complete a modified form of the Cornell medical index (CMI) (Rutter *et al.*, 1970), in which they were asked to give Yes–No answers on a questionnaire comprising 24 items tapping anxiety, depression and psychosomatic symptoms to give a "Malaise score". The mothers of the problem group revealed more psychological distress than control mothers in most of these measures. Thirty-six of the problem group mothers scored six or more on the modified CMI compared to 18 in the control group — a significant difference. Further, a higher proportion of the problem group mothers were rated as showing some degree of psychiatric disorder on the basis of their symptomatology — 37 of the problem group had at least a mild psychiatric disorder compared to 24 of the control group. The high rate of psychiatric disorder — mainly depression and anxiety — in the control group (24·4%) of mothers of non-disturbed three-year-old children should be noted.

Once again these figures gain meaning with illustrative examples of criteria used to rate different levels of severity of depression. The following three randomly selected examples of maternal depression may be helpful in this respect.

(a) Mild depression and anxiety

Mrs C. is normally cheerful, but since she saw her brother-in-law drown a few months previously she has felt low in spirit and often cries. She cannot concentrate or get on with her work and is reluctant to go out. She finds it difficult to get off to sleep. She has palpitations at night. Her appetite is poor and she has lost weight. Malaise score = 1

(b) Moderate depression

Mrs E. was in tears almost throughout the interview, and made numerous self-deprecatory remarks. She is a worrier especially about the children and does not like being separated from them. She insists on taking her child to school. She has been unwell and has lost two stone in weight. She is in poor physical health, having suffered from pneumonia twice in the last year and also sciatica. She has "menopausal" symptoms. She generally feels unwell and lacking in energy. She cannot enjoy life and is irritable all the time. She is taking sleeping tablets because she cannot get off to sleep and lies awake all night. She often wakes up feeling anxious with her heart thumping. She feels chronically anxious without knowing why and cannot understand her own level of anxiety. She fears a car crash all the time. She has stopped wanting to do anything or to go out. She feels everything is too much for her, often cries and wants to be alone. She spends a lot of time on her own and the father does most of the housework and child care. Her spirits lift only occasionally. She has had serious suicidal thoughts for about two weeks over the past year. She used to be energetic and happy. Malaise score = 13.

(c) Marked depression

Mrs D. is very depressed and totally apathetic. She cannot be bothered to do anything or look after herself. She has attended a psychiatrist in the past, but stopped attending 18 months ago because she was not improving. She was not able to participate in the interview and the father talked for her. She could not concentrate and has no confidence in herself. She is not relating to her husband or the children. She cries when the father goes to work, but is unable to talk about her problem. She is very irritable and shouts a good deal. She cannot get on with her work, and does not want to see people or go out. She spends a great deal of time sleeping. Clinical rating — Marked depression. Malaise score = 2.

Criticism and hostility towards the child by both mother and father were much more commonly present in the problem than in the control group. Thus 32 of the problem group mothers and 25 of the fathers showed a moderate or marked level of antagonism towards the child compared to eight of the mothers and eight of the fathers in the control group — highly significant differences. Similarly, control group mothers and fathers both looked warmer and sounded more affectionate when talking of their children. Thirty-five mothers and 20 fathers showed little or no warmth towards the children in the problem group compared to nine mothers and eight fathers in the control group (see Table 4.4.).

These higher levels of criticism and hostility were reflected in the amount of negative feelings and actions towards the child described by the mothers as having occurred over the previous few weeks. Thus, problem group mothers significantly more often described themselves as showing frequent irritability, smacking their children and having worrying thoughts of loss of control towards their children. Thirty-eight of the problem group mothers compared to fourteen of the controls either feared loss of control or had actually lost control of themselves with the child over the previous month. A similar picture was obtained for fathers, although here there were significant differences in irritability and smacking, but not fear of or actual loss of control.

An attempt was also made to assess the quality of the parental marriage by noting especially the warmth and affection with which the wife spoke of her husband, the positive remarks she made about him, the level of satisfaction she showed with the part he played in child rearing and household tasks, the number of activities jointly undertaken and the presence or absence of quarrels and arguments. "Good" marriages were characterized by warmth, affection, mutual satisfaction and a high level of shared activities, and "bad" marriages by an absence of these qualities and a high level of rows and

Table 4.4. *Differences between behaviour problem and control groups in family relationships at age 3 years*

Adverse family relationship	Percentage of children with adverse family relationship		
	Behaviour problem group (N = 94)	Control group (N = 91)	P^a
Mother moderately/markedly critical of child	34·0	8·9	<0·001
Mother shows little or no warmth to child	37·2	10·0	<0·001
Mother is irritated by child more than once a day	51·1	21·1	<0·001
Mother frequently fears or actually loses control of self with child	40·4	15·4	<0·001
Mother smacks child more than once a day	34·0	11·1	<0·001
Father moderately/markedly critical of child	27·2	8·9	<0·01
Father shows little or no warmth to child	21·7	8·9	<0·05
Father irritated by child at least once a day	33·7	6·7	<0·001
Father fears or actually loses control of self with child	14·3	7·7	N.S.
Father smacks child at least once a day	15·2	3·3	<0·05
Poor or very poor marital relationship	40·3	18·9	<0·01
Frequently disagree over punishing child	28·3	11·2	<0·01
Parents punish the child equally often	22·8	38·2	<0·05

^{a}Significance level of chi-square test, d.f. = 1.

disagreements. The problem group of children showed a higher level of "bad" marriages with 40% of the mothers describing marriages of this type compared to 19% of the control group mothers. It should be emphasized that the judgement whether a marriage was "bad" or not was made by the interviewer on the basis of factual information provided by the mother together with direct observations made by the interviewer of the mother's demeanour and manner of talking about different aspects of the marital relationship. Judgements of this type have been validated by follow up studies demonstrating the much higher rates of subsequent divorce and separation in marriages rated "poor" (Quinton *et al.*, 1976). Some random examples of our marital ratings are provided below.

(a) Marital relationship — very poor

The parents disagree over control especially over issues such as bed-time, sweets and general behaviour. Mrs G. is mainly left to get on with things. She disagrees with the way decisions are made in the family — father has made them in the past and mother is now trying to have "her own identity". They argue weekly over money, mother's work, and her need to feel more independent. Father has beaten her up on one occasion. Mrs G. is dissatisfied with his help and is unable to confide in him or talk things over with him. They do not enjoy each other's company and prefer to be with others. They have thought of getting a divorce for a few months and are now seeing a social worker. Mrs G. was very critical of her husband and showed no warmth towards him. Marital summary score = 0.*

(b) Marital relationship — average

Mr and Mrs H. disagree sometimes over the children and money. However, in general they decide things together. They have arguments less than monthly. Mrs H. would like more help with the children, but she is generally satisfied with the help she gets in the house. They can confide and talk things over together. Mrs H. is satisfied with the amount she goes out with her husband and they both enjoy going out together. Marital summary score = 12.

(c) Marital relationship — good

Mrs I. made many positive remarks about her husband, describing him for example as a "very patient man". She had no critical comments about him. The parents decide things jointly about their son as well as household and financial matters. They row less often than once a month. Mr I. helps a lot with the boy together with household tasks, and Mrs I. is satisfied with his help. They confide with each other and talk things over together. Mr I. goes out weekly to an evening class, but his wife is quite happy not to go out alone.

*Marital summary score less than 9 is indicative of an unsatisfactory marital relationship.

They rarely go out together but enjoy each other's company at home. Marital summary score = 16.

The poor quality of marriage in the problem group was reflected in aspects of child rearing such as discipline. Thus 26 of the problem group parents compared to 10 of the control group disagreed frequently over who should punish the child and how the child should be punished. There was also a greater tendency in the problem group for punishment to be administered more by one parent than another. Twenty-one of the problem group compared to 34 of the control group said that punishment was administered equally by both parents — a significant difference.

Stress on the family

The effects of stress have already been discussed on the basis of information obtained in the screening interview in the previous chapter. Here we examine stress based on the same information but comparing groups matched for sex and social class. As described earlier, factual information was obtained on the number of stresses acting upon the family in the year prior to interview. These ratings were not based on whether the informant perceived an event as stressful, but on the basis of objective accounts which the interviewer then rated depending on whether the criteria for the rating of a particular stress had been met. Thus, for example, housing stress was rated as present if accommodation was unduly cramped, or if part of it was uninhabitable due to damp etc. Ratings were made on stress produced by a recent birth in the family, the death of a relative or close friend, the death of a family pet, physical illness in a close relative or family friend, psychological disturbance in a member of the family, financial hardship, a serious problem related to father or mother's work, housing problems, quarrels with neighbours, legal problems, serious accidents to family or friends, and problems with other children.

The mean number of stresses was significantly greater in the problem compared to the control group (2·1 compared to 1·8), but it is perhaps more instructive to look at the areas of stress in which the two groups differed. These seemed particularly concerned with relationships and psychological disturbance rather than with material deprivation. Thus, the only individual stresses in which significant differences were found were quarrels with neighbours, difficulties with the other children and psychological disturbance in a member of the family. The problem group was indeed more likely to be stressed by material deprivation such as problems with housing, but because of the smaller numbers involved than in the findings presented in the previous chapter with the 705 sample, the differences were not present to a statistically significant degree.

Although the relationship of maternal employment to stress is unclear it may be appropriate to add here that the proportion of mothers going out to work in the two groups was almost identical — 27·0% of mothers in the control group were working at least part-time, and 26·6% of the mothers in the problem group.

Contacts with family and friends

These were examined separately in relation to the child and the parent and negative findings were obtained in both cases. Problem children appeared to have just as much contact with relatives and friends as the controls. Their range of contacts was also generally wide — in both groups over 70% had had social contact with three or more children outside play group over the previous month. As indicated below, the quality of social relationships was less satisfactory in the problem group, but there seem to have been no differences in the opportunity for such relationships to occur.

Similarly, there were no significant differences between the groups in the contacts the mothers had with close relatives or friends. Sixty-nine per cent of control group mothers saw their own mothers once a week compared to 60% in the problem group — a non-significant difference. There was also no difference in the degree to which mothers felt they could turn to close kin and friends for support in an emergency. Thus, although many of the problem mothers may well have felt more isolated because of the fact that they had to cope with a disturbed child and more frequently had signs of emotional disturbance and an unhappy marriage themselves, there is no evidence that they were any more socially isolated than control group mothers. Their social needs may have been greater but their social resources were at least no fewer in number.

Psychological testing

During the intensive interview, the parents were asked for permission for the project psychologist (J.S.) to come to the home to administer a battery of psychological tests. Subsequently testing was carried out in the child's home, nearly always within one month of the child's third birthday. The tester did not know whether the child had been selected as showing a behaviour problem or as a control.

In about half the testing sessions, which usually lasted 50 minutes to an hour the mother was present, and in the remainder the child was seen alone. In general good co-operation was obtained from the children while they were being tested.

The tests used and the test–retest reliabilities obtained with a retest interval of three weeks are provided in Table 4.5. These reliabilities were obtained prior to the main study by JS using a sample of 60 three-year-old children living in Waltham Forest. It will be seen that they comprise the English picture vocabulary test, and sub-tests taken from the Reynell developmental language scales (RDLS), the Illinois test of psycholinguistic ability (ITPA), the Hiskey–Nebraska test (H–N), and the Griffiths mental development scale (GMDS). It will be seen also that two of the ITPA tests (auditory and visual reception) showed low reliabilities and findings from these tests will not be reported further. The remaining test–retest reliability coefficients were regarded as sufficiently high to warrant placing some confidence in the results obtained, though it will be noted that the levels of

Table 4.5. *Test–retest reliabilities of the scores on the test battery for a sample of 3-year-old children (N = 60)*

Test	Reliability	P^a
English picture vocabulary test	0·42	<0·05
Reynell developmental language scales		
Expressive scale structure	0·47	<0·05
Vocabulary	0·30	N.S.
Content	0·80	<0·01
Total Scale	0·76	<0·01
Illinois test of psycholinguistic abilities		
Auditory reception	0·21	N.S.
Visual reception	0·38	<0·05
Auditory sequential memory	0·44	<0·05
Hiskey–Nebraska test		
Memory for colour	0·66	<0·01
Griffiths mental development scales		
Scale D — Hand eye coordination	0·70	<0·01
Scale E — Performance	0·78	<0·01

[a]Significance level of Pearson product moment correlation

reliability, though statistically significant, were sometimes, as in the RDLS Vocabulary Scale, disappointingly low.

In addition to these standardized tests, the child's behaviour was also assessed during the session on 14 three- or five-point scales devised by JS. These were test–task understanding, rapport, guessing, speed of response, spontaneous speech, speech directed to test–task, task orientation, motor activity, fidgetiness, persevering in response, need for tester praise, need for parental contact, habits and mood. Test–retest reliabilities on these scales were very high.

General ability — behaviour problem and control groups

The English picture vocabulary test (EPVT) is a test of verbal comprehension or vocabulary: the Griffiths scale D (a test of hand–eye coordination) and the Griffiths scale E (a test of non–verbal perceptual and perceptuo-motor ability) can be regarded as tests of general ability.

Table 4.6. *Comparison of the mean scores for the behaviour problem and control groups on developmental tests for 3 years*

| Developmental tests | Behaviour problem group | | | Control group | | | |
	N	Mean	Standard deviation	N	Mean	Standard deviation	P^a
Age at testing in months	94	36·2	0·7	91	36·2	0·7	N.S.
EPVT standard score	91	98·2	11·7	90	103·3	10·3	0·002
Griffiths scale D DQ	93	105·2	16·7	90	111.3	15·8	0·012
Griffiths scale E DQ	93	104·7	18·4	91	107·7	14·6	N.S.

^{a}Significance level of *t*-test

From Table 4.6 it can be seen that the behaviour problem group did less well than the control group on all three of these, and significantly less well on the EPVT and Griffiths scale D. When findings were examined separately for boys and girls, it was seen that the significant differences were confined to the boys, with smaller and less consistent differences occurring in girls (see Table 4.7).

It will be recalled that children in the problem group differed in their test

Table 4.7. *Comparison of mean scores for the behaviour problem and control groups separately for boys and girls on developmental tests at 3 years*

Developmental tests	Behaviour problem group			Control group			P^a
	N	Mean	Standard deviation	N	Mean	Standard deviation	
Boys							
Age at testing in months	52	36·3	0·7	50	36·3	0·9	N.S.
EPVT standard score	50	96·7	11·7	49	103·1	11·2	0·007
Griffiths scale D DQ	52	101·7	16·2	50	109·1	13·9	0·015
Griffiths scale E DQ	52	101·6	18·2	50	107·1	13·5	N.S.
Girls							
Age at testing in months	42	36·2	0·7	41	36·1	0·6	N.S.
EPVT standard score	41	100·1	11·7	41	103·6	9·2	N.S.
Griffiths scale D DQ	41	109·7	16·5	40	114·1	17·7	N.S.
Griffiths scale E DQ	41	108·7	18·0	41	108·5	16·0	N.S.

^{a}Significance level of t-test

behaviour, as well as in their test scores, from those in the control group. We wondered whether the low scores might be a result of artificial contamination of test performance by disturbed behaviour. In order to test for this possibility, a more complex statistical technique was performed in which two-way analyses of variance were calculated with control group v. behaviour problem group as one factor, and each of the ratings of test behaviour in turn as the other main factor. The main factor of behaviour problem group membership remains significant when each aspect of test behaviour was used as the other main factor, and there were no significant interactions in any of the analyses of variance. At this age, therefore, there was no support for the notion that disturbed behaviour was significantly affecting the performance of the child in the intelligence testing.

Developmental delays in the behaviour problem and control group

In addition to these comparisons between the two groups in their mean test scores, we also wished to determine whether the proportion of children with significant developmental delays was different in the two groups. Developmental delays are of two types — they may be specific with only one aspect of the child's functioning showing slowness of maturation, or they may be more general. We looked at the proportions of children with two types of general delay — in language and in non-verbal ability. We also looked at the rates of "specific" language delay: children in whom language was significantly less developed than their non-verbal abilities.

We defined children as having a delay by ascertaining whether their score fell below an arbitrary cut-off point on the test in question. This cut-off point was determined by examining the distribution of scores in a representative sample of children drawn from the general population (see Chapter 6), and the criterion point was taken as that below which roughly the lowest 10% of the population (i.e. the lowest decile) fell. Three types of maturational delay were thus defined:

1. *Low IQ.* The child was said to show low IQ if the developmental quotient on either the test of hand–eye coordination or the performance scale of the Griffiths mental development scales was below 85.

2. *General language delay.* The child's measured language age was compared to its chronological age. If the language age on the Expressive Scale of the Reynell developmental language scales (RDLS) was six months or more behind the chronological age, the child was regarded as showing mild general language delay, and if twelve months or more behind as showing severe language delay.

3. *Specific language delay.* A more complex statistical technique was used to define this group. A predicted language age taking into account the child's chronological age and general IQ (Griffiths performance DQ) was obtained by calculating a regression equation. The child's observed language age on the Expressive Scale of the RDLS was then compared to the predicted language age. If the observed language age was more than six months below the predicted language age the child was regarded as showing mild specific language delay, and if twelve months or more below as showing severe specific language delay. It should be noted that the Reynell developmental language scale is standardized separately for boys and girls.

It can be seen from Table 4.8 that there was no difference between the groups in the rates of low IQ, either in the total group or when the boys and girls were separately examined. The behaviour problem group did, however, contain a significantly higher proportion of children with both mild and severe general language delay, and the differences were significant for both boys and girls when severe general language delay was considered. Specific language delay was also more common in the behaviour problem group, but this was only significant within the case of mild specific delay. The differences between the groups were more marked in the boys than in the girls.

It was not possible to examine sex differences in rates of delay in other ways (e.g. to compare rates of boys in the control group with rates shown by

Table 4.8. *Percentage of the total groups, boys and girls, in the behaviour problem and control groups showing various developmental delays at 3 years*

Developmental delay	Behaviour problem group	Control group	P^a
Total	N = 94	N = 91	
Mild specific language delay	47·9	30·8	<0·05
Severe specific language delay	20·2	12·1	N.S.
Mild general language delay	52·9	31·9	<0·01
Severe general language delay	37·2	12·1	<0·001
Low developmental quotient (DQ)	19·4	11·1	N.S.
Boys	N = 52	N = 50	
Mild specific language delay	46·2	24·0	<0·05
Severe specific language delay	21·2	10·0	N.S.
Mild general language delay	50·0	30·0	N.S.
Severe general language delay	36·5	10·0	<0·01
Low developmental quotient (DQ)	25·0	10·0	N.S.
Girls	N = 42	N = 41	
Mild specific language delay	50·0	39·0	N.S.
Severe specific language delay	19·0	14·6	N.S.
Mild general language delay	54·8	34·1	N.S.
Severe general language delay	38·1	14·6	<0·05
Low developmental quotient (DQ)	12·2	12·5	N.S.

[a]Significance level of chi-square test, d.f. = 1

girls in this group) because the scales are standardized separately in the two sexes.

It will be recalled that the mean scores of the two groups were significantly different, and we wondered whether this mean difference might have been produced by the presence of a small number of highly deviant children. However, when we excluded children from both groups with severe language delay as defined above, the mean differences between the groups on the EPVT and Griffiths scales were still significant, so this is an improbable explanation.

Preliminary conclusions

Our group of problem behaviour children was compared with a comparison group after social class and sex and been controlled. It was therefore unlikely that great differences in material conditions between the groups would have been found. Bearing this in mind, what were the main conclusions which could be drawn from this comparison?

It seems that there is a wide range of factors which distinguish families with a disturbed child. Firstly, despite our attempts to control for social class by matching for parental occupation, the disturbed group nevertheless contained more evidence of material deprivation. Housing and financial stresses were commoner amongst the disturbed group. Secondly, the disturbed children came from larger families. Other differences in family structure or parental background were, however, not found. The parents were of similar age to parents of non-disturbed children and their level of education was comparable. There was no tendency for the disturbed group to have mothers who were more or less likely to be working.

A major difference between the groups was in the area of family relationships. The marital relationships of the parents in the disturbed group were distinctly less harmonious and the children were subjected to more criticism and hostility and enjoyed less affection and warmth. Their mothers were more likely to show signs of psychological disorder especially depression and anxiety. Few fathers demonstrated signs of psychological problems, and although there was a tendency for them to occur to a greater extent in the group of disturbed children, the differences were not great.

Relationships between factors associated with disturbance

In order to examine the circumstances in which adverse factors exerted their major effects, a different statistical technique was used — the coefficient of contingency, C^c (Everitt, 1974). This coefficient provides a measure of the size of the association between two variables. In contrast to the χ^2 test which is a measure of the significance of the difference in the proportions of two or more groups in the degree to which they share a particular characteristic, the magnitude of C^c is not dependent on the numbers in the groups. Thus coefficients of contingency for groups of different sizes can be compared. In our study we used C^c to compare the magnitude of the association with behaviour disturbance in eight different factors.

Table 4.9. *Association measured by the contingency coefficient, between eight major adverse factors and the presence or absence of behaviour problems at 3 years*

| | Percentage of children with adverse factor | | | |
| | Behaviour problem group (N = 94) | | Control group (N = 91) | Contingency coefficient C^c | P^a |
Adverse factor					
	N	%	N	%	
Marriage poor or very poor	37	40	17	19	0·23	<0·01
Mother at least somewhat critical	32	34	8	9	0·29	<0·001
Mother not showing marked warmth	35	37	9	10	0·30	<0·0001
Two or more stresses in the family over past year	53	56	47	52	0·05	N.S.
Housing other than owner occupied	56	60	55	60	0·01	N.S.
Below average expressive language scores	50	57	34	40	0·17	<0·05
Below average performance DQ	53	57	43	47	0·10	N.S.
Mother's mental status rated as at least dubious	37	39	24	26	0·14	N.S. (0·08)

[a]Significance level of chi-square test value on which the contingency coefficient is based, d.f. = 1

Table 4.9. shows the size of the C^c for each of the eight variables in their association with the presence of a behaviour problem. These eight variables were chosen either because of their likely importance or because, using the test of significance between proportions (χ^2), they showed the most marked links with the presence of a behaviour problem.

It can be seen that, using the C^c, the statistical procedure we are introducing at this point, three variables — the quality of the marriage, the mother's demonstrated warmth to the child, and the mother's demonstrated criticism of the child, showed the greatest level of association. C^c for these three variables ranged between 0·23 and 0·30. It should at this point be noted that the maximum possible value of C^c is in the region of 0·7. This suggests that although other factors, such as the mental state of the mother and environmental stress operating on the child and the family, are associated with the presence of the behaviour problem, the strongest associations are with those variables reflecting relationships in the family.

Using comparisons of C^c it was possible for us to examine in which circumstances the variables exerted their greatest effects. The results are presented in Table 4.10.

Table 4.10. *Association measured by the contingency coefficient, between seven main dichotomized variables and the presence or absence of behaviour problems at 3 years when each other variable and additional dichotomized variables are held constant in turn*

Values of variables held constant	*Main variables*						
	Sex	Social class	Marriage	Criticism	Warmth	Language	Mother Disturbed
Boys	—	03	18	24[a]	19	12	11
Girls	—	01	28[a]	36[a]	42[a]	23	17
Manual	01	—	24[a]	29[a]	33[a]	19[a]	13
Non-manual	02	—	18	30	19	05	12
Poor marriage	10	02	—	17	22	16	02
Good marriage	03	02	—	31[a]	28[a]	10	12
Mother critical	17	07	00	—	16	20	17
Mother not critical	04	01	23[a]	—	22[a]	19[a]	11
Mother not warm	25	08	07	15	—	04	01
Mother warm	09	03	21[a]	19[a]	—	16	15
Low expressive language	01	05	26	21	26[a]	—	08
High expressive language	10	06	18[a]	40[a]	31[a]	—	17
Mother disturbed	06	00	16	33[a]	24	10	—
Mother not disturbed	02	01	23[a]	26[a]	33[a]	19	—
High stress	01	02	24[a]	35[a]	36[a]	24[a]	21[a]
Low stress	01	04	20	22	22	06	02
Housing not owned	01	08	32[a]	33[a]	34[a]	23[a]	12
Housing owned	00	06	06	23	25	05	17
Low performance score	04	03	24[a]	19	26[a]	17	07
High performance score	05	04	20	34[a]	36[a]	11	20

[a]$P < 0.05$ for the chi-square test value on which the contingency coefficient is based, d.f. $= 1$

In this Table C^c is shown for each of seven variables when other factors are controlled. This is achieved by dividing the children into two groups, "favourable and "unfavourable" for all the eight factors, together with two additional factors, sex and social class. It is now possible to determine, by examining the size of C^c, whether the three major variables together with four others we have examined are more closely associated in "favourable" or "unfavourable" conditions of the other factors. For example it can be seen in Table 4.10 that the quality of the parental marriage is more closely associated with the presence of a behaviour problem in manual-class children ($C^c = 0.24$) than in middle-class children ($C^c = 0.18$). The size of the association is significantly greater than chance in the former ($P < 0.05$) but not the latter.

When the results of this analysis are examined overall, some of the results are surprisingly clear cut. All of the family relationship variables are most closely associated with disturbance in the presence of relative social adversity. Thus they are all more strongly linked to the presence of a behaviour problem when the child comes from a working-class family, has a high stress score, and is in relatively less privileged housing. In all cases the size of the association is statistically significant whereas when these social circumstances are "favourable", the associations are not significant. Adverse family relationships may therefore (and the findings are open to other interpretations) exert their maximum effect in the presence of social disadvantage.

By contrast, the links between the inter-personal variables themselves are less clear cut. The quality of the parental marriage is most strongly related to the presence of behaviour problems when the mother is relatively warm and uncritical towards her child and does not have a mental health problem, whilst warmth and criticism are rather inconsistently related to each other and to the mother's mental state.

When the links between family relationships and the level of development of the child are examined the results again become clearer. Absence of maternal warmth and high levels of criticism are most closely linked when the child's level of development is relatively advanced, whereas the marital relationship seems most important when there is relative developmental delay. Finally, girls are clearly more affected by adverse emotional relationships within the family than are boys.

Overall therefore a picture of the inter-linking of the variables has been built up by this statistical analysis. It suggests that the most marked adverse effects on behaviour are exerted by adverse relationships within the family and that these are more closely linked than social or developmental factors. On the other hand the major effects of adverse family relationships are seen in situations of social adversity — when families are stressed in other ways.

The results also suggest that girls are more vulnerable than boys in their response to adverse family relationships. By contrast, whether the child is developmentally relatively advanced in his language and other non-verbal functions does not seem to affect consistently the size of the association with the family relationship variables.

Summary

In this chapter we have examined the results obtained when a detailed comparison is made between a group of disturbed three-year-olds and a non-disturbed group matched for sex and social class. The groups differed over a wide range of behaviour and management problems as well as in their predisposition to accidents. The family background of the disturbed group was characterized especially by disharmonious parental marriages and by negative attitudes from parents to child. There were strong associations especially in boys between behavioural difficulties and both language and general intellectual development. Detailed analysis of the variables associated with disturbed behaviour suggested that while distorted family relationships were the factors most closely related to behaviour problems, the effect of these was significantly greater in girls than in boys and in children of both sexes living in socially disadvantaged circumstances.

In the next chapter we shall describe the implications of these findings for furthering our understanding of the causes of these problems.

5 The Pre-school Study: Implications

Prevalence

(1) Behaviour problems

A number of previous studies have examined rates of problem behaviour in the pre-school period. In spite of differences in methods and in criteria used to define the presence of a problem, our own findings are generally in line with those found by others. Probably the most comprehensive comparable study is that reported by MacFarlane *et al.* (1954), known as the Berkeley longitudinal study or the University of California Guidance Study. In this investigation, which will be referred to in more detail in discussion of our own longitudinal findings, the parents of 98 children were interviewed when the children were three years old. As an example of their findings, 18% of boys and 22% of girls were restless in their sleep, 37% of boys and 33% of girls were thought to show excessive activity, 69% of boys and 63% of girls had moderately frequent temper tantrums. Roberts and Schoellkopf (1951), in a group of 783 two-and-a-half-year-old children attending a well-baby clinic, found 29·6% had disturbed sleep, 10% were finicky with their food, 11·9% had bowel training problems, 40% were wet by day, and 43% were wet by night. In a population aged four years in a town in the Midlands in the UK, Newson and Newson (1970) found 30% of working class and 18% of middle-class children still wetting at least occasionally, and 14% to be regarded by their mothers as finicky eaters. Coleman *et al.* (1977), using the behaviour screening questionnaire devised by ourselves and described earlier in this book, found three-year-old boys living in the East End of London to have a mean behaviour score of 7·5 and girls 8·6. Thirty-five percent of these children were wet by night and 17% by day. Twenty-nine per cent had temper tantrums, 41% worried excessively and 28% were thought to be over-dependent. The findings presented on the rates of behaviour problems in our own sample are therefore rather comparable to those others have found, although in some respects, probably because different criteria are used, they are quite different. This suggests we were not dealing with an atypical population, nor that our methods were greatly out of line with those others have employed. Indeed, a cross-cultural replication of our procedure (Earls, 1980) has shown that the overall prevalence rates of behaviour problems as well as of individual items of behaviour are very similar in a rural American population.

However, our interest in this part of the study lay less in the individual items of problem behaviour than in identifying the proportion of children who might be regarded as having an accumulation of problems which, by virtue of their extent and severity, could be regarded as of such concern as to require attention from professional sources. In this respect our prevalence data for the rate of disorders are most relevant. The fact that 15% of three-year-olds turned out to have mild problems, 6·2% problems of moderate severity, 1·1% severe problems, seems to us to suggest a widespread and hitherto largely unrecognized source of suffering involving young children and their families. The seriousness with which society should view these figures depends, in large measure, on the impact made by the illustrative descriptions we have provided in Chapter 3. If these are seen as unremarkable and readily acceptable examples of child behaviour, then clearly no legitimate reason for attempting prevention or intervention exists. The figures may, however, be seen, as we see them, as reflecting a poor quality of existence for many children and parents. They call for serious consideration of the circumstances in which families with young children are living and how such distressing circumstances could be ameliorated.

(2) Maternal depression

Our findings in terms of rates of mental distress in mothers suggest a strikingly high rate — approximately 30% of mothers have a significant mental health problem. At the time our study was undertaken such a figure would have been regarded as unrealistically high. However, other work, undertaken at round about the same time, especially by George Brown and his co-workers (Brown and Harris, 1978), has suggested roughly similar figures, and indeed has confirmed that, although rates of depression and anxiety are generally high in women, they are especially so in mothers of young children. Rates appear to be highest where there are three children under the age of 14 years, and at least one child under the age of six years.

(3) Language

The rates of language delay we found are in general somewhat higher than those found in other surveys, especially when estimates are based on referrals made to speech therapists. However, Randall *et al.* (1974), studying a normal population in another part of North London, also found a high but somewhat lower rate in a general population of three-year-olds. Kolvin *et al.* (1979), by contrast, found a distinctly higher rate (4%) in a population of three-year-olds, using a less stringent definition, viz. "failure to use three or more words strung together to make some sort of sense" — a judgement made on maternal report. It is likely that the reason for the differences lies in the different criteria used to identify a language problem, and further work may clarify which standards are most appropriate to apply.

Screening

(1) Behaviour

The behaviour check-list (BCL) is a simple screening device which takes the mother only a few minutes to complete and could easily be administered by health visitors, clinic doctors or general practitioners. It is not as sensitive or as specific as the BSQ, but could nevertheless be used as part of a rapid clinical assessment in the individual child, and results from it could indicate whether further enquiries about the child's behaviour should be made. The behaviour screening questionnaire (BSQ) is a more time-consuming procedure, taking 30 to 45 minutes to administer. It involves more experience to administer and to interpret. It is, however, a reliable and valid instrument and produces very few false negative responses, and none at all if moderate or severe problems are taken as a criterion. Unlike the BCL, which would miss a small number, the BSQ would identify all moderate and severe problems. The BSQ appears most suitable for research and training procedures and could serve an especially useful function in other survey work.

(2) Language

Using two relatively simple screening tests, which again could easily be applied by health visitors and doctors, it is possible to identify most children (83%) whose language is markedly delayed at three years. Our work suggests that any child who scores less than two points on the screening test, cannot be tested, or is reported by the parents not to speak in three-word phrases, should be referred for further assessment and, if necessary, further treatment. If screening procedures for behaviour problems accompany these language tests, it is likely from our findings that virtually complete coverage of children with language delay will be achieved.

Causation of behaviour and emotional problems

(1) The wider environment

The association between council housing and particularly high-rise flat accommodation, and the presence of behaviour problems, draws attention to the possible importance of aspects of the urban environment in the development of such problems in young children. It is of course possible, as we have already indicated, that families in poor and unattractive housing have been selectively placed in such accommodation because they are showing social problems which make housing departments unlikely to find better facilities for them. It could be the social problems therefore, rather than the poor housing, which are responsible for the higher rates of behaviour problems, and our data do not allow us to rule out this possibility. Nevertheless, our findings are of interest for others have suggested that flat-living is unfavourable to the upbringing of young children (Stewart, 1970; Jephcott, 1971).

Our impression, linked with the work of others, suggests various reasons why flat-living might be associated with high rates of behaviour problems. The fact that, at least as far as children from non-manual classes were concerned, the association was limited to boys whose expectation of physical activity was likely to be higher, suggests that constriction of space may be important. High-rise accommodation is usually lacking in accessible space for play, especially important in young children who need close supervision, and the absence of such space for active play might well result in boys being more adversely affected than girls. A more indirect effect might occur through the impact of living in high-rise accommodation on the mother's mental state. In an earlier investigation (Richman, 1974), as well as in the analysis of data derived from the present study (Richman, 1977), we have found an association between type of housing and maternal depression, with higher rates of depression in women living in council estates, especially blocks of flats. It seems likely that flat-living, with the extra difficulties this brings in the lack of opportunity for casual social contacts across the street or over the garden fence results not infrequently in more social isolation and depression than is the case with other types of housing.

Of course flat-living is not by any means necessarily associated with high rates of disturbance. In many large cities in developing countries, for example, it is in the low-level shanty town areas rather than in the rather more prosperous blocks of residential accommodation that psychological problems are likely to be particularly prevalent. Further, for centuries, middle-class children in most countries in continental Europe have been reared in flats without apparent serious difficulties. Clearly other factors must be involved, and we would suspect that the expectations which British parents have of a separate garden and a personal, private entrance onto a street may be of importance.

It seems probable that both high rates of behaviour problems in children and the high delinquency rates with which they are associated (Gath *et al.*, 1977) are likely to be due to factors contributing to the low morale found on some large council estates. The relative absence of a sense of community, linked to the presence of large areas of poorly maintained public space, is likely to lead to vandalism of property and, at any rate, on some estates, a sense of insecurity amongst inhabitants which will militate against the provision of the settled atmosphere needed for the rearing of young children (Yancey, 1971; Clarke, 1978).

(2) The marital relationship

We also found that the quality of the marital relationship was associated with the presence of behaviour problems in the children we studied. In the marriages we rated as poor, there was likely to be a good deal of open quarrelling or tension between the parents which the children would probably have witnessed on a number of occasions. Given these criteria, it is perhaps notable that even in our control group, nearly one in five children has parents whose marriage was rated as poor, and not surprising that with problem children the rates are nearly twice as high (37%). Although our marital ratings were based largely on mothers' accounts, other work (e.g. by Brown and Rutter, 1966) suggests that fathers' accounts of the marriage usually agree rather well with mothers'. Further, the predictive validity of the ratings made in this way has been confirmed by follow-up studies, especially that of Quinton *et al.* (1976) and our own reported later in this volume.

Various ways in which unhappy marital relationships can lead to disorders in children are fairly obvious. Young children are likely to be confused or frustrated by inconsistencies in care when their parents cannot agree how to handle them. They may be involved in parental conflict with, for example, a father provoking disturbed behaviour in a child and then accusing his wife of being unable to cope with it. Alternatively, children may be treated as allies in marital disputes, with a mother, for example, inappropriately coming to rely on her child for emotional support because her husband refuses or is unable to provide it. Parents may also act as inappropriate models of behaviour — the shouting and screaming of instructions and commands comes for some children to be the only model of communication that is available for them to imitate, and it is not surprising if, in these circumstances, they show themselves unable to communicate in more socially acceptable ways. Others (e.g. Brown and Harris, 1978) have found that the lack of a confidant, whether spouse or cohabitee, predisposes women to depression when stressful events occur, and it is likely that, in our families too, this had an important effect mediated through the mother's mental state.

(3) Maternal attitudes and mental state

We consider together the effects of maternal attitude and mental state because so often mental state reflects attitudes and vice versa. The overwhelming number of women who showed a mental health problem in our sample were suffering from deep and prolonged depressive feelings, from excessive anxiety, or from a combination of these. Mental states of this type are commonly characterized by a change in the quality of relationships with others, especially by a tendency to show irritability in mildly frustrating circumstances. Young children, par excellence, are likely to be sources of minor frustration — their demands can easily be seen as excessive and their dependence on help for even small achievements is likely to lead to a woman who is already stretched in her emotional resources becoming intolerant and impatient. Emotional and physical withdrawal represents a further behavioural reaction common in depression, which is likely to have a similar obviously deleterious effect on the mother's attitude to her child. Commonly, women who are suffering from depression and anxiety show an alternating or mixed pattern of excessive irritability and withdrawal.

In our study we found maternal psychiatric status to be much more commonly problematic in our disturbed than in our control group. On the malaise inventory, the self-rating measure of mental distress, the percentage of mothers scoring six or more was 38%, compared with 20% in the control group. Approximately 40% of the problem group mothers had at least a mild psychiatric disorder, compared to 26% in the control group. Problem group mothers were significantly more critical of their children, were irritated by them, feared losing control or actually had lost control of their tempers in dealing with them more frequently, and, in the interview, were less warm when describing their children. The indirect information we have regarding paternal attitudes is, of course, likely to be less valid, but in so far as it can be taken to be worthy of consideration, a similar picture emerges when considering differences between paternal attitudes in the two groups.

An immediate problem which arises in considering the relevance of these findings to a discussion of the causes of childhood behaviour problems is the question of cause and effect. Firstly, there is the problem of validity of the measures involved. Women, when they are describing children who have objectionable behaviour, might well *sound* more critical in interview than women whose child's behaviour was more acceptable, even though there was very little difference between them in life outside the interview situation. Some light may be shed on this problem, and we describe an attempt to do so, by examining the outcome of non-disturbed children whose mothers are nevertheless critical of them. However, even if mothers of problem children are more critical, less warm and more depressed and anxious than mothers of non-problem children, the question still arises as to the direction of the cause or connection. Do angry, unhappy women produce disturbed children or do disturbed children produce anger and unhappiness in their mothers? We consider the child's own contribution to problem situations which arise in a later section, but even at this point it is evident that a single direction of causation is improbable. Again, our follow-up study of non-disturbed children clarifies this issue to some degree.

The mechanics whereby depressed women might engender behaviour problems in their children have been considered by Weissman *et al.* (1971). Using a theoretical framework derived from the work of Parsons and Bales, they divided family roles into two types — instrumental roles which were important in adapting to extra-familial, wider society, and expressive roles concerned with integrative roles and affectional relationships within the family group. They compared a sample of depressed women with a group of normal women drawn from the general population, and compared them in their role performance in both these respects. They found that, while the instrumental role was certainly affected by depression, the greatest differences were found in measures of the expressive functions carried out in relation to spouse and children.

There are various alternative frames of reference for considering the relationship between negative parental attitude, maternal depression and problem behaviour in children. Considering the family as a single unit, the disturbed mother–child relationship can be seen as a malfunctioning system in which, for example, persistent communication from the mother that she is just not coping with her domestic responsibilities may bring out, not increased support from her husband, but a tendency on his part to opt out even further from family responsibilities. Constant maternal irritability may alternate with withdrawal in an increasing and unsuccessful attempt to find a strategy which will elicit emotional support when none is forthcoming. Learning theory provides further types of explanation. Depressed mothers may fail to provide appropriate reinforcement for appropriate behaviour. An irritable mother is likely to reward, and thus reinforce, obnoxious behaviour with attention, whereas she may feel that acceptable behaviour is only her due and ignore it, thus failing to make it more likely to persist and recur. Finally, there are theories which put emphasis on the need for satisfactory "transactional" relationships between mothers and young children with a constant transmission and reception of messages. A depressed, anxious mother who is not "in tune" with her child will fail to respond to the young child's communications and will fail to transmit her own messages if her child is not in a receptive frame of mind.

(4) External stress

It is notable that although, as seen in Chapter 3, the mean number of family stresses in children with problems was not higher than that of children in the general population, once social class had been controlled (as in the analysis described in Chapter 4), the mean level of stress in the problem group was significantly higher. When the effects of stress acting on the child were considered, they seemed to be greatest when they concerned personal relationships, e.g. difficulties with another child, psychological disturbance in another member of the family, and quarrels with neighbours. When, however, stress was considered in relation to a combination of maternal depression and childhood behaviour problems, more material factors seem to enter into account. Severe money problems, usually involving prolonged indebtedness, were related. We rated housing stress as present if there was evidence of a poor physical environment, e.g. rooms unusable because of damp, lack of electricity or hot water. Both severe money and housing stress were significantly related to the presence of an associated child behaviour problem and maternal depression (Richman, 1977).

Although it is generally assumed that children are responsive to externally stressful circumstances, either as a result of direct report or indirectly through their parents, there is in fact rather little scientific evidence to support this view or to clarify the mechanisms through which stress might operate. Douglas (1973) found that failure to achieve bladder continence was associated with stress events in the first four years of life, and Dunn and Kendrick (1980) have chronicled the impact of the birth of a younger sib on the behaviour of an older child. The fact that material deprivation is most closely associated when the mother shows an adverse mental reaction as well as the child, suggests that the effect of stress of this type is largely mediated by parental reaction. It is unclear whether what is important here is the level of absolute deprivation or the experience of subjective deprivation experienced by parents who see themselves as relatively deprived in relation to others or in relation to their own expectations. Material standards of living, for example, have steadily risen over the last generation, but expectations may well have risen faster still. Levels of housing dissatisfaction may, paradoxically, have risen despite considerable improvement in the quality of the housing stock. It is unlikely that children would be directly involved in an emotional response to material deprivation, and more probable that the depression experienced by a mother attempting without success to change her house or flat, or to combat rising damp, would be communicated to her child in an upsetting manner. Stresses involving personal relationships may be present to an excessive degree in the background of disturbed children for rather similar reasons, and again it is difficult to be categorical regarding the direction of causality. It is certainly possible that difficult children adversely influence their parents' mental state so as to make them more irritable with neighbours and less competent to deal with problems occurring with other children. More probably, there is an interaction between external stress and maternal depression with demoralized women finding it more difficult to cope with their children when living in unfavourable circumstances or when other personal relationships are not going smoothly.

One particular aspect of maternal care and possible stress which has been subject to variable interpretation over the years, concerns maternal employment. Twenty years ago it was assumed by many experts in child development that the repeated separations and relative deprivation in care which, it was postulated, resulted when a woman went out to work, meant that this situation should be avoided wherever possible. However, when this view was examined systematically (e.g. by Yudkin and Holme, 1963), it rapidly became apparent that the subject was far more complex than had originally been thought to be the case. More recent reviews (Wallston, 1973) suggest that the concept of maternal deprivation is inappropriate to apply to the children of working mothers, many of whom have an enriched experience as a result of the substitute care they enjoy while their mothers are working. However, some children *are* deprived of stimulation and care because their mothers, for reasons of economic necessity, have to go to work even though the alternative care they can arrange for their children is inadequate.

Our own findings suggest that, in the population we studied, as far as the children were concerned, the advantages just about balance the disadvantages in that the proportion of women working (about 20%) was almost exactly the same in both the disturbed and non-disturbed groups. Our impressions confirm the findings of Harrell and Ridley (1975) that among working mothers of young children, the quality of mother–child interaction is positively related to the amount of satisfaction the mother obtains in her work outside the home.

(5) Pre-school facilities

Controversy over the value and possible dangers of pre-school facilities in the personality development of young children has perhaps also obscured certain important issues. Concern was expressed early over the care experienced by very young infants and toddlers placed for long periods of the day in day-nurseries with young, inexperienced and often temporary staff look-ing after them. Such a situation is very different from that in which most of the children in our study were placed. These were older children, usually spending two or three half-days a week at a play-group, not because of any particular need for substitute care, but because their parents thought the experience would enhance their social and intellectual development.

The fact that overall there was no association between attendance at play-group or other pre-school facility and the presence of a behaviour problem may mask important differences which did exist. Firstly, we know that children of unmarried mothers were over-represented and they might be expected to have a higher rate of problems. However, counter-balancing this, we also know that, amongst children whose parents were together, those from middle-class families were more likely to be attenders than those from working-class families, and, as reported in Chapter 3, middle-class children are likely to show slightly lower rates of disturbance.

We shall discuss the policy implications of our findings in relation to pre-school facilities in Chapter 14 when we have considered the outcome of attenders and non-attenders.

The child's contribution

Language development

The relationship between language delay and factors in the family such as social class and the quality of stimulation provided by the mother, has received much attention. Similarly, the links between behaviour problems in young children and factors in the family background such as maternal attitudes and parental mental health have also been extensively investig-ated. However, except in the case of childhood autism, the associations between behaviour disturbance in young children and their ability to com-prehend and express themselves has been very little investigated. In autism there is increasing acceptance of the view that much behaviour disturbance is produced by the failure of the child to adapt to his world because of a virtual absence of the capacity to integrate sensory experiences in a meaningful manner. In non-autistic children with language delay, the mechanism whereby they suffer high rates of behaviour problems remains much more uncertain (Cantwell *et al.*, 1980).

Comparing the background of children with language delay and those with behaviour problems, there is a strong link with social deprivation in language-delayed children and a strong component of distorted family re-lationships in children with behaviour problems. Yet the overlap remains considerable. We can perhaps clarify this issue by citing some of the available evidence. In the genesis of language delay it seems probable that the quality of stimulation from parents is of importance. Brown and Hanlon (1970) found that phonetic and semantic development were enhanced by appropriate parental reinforcement. Cazden (1966) found that language development was promoted more by the opportunity for stimulating interaction with adults than by contact with other children. The capacity of a depressed or overworked mother to provide such appropriate reinforcement and stimulating interaction is likely to be reduced, and it is therefore conceivable that the same type of factors are responsible, directly or indirectly, for language delay as for behaviour problems. In a later chapter we shall consider the possible influence of an adverse emotional environment in the pre-school child and later language development in the sphere of reading. If this association is substantiated, it seems likely to be mediated through an effect on language development occurring initially in the pre-school period.

A further thread of evidence which seems relevant is provided by links which have been demonstrated between the hyperkinetic syndrome and learning difficulties, including those involving language functions. These have been reviewed by Cantwell (1976). He points to three possibilities to explain the linkage — the possibility that neurological impairment causes both the behavioural syndrome and the cognitive disabilities; that overactivity interferes with attention and the acquisition of information; and that hyperkinetic children make decisions too quickly. All of these interactions are readily observable in clinical practice, and, at this stage, it does not seem possible to select any one as likely to be of paramount importance. Hyperkinesis is not, of course, the only behavioural problem which could be associated with language retardation. Shy, withdrawn children receive reduced adult–child or child–child interaction, and thus less language stimulation. Apart from rare cases of elective mutism in which language itself is not affected but the use of language is inhibited for emotional reasons, there is a lack of evidence linking shy behaviour with delayed language development. In older children it is now well established that the shy, anxious child is not particularly prone to retardation in reading ability or other types of educational failure.

Our own study provides some support for the view that different factors are responsible for the development of language delay and behaviour problems, in that social deprivation seems heavily inculpated in the former and distortion of family relationships in the latter. However, the overlap between these two types of problem suggests that, once established, each type of problem may be at least partly responsible for giving rise to the other through one or other of the mechanisms already described. We shall return to this issue in Chapter 13 when we discuss the antecedents of reading retardation.

We did not in fact assess the child's contribution by virtue of his temperament in our study, but the work of others, and indeed some of our own previous work suggests it is likely to be of importance, and this seems an appropriate point for discussion of this topic. The role of temperament has been explored particularly thoroughly by the New York Longitudinal Study investigators who have examined temperamental characteristics in a group of children studied from infancy to adolescence (Thomas and Chess, 1977). From interviews with mothers they have obtained information about the child's everyday behaviour which is then rated along pre-determined lines on one of nine temperamental categories — activity level, rhythmicity, approach/withdrawal, adaptability, intensity of reaction, threshold of responsiveness, quality of mood, distractability, attention span and persistence. The investigators have claimed (Thomas *et al.*, 1968) that significant continuity of temperament can be identified over time. They also claim that clusters of particular manifestations of temperament allow children to be described as "difficult", "easy", and "slow to warm up", and that these clusters are predictive of whether the children will show behaviour disorders later on, and, if they do, the type of disorder which they will develop.

This work is open to methodological criticism (Blennow-Persson and McNeil, 1979; Bates, 1980), and it is not free from conceptual problems. Thus the degree of continuity from year to year in individual characteristics is often rather slender, rendering the concept of enduring personality traits a rather tenuous one. Work recently reported (Vaughn *et al.*, 1980) suggests that the temperamental characteristics of the child can be predicted before the child is born by examining the attitude of the mother during the pregnancy to her as yet unborn child. This suggests either that children reported to have negative temperamental characteristics are really behaving in the same way as other children, but are merely perceived negatively by their mothers, or that temperament is largely conditioned by maternal attitudes and child-rearing practices. In either event the concept of constitutionally determined "temperament" is called in question. A further problem arises in tracing continuity from personality traits to behaviour problems, in that it is often difficult to tell where one ends and the other begins. Presumably temperamental characteristics are enduring traits, not in themselves socially handicapping provided parental care is appropriate. By contrast, behaviour problems would tend to be more episodic and defined more by the presence of handicap. But is there really any qualitative difference between one child who is temperamentally "difficult" and another who has a behaviour disorder characterized by irritability, temper tantrums and disobedience? The fact that findings in relation to predictability of behaviour have been confirmed on an independent sample (Graham *et al.*, 1973) suggests that an important degree of continuity exists at least between one type of behaviour problem and another, however these are conceptualized. Further, whatever turns out to be the final precise interpretation of the work carried out by the New York investigators it is clear that the undeniable contribution of the child's own personality to parent–child interaction must not be overlooked in any discussion of the development of behaviour problems.

An important aspect of the child's contribution to a disturbed inter-actional process is the type of problem behaviour which may be present. It would be surprising if specific types of problem did not elicit rather characteristic behaviour in parents. A child waking every night with a sleep problem may produce parental exhaustion and irritability during the day. Restlessness and overactivity is similarly exhausting to cope with. By contrast, a depressed, anxious child may, more commonly, elicit overprotective rather than rejecting parental behaviour.

A synthetic view of the causation of behaviour problems

Even at three years of age, present evidence suggests that children and their behaviour problems can only be understood with reference to the long and complex series of processes involving them, their caretakers, and others in their environment over the whole of the preceding period of their existence. By focusing on the environmental contribution, the parental contribution, and finally on the child's own contribution, it is more than possible that the crucial aspects of development have been overlooked, namely the dynamic interaction between all three of these.

From the first few days of life, as Condon and Sander (1974) have indicated, the behaviour of neonates is closely linked to that of adults, for even babies of this age move synchronously in relation to adult speech. Subsequently, in what Shaffer (1977) refers to as a process of social enmesh-ment, patterns of interchange become more complicated. Stern (1974) has described how three-month-old babies and their mothers, when involved in mutual interaction, move their heads in time with each other — the baby playing his part just as much as his mother. Brazelton *et al.* (1974) observed mother–infant dyads, and commented on the way in which mothers and babies had to learn about each other as follows:

> Each member seemed to need to "learn" the nuances of the other member of the dyad . . . Flexibility and change were necessary for maintaining optimum interaction . . . One of the most important rules was concerned with the mother's sensitivity to the baby's capacity for attention and non-attention.

The importance of achieving reciprocity in these dyadic relationships for the avoidance of behaviour and emotional problems and for maturation of language remains to be demonstrated, but it seems highly plausible that, if either of the parties brings deficiencies to the playing of their part, then difficulties in either or both of these might arise. The child with adverse temperamental characteristics who is restless and fails to pay attention, will not vocalize in response to his mother's words because he will not have assimilated them. The depressed or anxious mother will not bring to the task *her* attention so that the baby's messages will not be ignored or misinterpreted. A further implication of this model is that exceptionally good performance by one or other member of the dyad might be expected to make up for the poor performance of the other. Thus, a difficult baby with a mother exceptionally attuned to receiving messages, even though these were transmitted in haphazard fashion, will have a smoother time than a similar baby with a less gifted mother. Incidentally, the emphasis on the mother–child dyad here may be misleading. The adult member of the dyad may be the father. Further, although it is reasonable to think that a large number of different adults will not all be able to tune themselves to a particular child's pattern of responsiveness, it may well be perfectly possible for four or five different adults — both parents and two or three substitutes — to achieve this skill (Rutter, 1980).

These suggestions for integrating our findings regarding causation with evidence available from the child development literature do, of course, have implications for prevention and treatment services, for counselling of mothers, health education, and for the training of professionals. It is to this theme, therefore, that we shall return when we discuss the implications of our follow-up studies, which we now go on to describe.

6 Follow-up Study: Introduction and Methods

We have already indicated our twofold reasons for wishing to carry out a follow-up study of the children we had studied at three years — namely to determine the course of the disorders we had identified and to attempt to understand better the roots of disorder occurring in school-aged children.

The study of behaviour over a period of time can be undertaken in various ways depending on the questions one is trying to answer. To begin with, one needs to decide whether one is interested in children with unusual behaviour, with behaviour falling at one or other extreme of the normal range, or whether behaviour across the whole range is of most concern. One approach may be appropriate, for example, when asking whether quite unusually active pre-school children have difficulties later on. A different approach may be necessary to determine whether a preschooler with an above-average level of activity is likely to continue to be above average in this respect in his school years. In general we ourselves have been more interested in the extremes of behaviour, and this derives from our clinical concern for children with significant levels of disorder.

Developmental studies can focus on the frequencies of problems at different ages. Some types of problem are likely to disappear with age, and others to remain relatively stable. A knowledge, for example, of the frequency of bed-wetting at different ages, can be relevant when considering at what age to regard a problem as calling for clinical concern. A further issue which can be examined is the consistency with which individuals showing a particular type of behaviour are affected over a period of time. Thus, for example, the rate of depressive symptoms may be very similar over a particular time span. Yet, if the symptoms are only experienced episodically, the individuals showing depression at one age period may be almost entirely different from those suffering from this problem at a later point in time. Such information could be very relevant to anyone wanting to know for how many individuals services are required. Our own interest, although encompassing those described above, lay particularly in answering questions related to the outcome of disorders, together with the factors influencing outcome. We considered influential factors as likely to be of two main types — those exerting an external effect on the child, such as the quality of family relationships, and, on the other hand, aspects of the child's own functioning such as his level of language development which might also provide an aggravating or protective influence. Examining the links between two variables, say a particular behavioural characteristic A (such as the presence of a significant behaviour problem), and an external or internal characteristic B (such as maternal depression) over a period of time from T_1 to T_2 is potentially an alarmingly complicated exercise. We first needed to ask whether the two were associated at point of time T_1. If they were, how could we explain this association? Were there common factors influencing both, or did the association persist even when other factors had been considered so that an influence of one upon the other was more probable? Next we needed to consider whether at point in time T_2 they were still associated. Even if they were not it is still possible that the influence of, for example, A upon B at time T_1 may have had an enduring effect.

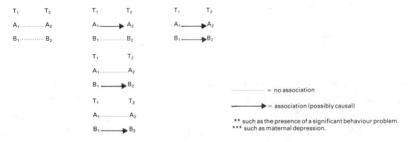

Figure 6.1. *The pattern of associations for the T_1 and T_2 values for two variables (A^{**} and B^{***}) measured at two time points (T_1 and T_2)*

Figure 6.1. shows possible patterns of association between A_1 and A_2, and B_1 and B_2 at two different points in time. Each of these patterns however, may be associated with four different levels of association between A and B at one point in time (Fig. 6.2).

Each of these sixteen different combinations may also be linked to associations between A and B at the two different points in time. This can also occur in four different ways (Fig. 6.3).

The number of ways in which just two variables can be associated is therefore very considerable. Each pattern has different implications for our understanding of the way in which each variable develops over time.

Although this method of examining continuities, patterns of association and possible chains of causation is complex, we felt it was very relevant to

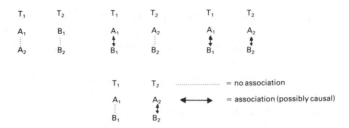

Figure 6.2. *The pattern of associations between A and B at the same time point for two variables (A and B) measured at two time points (T_1 and T_2)*

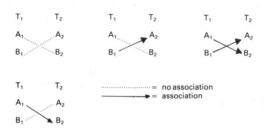

Figure 6.3. *The pattern of associations between A and B at different time points for two variables (A and B) measured at two time points (T_1 and T_2).*

many of the issues with which we were concerned.* Thus we wished to know what the chances were of different types of behaviour persisting or clearing up once the child went into school. We knew that adverse social factors were, in the pre-school period, linked to behaviour disturbance. Did it make any difference to outcome if such social adversity itself persisted, or did it seem as if, once the problem had occurred, it tended to persist regardless of whether the child's social circumstances improved? Did social adversity itself show continuity? For example if the mother was depressed when the child was pre-school, was she likely to be still depressed when the child had moved into school? We knew that many parents of disturbed school-age children said their children had been disturbed before they entered school. Doubtless this was sometimes the case, but was it more common for children to become disturbed *de novo* after entering school, or were long-standing persistent disorders the rule rather than the exception? Many children are known to remain non-disturbed despite the presence of serious adversity in their background. Could we identify factors present at an early stage of their lives which seemed to protect them from subsequently developing dis-

*It was not possible for us to examine all these permutations and combinations. We had to focus on those likely to be of relevance.

orders? It was because we felt it was worthwhile attempting to answer these questions that we embarked on our follow-up study.

Methods involved in follow-up study

Between six and eight weeks before the child's fourth birthday, and again before the eighth birthday, parents in our intensively studied behaviour problem and control groups (198 in all) were contacted by letter and asked if they would agree to further interviews. As, between four and eight years, over half the families had moved, tracing them at the later age proved a challenging task. Nevertheless with the cooperation of general practitioners and schools, we were able to trace 91 and 94% of the original control and problem groups at four years, and 90 and 93% of those who had been seen at four years when they were eight years old. Among those traced there were only two refusals at four years and none at all at eight years. The interviewers were, in general, all different at the three ages and they were ignorant of the data gathered earlier. They were graduates in social sciences, and all received individual training in the administration of the interview.

The interview was semi-structured and similar to that carried out when the child was three years old. As before, the principal areas covered included the physical health and behaviour of the child, details of the family background and especially the quality of relationships within the family, the mental and physical health of the parents, stresses operating on the family, social contacts with family and friends, housing conditions and contacts with services. When the child was eight years old additional questions were asked about the child's school experience, difficulties at school in behaviour or learning, parental attitudes to the school and parental interest, and parental involvement in the child's education.

At four years the same measures of behaviour were used as in the initial phase of the survey, namely the behaviour screening questionnaire (BSQ), the behaviour check-list (BCL) and the clinical rating of behaviour based on the information obtained during the BSQ. At eight years the behavioural section of the interview was based on the interview developed by Graham and Rutter (1968) for ten- and eleven-year-old children, but also included the behavioural items in the behaviour screening questionnaire. The parent in addition completed a parent behaviour questionnaire (Rutter *et al.*, 1970) and the mother completed a self-rating malaise inventory, a modified form of the Cornell medical index (Rutter *et al.*, 1970). At this age also, teachers were asked to complete a behaviour questionnaire (Rutter, 1967).

In between two-thirds and three-quarters of these interviews the informant was the mother alone, and in the great majority of the remainder either both parents or, more rarely, the father alone, were interviewed. At eight years, in 47 (24 control and 23 problem group) consecutively sampled boys, fathers were separately interviewed using a modified version of the same parental interview. These fathers also completed a child behaviour questionnaire. These interviews were all carried out by one of us (P.G.) in ignorance of the information obtained at the other interviews.

The arrangements for test administration at four years for the children were identical to those made at three years, i.e. the mother's permission was obtained during the interview, and subsequent testing took place within a month of the child's fourth birthday, Again, the tester was blind as to the behavioural status of the child at three or four years. The place of testing was the child's home, and the procedures for test administration were as at three years.

At four years, the children were again given the English picture vocabulary test, the expressive scale of the Reynell developmental language scales, and the two sub-scales of the Griffiths mental development scales (hand–eye coordination and performance). The sub-tests from the Illinois test psycholinguistic ability and the memory for colour scale from the Hiskey–Nebraska test were dropped from the battery at four years. They were replaced by the administration of the complete Weschler Pre-school and Primary Scale of Intelligence (WPPSI). On this occasion, the inclusion of the complete WPPSI meant that the test session lasted an hour to an hour-and-a-quarter.

The same 14 items of behaviour during testing as had been rated at three years were also rated at four years. When the children were eight years of age, the families were first contacted by the interviewer. The interviewer obtained parental permission for the child to be seen by the psychologist at the school it was attending if it was still living within the borough of Waltham Forest, and for the child to be seen at home if it was living outside the borough. The psychologist then assessed the child at school or home within two months of the child's eighth birthday.

The tester was again blind as to the child's behaviour at ages three, four and eight years. If the testing took place in the school a room or area of the school was found away from the child's classroom and other children. The testing took place according to the instructions laid down in the standardized manuals, and at this age utilized a table rather than the floor for the surface on which the material was displayed. When testing in the child's home, a table was found away from the main activities in the home, and on this occasion the mother was encouraged not to be present for the testing.

We were concerned at eight years to get a measure of overall intellectual ability, a measure of reading attainment and to rate the child's behaviour during testing. The shortened form of the Wechsler intelligence scale for children (WISC) was used; this included the sub-tests — vocabulary, similarities, object assembly, and block design. To assess reading attainment the Neale analysis of reading ability was given to the children and the scores on accuracy and comprehension obtained. The measure of speed which is available with the Neale analysis of reading ability was not used.

Finally a modified version of the earlier unstandardized rating of behaviour during testing was made at the end of the test session. The full test battery also included a repertory grid to assess the child's perception of various school activities, but the results of the grid investigation will not be included in the current report. The complete test battery took an hour to administer.

A representative sample

By the time data collection had been completed when the children were eight years old, we had therefore obtained information at three ages (three years, four years and eight years), on 185 children (94 problem group and 91 controls). This information would allow us to examine the outcome of disturbed and non-disturbed children and to compare these on a wide variety of measures. However, in addition to this information we wished to know how children *in general* developed behaviourally over the years, and in order to obtain insights into this issue we needed data from a representative sample of the *whole* population. Ideally we should have carried out a follow-up study of our total original 705 one in four sample, but we did not have the resources to do this. Clearly our original total intensively studied group of 198 children could not be regarded as representative of the original random sample since it contained 99 children with problems and 99 control children matched for sex and social class. To overcome this problem we reconstituted a representative sample of 98 children from the 202 intensively studied group in order to have approximately the same distribution of sex, social class and behavioural difficulties as the original 705 randomly selected samples. Characteristics of the original 705 sample and of the representative sample of 98 children derived from the intensively studied group are shown in Table 6.1, and the two groups do not differ on the great majority of variables, though, because of the exigencies of sampling, more girls in the representative sample scored 10 or more on the BSQ.

Presentation of findings

In the following chapter we describe the characteristics of this representative sample of children at three, four and eight years, in order to indicate how

Pre-school to School

Table 6.1. *Comparison between the original sample (N = 705) and the reconstituted representative sample (N = 98) of sex, social class and BSQ scores*

	Original sample (N = 705)	Reconstituted representative sample (N = 98)
Percentage of boys	49	52
Percentage in manual social class	66	72
Percentage of boys in manual social class	68	65
Percentage of girls in manual social class	66	79
Percentage with BSQ scores of 10 or more	14	16
Percentage of boys with BSQ scores of 10 or more	18	12
Percentage of girls with BSQ scores of 10 or more	12	21

children develop behaviourally over this period. These data enable us to indicate the value or otherwise of pre-school screening for behaviour disturbance in the identification of learning and behaviour problems arising in the school years. Then in Chapter 8 we compare the outcome of the problem group with that of children in the control group. In Chapter 9 we provide a general overview of the factors associated with persistence of and recovery from disorders in the problem group, as well as factors associated with development and non-development of disorders in the control group children — none of whom were, by definition, showing disturbance at three years of age. In Chapter 10 we examine the differences in outcome according to the sex of the child. In Chapter 11 we describe outcome in terms of types of problems the children showed at three years and the types of difficulties they had developed at eight years. In Chapter 12, using data from our three samples (representative, problem and control) we descibe our analysis of continuity and discontinuity in family and social factors. In Chapter 13 using data derived from the representative sample, we attempt to identify factors later associated with poor intelligence and educational achievement, at eight years, and finally in Chapter 14 we describe the implications of our study both for achieving understanding of processes in psychological development and for social and health policy.

7 Individual Items of Behaviour at Three, Four and Eight Years: Continuity and Discontinuity

In this chapter we present the information we have obtained on individual items of behaviour over the period of study. Information of this type can be useful in a variety of ways. In child welfare clinics, for example, when a health visitor or doctor discovers that a particular problem exists, it is useful to have some idea whether the difficulty is likely to persist either in the short — or in the long-term. Information obtained on our representative sample of children provides an indication of how children in general might be expected to fare. However, it is possible that if the particular behaviour problem is occurring as an isolated manifestation, the outcome might well be different from when behaviour is part of a more widespread disturbance. For this reason we have provided information from our control and problem groups.

In Table 7.1. the percentage of children with particular types of behaviour problems at three, four and eight years are provided. To be counted for this purpose, behaviour had to be rated as definitely present on the behaviour screening questionnaire (BSQ) at three or four years, or on the parental interview at eight years. The percentages are separately provided at each age group on the representative, behaviour problem and control groups. Despite the fact that there may well be maturational changes in the way individual items of behaviour are shown, we believe these comparisons are meaningful because we made considerable attempts to ensure that information was collected in a comparable way at each of these ages.

It can be seen that appetite problems and food faddiness are fairly stable throughout the period in question, although there is a tendency for faddiness to peak at four years and subsequently to decline. In the previous study most

Table 7.1. *Percentage of children with specific items of problem behaviour definitely present in the representative, behaviour problem and control groups at 3, 4 and 8 years*

Specific items of problem behaviour	Representative Group (N = 98)			Behaviour Problem Group (N = 94)			Control Group (N = 91)		
	3 years	4 years	8 years	3 years	4 years	8 years	3 years	4 years	8 years
Poor appetite	19	20	13	45	39	22	14	15	9
Faddy eating	15	24	15	31	44	29	14	22	12
Difficulty settling at night	16	15	12	29	26	31	11	11	9
Waking at night	14	12	3	29	19	5	11	8	2
Sleeping in parents' bed	10	6	5	20	20	3	12	14	1
Large number of habits	17	14	1	27	12	2	12	14	1
Overactive, restless	17	13	11	55	40	17	9	9	11
Poor concentration	9	6	7	26	17	18	1	2	5
Attention seeking	9	10	7	40	23	16	2	3	5
Dependency	6	5	8	17	7	14	7	3	5
Difficult to control	11	10	10	53	39	18	2	5	9
Tempers	5	6	9	22	28	21	2	3	5
Unhappy mood	4	7	7	17	15	15	1	4	5
Worries	4	10	21	6	17	38	2	5	19
Fears	10	12	2	21	24	0	7	7	2
Relations with sibs	13	19	19	35	38	33	8	14	20
Relations with peers	4	6	8	26	11	20	0	6	3
Day wetting	26	8	2	32	17	0	25	8	3
Night wetting	34	19	4	49	31	12	33	19	5
Soiling	16	3	4	27	9	3	15	1	3

comparable to our own, the Berkeley Guidance Study (Macfarlane *et al.*, 1954) in which children over the same age range were studied in the 1930s, nearly 50 years previously, a very similar finding was obtained. Our peak at four years was found in all three groups, but it is important to remember that, although the problem and control groups are separate, the representative group consists entirely of children drawn from the other two groups and cannot be considered as an independent sample. It is therefore not surprising that it shows very much the same developmental trend as the other two groups.

Failure to control bowel and bladder function declined sharply with age in all three groups, but it is noticeable that the decline is less marked in those children who also have a variety of other problems. Thus, in the behaviour problem group at four years the rate of bedwetting remains at 31% compared to 19% in both the representative and control groups. Soiling shows the same tendency except that here the decline in the problem group is nearly as sharp as in the other two groups. In the Berkeley study, the findings are somewhat similar except that the rate of day wetting appeared lower to begin with. The continuity of sleep problems varied with the nature of the difficulties studied. Thus, problems in getting children to bed and off to sleep occurred with roughly the same frequency in all three groups, whereas restlessness at night and waking during the night, were nearly as common at four as three years, and dropped sharply in frequency by the time the children were eight years old. Spending time during the night in the parents' bed was only common in the problem group at three and four years, and was uncommon even in that group by eight years. It is interesting to note that, in the Berkeley study, although restlessness in sleep was rated, it was not thought warranted to obtain information on night waking or spending time in the parental bed. It seems quite possible that these problems were not so widespread half a century ago as they are today.

Habits, such as thumb sucking and nail biting tended to remain fairly static in prevalence from three to four years and then to decline fairly sharply. In the Berkeley study nail biting increased quite markedly over this period and thumb sucking declined. Our codings did not enable us to distinguish between different types of habits at the three ages.

The level of activity is known to decrease in hyperkinetic children in whom this type of behaviour has been seriously problematic, although the overactivity in these cases is often replaced by other problems (Minde *et al.*, 1972). This was confirmed in our own study with a particularly sharp decline in overactivity in our problem group children. In view of the subsequent fate of the problem group (described in more detail in subsequent chapters) it is evident that overactivity in this group must indeed be replaced by other problems.

Difficulties such as attention seeking, over dependency and disobedience, or difficulties over management (which might all be regarded as reflecting disturbances in parent–child relationships), tended to show a rather similar pattern of development. They were infrequent in the representative and control groups and remained so during the period in question. In the problem group children they were much more prevalent originally and then declined slowly but remained fairly common. The Berkeley study obtained rather similar results except that attention seeking in that investigation declined at four years and rose again in frequency. Temper tantrums which were found to decrease slowly with age both in the Berkeley study and in the classic work of Goodenough (1931) also declined in our representative group, but remained remarkably stable over time in our problem group. Behaviour arising out of adverse parent–child relationships or an inability to withstand frustration is therefore distinctly less likely to decline with age in children who show generalized emotional or behaviour disturbance.

Problems relating to emotional life have a rather mixed course depending on their nature. Thus mood disturbances, mainly tendencies to prolonged sadness and misery, were uncommon throughout in the population generally, but were somewhat more common in the problem group and remained so. Worries increased steadily in all three groups, and this may well be a function of increasing ability with age to express anxieties. When the children were three-years-old, some mothers expressed surprise that we might think that children so young could experience worry. Fears are more openly and obviously manifest however and here the position is exactly reversed with a remarkably low level of specific fears manifest at eight years in all three groups. This finding is supported by other studies (e.g. Lapouse and Monk, 1959; Gersten *et al.*, 1976) which have not investigated children as young as we did, but which have identified a decline in the presence of specific fears from six years onwards.

Rates of problems in relationships with sibs appeared uniformly rather high in our problem group, and similarly steady but at a rather lower level in our other two groups. As far as relationships with other children were concerned, there was a slightly more marked difference with even lower levels of problem in this area in the representative and control groups.

Continuity of problems within children

So far we have been considering similarities and differences in overall rates of problems at the three ages we have studied our children. As we have seen, it is possible to determine different trends depending on which symptoms or items of behaviour are examined. We have also been assuming that when rates of a problem in a particular group rise or fall, the chances of a child identified with a problem at the earlier age showing it at a later age are increased or diminished accordingly. It is, however, possible to examine the outcome further to determine whether, for example, when rates remain static over a period of time, it is the same or different children who suffer. We have examined our data to investigate this problem in each of our three groups (problem, control and representative) over three different time periods, three to four years, four to eight years, and three to eight years.

(a) Persistence of problems from three to four years

Tables 7.2 to 7.4 contain information on persistence and continuity of behavioural items from three to four years in each of the three groups. An

Table 7.2. *Persistence of specific items of problem behaviour from 3 to 4 years in the representative group (N = 98)*

Specific item of problem behaviour	Percentage of children with item of problem behaviour definitely present at various ages (Numbers in brackets)							
	3 years only		3 and 4 years		4 years only		Neither age	
Poor appetite	5	(5)	14	(14)	6	(6)	74	(73)
Faddy eating	5	(5)	10	(10)	14	(14)	70	(69)
Difficulty settling at night	12	(12)	4	(4)	11	(11)	72	(71)
Waking at night	9	(9)	5	(5)	7	(7)	79	(77)
Sleeping in parents' bed	9	(9)	1	(1)	5	(5)	85	(83)
Large number of habits	14	(14)	3	(3)	11	(11)	71	(70)
Overactive, restless	10	(10)	7	(7)	6	(6)	76	(75)
Poor concentration	7	(7)	2	(2)	4	(4)	87	(85)
Attention seeking	5	(5)	4	(4)	6	(6)	85	(83)
Dependency	6	(6)	0	(0)	5	(5)	88	(86)
Difficult to control	6	(6)	5	(5)	5	(5)	83	(82)
Tempers	3	(3)	2	(2)	4	(4)	91	(89)
Unhappy mood	3	(3)	1	(1)	6	(6)	90	(88)
Worries	3	(3)	1	(1)	9	(9)	87	(85)
Fears	7	(7)	3	(3)	9	(9)	80	(78)
Relations with siblings	6	(5)	6	(5)	13	(10)	74	(59)
Relations with peers	4	(4)	0	(0)	6	(6)	90	(85)
Day wetting	19	(19)	7	(7)	1	(1)	72	(71)
Night wetting	21	(21)	12	(12)	7	(7)	59	(58)
Soiling	14	(14)	2	(2)	1	(1)	83	(81)

Table 7.3. *Persistence of specific items of problem behaviour from 3 to 4 years in the behaviour problem group (N = 94)*

Specific item of problem behaviour	Percentage of children with item of problem behaviour definitely present at various ages (Numbers in brackets)							
	3 years only		3 and 4 years		4 years only		Neither age	
Poor appetite	18	(17)	27	(25)	12	(11)	44	(41)
Faddy eating	10	(9)	21	(20)	22	(21)	47	(44)
Difficulty settling at night	16	(15)	13	(12)	13	(12)	59	(55)
Waking at night	20	(19)	9	(8)	11	(10)	61	(57)
Sleeping in parents' bed	11	(10)	10	(9)	11	(10)	69	(65)
Large number of habits	19	(18)	8	(7)	4	(4)	69	(64)
Overactive, restless	26	(24)	31	(29)	10	(9)	34	(32)
Poor concentration	18	(17)	7	(7)	10	(9)	65	(61)
Attention seeking	27	(25)	14	(13)	10	(9)	50	(47)
Dependency	16	(15)	1	(1)	6	(6)	77	(72)
Difficult to control	24	(23)	29	(27)	11	(10)	36	(34)
Tempers	12	(11)	11	(10)	17	(16)	61	(57)
Unhappy mood	11	(10)	6	(6)	9	(8)	74	(70)
Worries	4	(4)	2	(2)	15	(14)	79	(74)
Fears	12	(11)	10	(9)	15	(14)	64	(60)
Relations with siblings	15	(12)	20	(16)	18	(14)	48	(38)
Relations with peers	20	(18)	6	(5)	6	(5)	69	(62)
Day wetting	23	(22)	9	(8)	9	(8)	60	(56)
Night wetting	23	(21)	27	(25)	4	(4)	47	(44)
Soiling	20	(19)	6	(6)	2	(2)	71	(67)

example may be helpful here. In the representative group (Table 7.2) of the 19 children who had an appetite problem at three years, 14 (74%) still had such a problem at four years. Further, of the 20 children who had such a problem at four years, 14 (70%) have had such a problem when they were three years old. These percentages provide probably the best guide we can give to the likelihood of a particular problem persisting in a particular child, as well as the chances of a problem at a later date being present at the earlier age.

Table 7.5 therefore presents the percentages for the three groups over the period in question calculated as in the example above. In summary the findings are as follows. Appetite disturbance and faddiness persist for one year in about two-thirds of children showing these problems at three years.

Table 7.4. *Persistence of specific items of problem behaviour from 3 to 4 years in the control group (N = 91)*

Specific item of problem behaviour	Percentage of children with item of problem behaviour definitely present at various ages (Numbers in brackets)							
	3 years only		3 and 4 years		4 years only		Neither age	
Poor appetite	5	(5)	9	(8)	7	(6)	79	(72)
Faddy eating	3	(3)	11	(10)	11	(10)	75	(68)
Difficulty settling at night	9	(8)	2	(2)	9	(8)	80	(73)
Waking at night	8	(7)	3	(3)	4	(4)	85	(77)
Sleeping in parents' bed	8	(7)	0	(0)	4	(4)	88	(80)
Large number of habits	10	(9)	2	(2)	12	(11)	76	(69)
Overactive, restless	7	(6)	2	(2)	7	(6)	85	(77)
Poor concentration	1	(1)	0	(0)	2	(2)	97	(88)
Attention seeking	2	(2)	0	(0)	3	(3)	95	(86)
Dependency	2	(2)	0	(0)	3	(3)	95	(86)
Difficult to control	1	(1)	0	(0)	5	(4)	93	(85)
Tempers	2	(2)	0	(0)	3	(3)	95	(86)
Unhappy mood	1	(1)	0	(0)	5	(4)	94	(86)
Worries	2	(2)	0	(0)	6	(5)	92	(84)
Fears	6	(5)	1	(1)	6	(5)	87	(79)
Relations with siblings	4	(3)	4	(3)	10	(7)	82	(58)
Relations with peers	0	(0)	0	(0)	6	(5)	94	(82)
Day wetting	19	(17)	7	(6)	1	(1)	74	(67)
Night wetting	22	(20)	11	(10)	8	(7)	59	(54)
Soiling	14	(13)	1	(1)	0	(0)	85	(77)

Day wetting only persists for a year in a quarter of the children and it makes no difference in this symptom whether the child had a behaviour problem at three years or not. Night wetting, by contrast, persists in half the generally disturbed children but in only about a third of the non-disturbed. In most, but not quite all other problems, the trend is as with night wetting — that is difficulties tend to persist more in the problem group than in the control or representative group. The persistence of individual items of behaviour in children who are generally disturbed is seen in particularly marked form in those children spending time in the parental bed and in those showing temper tantrums. It is not evident at all or evident very little in management difficulties or in relationships with sibs.

When one considers the contribution made to behavioural items present at four years by children who were showing the same problem at three years,

Table 7.5. *Relative persistence of specific items of problem behaviour from 3 to 4 years in the representative, behaviour problem and control groups*

Specific item of problem behaviour	Percentage of representative group not showing item of problem behaviour at 3 or 4 years	Percentage of children with item of problem behaviour at 3 years still showing the problem at 4 years			Percentage of children with item of problem behaviour at 4 years who showed the problem at 3 years		
		Representative group	Behaviour problem group	Control group	Representative group	Behaviour problem group	Control group
Poor appetite	74	74	60	60	70	75	57
Faddy eating	70	67	69	77	42	49	50
Difficulty settling at night	72	25	44	20	27	50	20
Waking at night	79	36	30	30	42	44	43
Sleeping in parents' bed	85	10	47	0	17	47	0
Large number of habits	72	18	28	18	21	64	15
Overactive, restless	77	41	55	25	54	76	25
Poor concentration	87	22	29	0	33	44	0
Attention seeking	85	44	34	0	40	59	0
Dependency	89	0	6	0	0	14	0
Difficult to control	84	45	54	50	50	73	20
Tempers	91	40	48	0	33	38	0
Unhappy mood	90	25	38	0	14	43	0
Worries	87	25	33	0	10	23	0
Fears	80	30	45	17	25	39	17
Relations with siblings	74	50	57	50	33	53	30
Relations with peers	90	0	22	0	0	50	0
Day wetting	72	27	27	26	88	50	86
Night wetting	59	36	54	33	63	86	59
Soiling	83	13	24	7	67	75	100

the trends are perhaps less clear cut. There is however a definite tendency for relationship problems, when they are present at four years, to be the aftermath of similar earlier difficulties in the problem group, but to be arising *de novo* in the control and representative groups. In all the groups sphincter problems at four years are very likely to be the continuation of a similar problem a year previously.

(b) Persistence of problems from four to eight years

Similar data are presented for the period four to eight years in Table 7.6 to Table 7.9. In many items continuity is less marked, but between a quarter and a half of the children persist in showing most individual items, and, by this stage, the tendency for persistence is not so obviously more marked in

Table 7.6. *Persistence of specific items of problem behaviour from 4 to 8 years in the representative group (N = 98)*

Specific item of problem behaviour	Percentage of children with item of problem behaviour definitely present at various ages (Numbers in brackets)							
	4 years only		4 and 8 years		8 years only		Neither age	
Poor appetite	12	(12)	8	(8)	5	(5)	74	(73)
Faddy eating	16	(16)	8	(8)	7	(7)	68	(67)
Difficulty settling at night	9	(9)	6	(6)	6	(6)	79	(77)
Waking at night	10	(10)	2	(2)	1	(1)	87	(85)
Sleeping in parents' bed	4	(4)	2	(2)	3	(3)	91	(89)
Large number of habits	14	(14)	0	(0)	1	(1)	85	(83)
Overactive, restless	10	(10)	3	(3)	8	(8)	79	(77)
Poor concentration	3	(3)	3	(3)	4	(4)	90	(88)
Attention seeking	8	(8)	2	(2)	5	(5)	85	(83)
Dependency	4	(4)	1	(1)	7	(7)	87	(85)
Difficult to control	8	(8)	2	(2)	8	(8)	82	(80)
Tempers	3	(3)	3	(3)	6	(6)	88	(86)
Unhappy mood	6	(6)	1	(1)	6	(6)	87	(85)
Worries	6	(6)	4	(4)	17	(17)	72	(71)
Fears	12	(12)	0	(0)	2	(2)	85	(83)
Relations with siblings	10	(8)	9	(7)	10	(8)	71	(56)
Relations with peers	5	(5)	1	(1)	7	(7)	86	(82)
Day wetting	7	(7)	1	(1)	1	(1)	91	(89)
Night wetting	15	(15)	4	(4)	0	(0)	81	(79)
Soiling	2	(2)	1	(1)	3	(3)	94	(92)

Table 7.7. *Persistence of specific items of problem behaviour from 4 to 8 years in the behaviour problem group (N = 94)*

Specific item of problem behaviour	Percentage of children with item of problem behaviour definitely present at various ages (Numbers in brackets)							
	4 years only		4 and 8 years		8 years only		Neither age	
Poor appetite	21	(20)	17	(16)	5	(5)	56	(53)
Faddy eating	27	(25)	17	(16)	12	(11)	45	(42)
Difficulty settling at night	13	(12)	13	(12)	18	(17)	56	(53)
Waking at night	16	(15)	3	(3)	2	(2)	79	(74)
Sleeping in parents' bed	18	(17)	2	(2)	1	(1)	79	(74)
Large number of habits	12	(11)	0	(0)	2	(2)	85	(80)
Overactive, restless	30	(28)	11	(10)	9	(8)	51	(48)
Poor concentration	10	(9)	7	(7)	11	(10)	72	(68)
Attention seeking	17	(16)	6	(6)	10	(9)	67	(63)
Dependency	6	(6)	1	(1)	13	(12)	80	(75)
Difficult to control	29	(27)	11	(10)	7	(7)	53	(50)
Tempers	18	(17)	10	(9)	12	(11)	61	(57)
Unhappy mood	11	(10)	4	(4)	11	(10)	74	(70)
Worries	6	(6)	11	(10)	28	(26)	55	(52)
Fears	24	(23)	0	(0)	0	(0)	76	(71)
Relations with siblings	15	(12)	23	(18)	10	(8)	53	(42)
Relations with peers	7	(6)	4	(4)	16	(14)	73	(66)
Day wetting	17	(16)	0	(0)	0	(0)	83	(78)
Night wetting	20	(19)	2	(2)	1	(1)	68	(64)
Soiling	6	(6)	2	(2)	1	(1)	90	(85)

the problem group. When one looks at the population of children at eight years with a particular problem who were showing the same problem earlier on, it is clear that night wetting is nearly always the aftermath of a similar problem manifest earlier. So-called onset wetting is clearly very unusual between four and eight years. Certain problems, such as habits and some fears appear virtually always to clear up between four and eight years, and are very rare at the latter age.

Persistence of problems from three to eight years

Continuity of behaviour over this time period is shown in Tables 7.10 to 7.13. Appetite problems and food faddiness persist over five years in about a third

Table 7.8. *Percentage of specific items of problem behaviour from 4 to 8 years in the control group (N = 91)*

Specific item of problem behaviour	Percentage of children with item of problem behaviour definitely present at various ages (Numbers in brackets)							
	4 years only		4 and 8 years		8 years only		Neither age	
Poor appetite	12	(11)	3	(3)	5	(5)	79	(72)
Faddy eating	16	(15)	5	(5)	7	(6)	71	(65)
Difficulty settling at night	7	(6)	4	(4)	4	(4)	85	(77)
Waking at night	7	(6)	1	(1)	1	(1)	91	(83)
Sleeping in parents' bed	2	(2)	2	(2)	3	(3)	92	(84)
Large number of habits	14	(13)	0	(0)	1	(1)	85	(77)
Overactive, restless	9	(9)	3	(3)	8	(7)	84	(76)
Poor concentration	1	(1)	1	(1)	4	(4)	93	(85)
Attention seeking	3	(3)	0	(0)	5	(5)	91	(83)
Dependency	2	(2)	1	(1)	4	(4)	91	(83)
Difficult to control	4	(4)	1	(1)	8	(7)	87	(79)
Tempers	2	(2)	1	(1)	4	(4)	92	(84)
Unhappy mood	4	(4)	0	(0)	5	(5)	90	(82)
Worries	4	(4)	1	(1)	18	(16)	77	(70)
Fears	7	(6)	0	(0)	2	(2)	90	(82)
Relations with siblings	7	(5)	7	(5)	13	(9)	73	(52)
Relations with peers	6	(5)	0	(0)	3	(3)	91	(79)
Day wetting	7	(6)	1	(1)	1	(1)	91	(83)
Night wetting	14	(13)	4	(4)	1	(1)	80	(73)
Soiling	1	(1)	0	(0)	3	(3)	95	(87)

of the children who initially show them. A small appetite is more likely to persist in generally disturbed children than in controls, but this is not the case with food faddiness. Day wetting disappears in nearly all children regardless of whether they are generally disturbed or not, but night wetting is more likely to persist in disturbed children. Contrary to expectation soiling persists in about one in six children and the degree of general disturbance shown initially is unimportant. About half the problem children who had difficulty in getting off to sleep at three years still had such a problem at eight years, but the number of children who continued to wake at night was small in all three groups. As we have already noted, habits and fears were very uncommon by eight years, so inevitably the great majority of children who had shown these problems at three years were no longer doing so by eight years. Most of the other problems, such as activity level, emotional problems and

Table 7.9. *Relative persistence of specific items of problem behaviour from 4 to 8 years in the representative, behaviour problem and control groups*

Specific item of problem behaviour	Percentage of representative group not showing item problem behaviour at 4 or 8 years	Percentage of children with item of problem behaviour at 4 years still showing the problem at 8 years			Percentage of children with item of problem behaviour at 8 years who showed the problem at 4 years		
		Representative group	Behaviour problem group	Control group	Representative group	Behaviour problem group	Control group
Poor appetite	74	40	44	21	61	76	38
Faddy eating	68	33	39	25	53	59	45
Difficulty settling at night	79	40	50	40	50	41	50
Waking at night	87	17	17	14	67	60	50
Sleeping in parents' bed	91	33	11	50	40	67	40
Large number of habits	85	0	0	0	0	0	0
Overactive, restless	79	23	26	38	27	56	30
Poor concentration	90	50	44	50	43	41	20
Attention seeking	85	20	38	0	29	40	0
Dependency	87	20	14	33	13	8	20
Difficult to control	82	20	27	20	20	59	13
Tempers	88	50	35	33	33	45	20
Unhappy mood	87	14	29	0	14	29	0
Worries	72	40	63	20	19	28	6
Fears	85	0	0	0	0	—	0
Relations with siblings	71	47	60	50	47	69	36
Relations with peers	86	17	40	0	13	22	0
Day wetting	91	13	0	14	50	—	50
Night wetting	81	27	34	24	100	91	80
Soiling	94	33	25	0	25	67	0

relationships with parents and other children, also tended to decline with age just as markedly, and sometimes more markedly in the problem as in the other two groups. Temper tantrums and difficult relationships with brothers and sisters showed a somewhat similar decline as other types of problems.

Implications

The data provided here suggest that there is indeed a moderate degree of continuity over time in many of the types of individual behaviour problems studied. Difficulties were, on the whole, more likely to persist in those children who were initially in the problem group, but this trend was not universally shown.

Continuity and discontinuity have been previously studied in two main types of investigation — those considering the stability of personality characteristics over time, and those, such as the Berkeley Guidance Study to which we have already made reference in this chapter, that have examined the stability of problem behaviour.

Continuity of temperamental characteristics has been extensively investigated by the New York longitudinal study investigators (Thomas and Chess, 1977) and others whose work this study has inspired, e.g. Carey and McDevitt (1978). Continuities in temperamental characteristics over time are generally rather low, although attributes such as level of activity and threshold of responsiveness are correlated over time to a greater degree than one would expect by chance. By contrast, problem behaviour shows a greater level of continuity. Others, such as Minde and Minde (1977) who have used an approach very similar to that employed here, have also discovered stable patterns of abnormal or problematic behaviour over time. Further, the longitudinal significance of personality characteristics is much enhanced when they are considered as predictors of disturbance (Thomas *et al.*, 1968, Graham *et al.*, 1973). Children characterized as "difficult" in their early years are more likely to show aggressive or acting out types of behaviour disturbance; "slow to warm up" children later have a high level of behaviour characterized as withdrawal and inhibition, and "easy" children are little prone to any type of emotional or behavioural problem.

We hope that the data provided in this chapter might provide some prognostic indicators for those, such as health visitors, and general practitioners, dealing with disturbed children in clinical situations. They provide at least a rough guide to the outcome that might be expected when a child presents with a particular difficulty. It may be however that prognostic ability can be achieved to a greater degree by looking more closely at the way in which children showed their problems at three years and it is to this possibility that we now turn.

Cluster analysis

We decided to examine the possibility that prediction of outcome could be improved by developing a classification of problems occurring at three years. Up to this point we have assumed that, although it is possible to distinguish disorders in young children by their level of severity, it is more difficult or perhaps impossible to provide an adequate typology of disorders at this age. By eight years of age, as we shall describe in Chapter 11, some distinction between types of disorder is feasible, and, in particular, as we shall discuss, a useful distinction can be made between antisocial or conduct problems on the one hand and emotional or neurotic disorders on the other. At this stage we will, however, present information which suggests that it

Table 7.10. *Persistence of specific items of problem behaviour from 3 to 8 years in the representative group (N = 98)*

Specific item of problem behaviour	Percentage of children with item of problem behaviour definitely present at various ages (Numbers in brackets)			
	3 years only	3 and 8 years	8 years only	Neither age
Poor appetite	13 (13)	6 (6)	7 (7)	73 (72)
Faddy eating	11 (11)	4 (4)	11 (11)	73 (72)
Difficulty settling at night	12 (12)	4 (4)	8 (8)	76 (74)
Waking at night	13 (13)	1 (1)	2 (2)	84 (82)
Sleeping in parents' bed	7 (7)	3 (3)	2 (2)	88 (86)
Large number of habits	17 (17)	0 (0)	1 (1)	82 (80)
Overactive, restless	13 (13)	4 (4)	7 (7)	76 (74)
Poor concentration	8 (8)	1 (1)	6 (6)	85 (83)
Attention seeking	8 (8)	1 (1)	6 (6)	85 (83)
Dependency	5 (5)	1 (1)	7 (7)	85 (84)
Difficult to control	7 (7)	4 (4)	6 (6)	83 (81)
Tempers	1 (1)	4 (4)	5 (5)	90 (88)
Unhappy mood	2 (2)	2 (2)	5 (5)	91 (89)
Worries	3 (3)	1 (1)	20 (20)	76 (74)
Fears	10 (10)	0 (0)	2 (2)	87 (85)
Relations with siblings	9 (7)	4 (3)	15 (12)	72 (57)
Relations with peers	3 (3)	1 (1)	7 (7)	88 (84)
Day wetting	25 (25)	1 (1)	1 (1)	72 (71)
Night wetting	32 (32)	1 (1)	3 (3)	63 (62)
Soiling	13 (13)	3 (3)	1 (1)	83 (81)

Table 7.11. *Persistence of specific items of problem behaviour from 3 to 8 years in the behaviour problem group (N = 94)*

Specific item of problem behaviour	Percentage of children with item of problem behaviour definitely present at various ages (Numbers in brackets)							
	3 years only		3 and 8 years		8 years only		Neither age	
Poor appetite	27	(25)	18	(17)	4	(4)	51	(48)
Faddy eating	22	(21)	9	(8)	18	(19)	49	(46)
Difficulty settling at night	15	(14)	14	(13)	17	(16)	54	(51)
Waking at night	26	(24)	3	(3)	2	(2)	69	(65)
Sleeping in parents' bed	19	(18)	1	(1)	2	(2)	78	(73)
Large number of habits	26	(24)	1	(1)	1	(1)	71	(67)
Overactive, restless	41	(39)	13	(12)	4	(4)	39	(37)
Poor concentration	20	(19)	5	(5)	13	(12)	62	(58)
Attention seeking	31	(29)	10	(9)	6	(6)	53	(50)
Dependency	12	(11)	5	(5)	9	(8)	74	(70)
Difficult to control	38	(36)	15	(14)	3	(3)	44	(41)
Tempers	13	(12)	10	(9)	12	(11)	66	(62)
Unhappy mood	12	(11)	5	(5)	10	(9)	73	(69)
Worries	2	(2)	4	(4)	34	(32)	60	(56)
Fears	21	(20)	0	(0)	32	(30)	79	(74)
Relations with siblings	19	(15)	16	(13)	16	(13)	49	(39)
Relations with peers	18	(16)	8	(7)	12	(11)	62	(56)
Day wetting	32	(30)	0	(0)	0	(0)	68	(64)
Night wetting	38	(36)	11	(10)	1	(1)	50	(47)
Soiling	23	(22)	3	(3)	0	(0)	73	(69)

may similarly be useful to classify problems when children are three years of age.

The technique we used to investigate the classification of problems at three years is known as cluster analysis. The purpose of using this technique is to determine whether there are hidden but identifiable relatively homogeneous sub-groups within a mass of apparently amorphous data. The method requires that a large number of measures have been taken on a number of potentially related items. In this case we have available information on the individual items of behaviour on a questionnaire, and we wished to see whether there were any underlying patterns of disturbance. Using Ward's method (Everitt, 1974), a computer search is made for the two individuals whose scores were the most similar. Their high level of similarity is tested by determining that their pairing has least effect on the total variance within the group, i.e. the overall pattern of variation within the whole group is least changed. A search is then made for the pairing which has the next smallest effect on the whole pattern. This may involve linking two previously unpaired individuals or it may mean linking one unpaired child with the already existing pair. The process of linking the most similar children continues, and may logically proceed until all the children have been linked up again. In using the method, however, one may examine the groupings stage by stage and stop grouping at the point when the individuals in the same group appear to have meaningful similarities but individuals in different groups are so unlike as to make further linking of groups no longer meaningful.

For the purposes of our cluster analysis we examined in this way the

Table 7.12. *Persistence of specific items of problem behaviour from 3 to 8 years in the control group (N = 91)*

Specific item of problem behaviour	Percentage of children with item of problem behaviour definitely present at various ages (Numbers in brackets)							
	3 years only		3 and 8 years		8 years only		Neither age	
Poor appetite	13	(12)	1	(1)	8	(7)	78	(71)
Faddy eating	10	(9)	4	(4)	8	(7)	78	(71)
Difficulty settling at night	9	(8)	2	(2)	7	(6)	82	(75)
Waking at night	11	(10)	0	(0)	2	(2)	87	(79)
Sleeping in parents' bed	4	(4)	3	(3)	2	(2)	90	(82)
Large number of habits	12	(11)	0	(0)	1	(1)	87	(79)
Overactive, restless	5	(5)	3	(3)	8	(7)	83	(76)
Poor concentration	1	(1)	0	(0)	5	(5)	93	(85)
Attention seeking	2	(2)	5	(5)	5	(5)	92	(84)
Dependency	2	(2)	5	(5)	5	(5)	91	(83)
Difficult to control	1	(1)	1	(1)	8	(7)	90	(82)
Tempers	1	(1)	1	(1)	4	(4)	93	(85)
Unhappy mood	1	(1)	0	(0)	5	(5)	93	(85)
Worries	2	(2)	0	(0)	19	(17)	79	(72)
Fears	7	(6)	0	(0)	2	(2)	90	(82)
Relations with siblings	4	(3)	4	(3)	15	(11)	76	(54)
Relations with peers	0	(0)	0	(0)	3	(3)	97	(84)
Day wetting	24	(22)	1	(1)	1	(1)	73	(67)
Night wetting	32	(29)	1	(1)	4	(4)	63	(57)
Soiling	13	(12)	2	(2)	1	(1)	73	(67)

Table 7.13. *Relative persistence of specific items of problem behaviour from 3 to 8 years in the representative, behaviour problem and control groups*

Specific item of problem behaviour	Percentage of representative group not showing item of problem behaviour at 3 or 8 years	Percentage of children with item of problem behaviour at 3 years still showing the problem at 8 years			Percentage of children with item of problem behaviour at 8 years who showed the problem at 3 years		
		Representative group	Behaviour problem group	Control group	Representative group	Behaviour problem group	Control group
Poor appetite	73	32	40	8	46	81	13
Faddy eating	73	36	28	31	27	30	36
Difficulty settling at night	76	25	48	20	33	45	25
Waking at night	84	7	11	0	33	60	0
Sleeping in parents' bed	88	30	5	43	60	33	60
Large number of habits	82	0	4	0	0	50	0
Overactive, restless	76	24	24	38	36	75	30
Poor concentration	85	11	21	0	14	29	0
Attention seeking	85	11	24	0	14	60	0
Dependency	87	17	31	71	12	38	50
Difficult to control	83	36	28	50	40	82	13
Tempers	90	80	43	50	44	45	20
Unhappy mood	91	50	31	0	29	36	0
Worries	76	25	67	0	5	11	0
Fears	88	0	0	0	0	—	0
Relation with siblings	72	30	46	50	20	50	21
Relation with peers	88	25	30	0	12	39	0
Day wetting	72	4	0	4	50	—	50
Night wetting	63	3	22	3	25	91	20
Soiling	83	19	12	14	75	100	67

behavioural ratings of 205 children who comprised the problem group (99), the control group (99), and a small number of additional children selected because they had language delay alone. In many ways it would have been preferable to take a random sample from the total group, but the representative sample which we have just described was too small to allow a useful analysis to be carried out, and we had no access to longitudinal data on a larger representative group.

In our analysis we chose to stop clustering when there were five groups of children remaining. This number of clusters was selected partly because this seemed a meaningful decision on inspection of the data, and partly because we wished to make our data comparable with those of Wolkind and Everitt (1974) who had conducted a similar statistical analysis on children of the same age using approximately the same questionnaire.

From Table 7.14 we can examine the nature of the clusters identified. It can be seen that there are three rather clear cut groups and two that are more broadly defined. The clear cut clusters were roughly the same size and consisted of a "disturbed/widespread sphincter control problem group" with day and night wetting as well as soiling (24%), a normal group with few symptoms (21%) and a group wetting at night only (22%). Of the two more broadly defined groups the first, which we have called the "disturbed/night wetting/conduct problem" (DNC) group contained 10% of the children and the second which we have called "disturbed/restless/food fads" (DRF) contained 23% of the children. These five groups accounted for all the 205 children. These groups corresponded reasonably well with those identified by Wolkind and Everitt (1974) who found two principal clusters and three less well defined clusters in their study of three-year-olds attending nursery school and "in special care". Their first cluster consisted of children showing fears and habits, sleeping and eating problems, and their second cluster comprised children with bed wetting, tantrums and management problems. A high proportion of children "in care" were in this second group, whereas they were absent from the first group.

Our cluster analysis suggests that, at the age of three years, it is possible to distinguish four types of disturbance which may be broadly categorized as (a) disturbed/widespread sphincter control problem, (b) nocturnal bladder incontinence, (c) general disturbance with nocturnal bladder incontinence, (d) overactivity with food faddiness and restlessness. It should be noted that there is no hint of a neurotic or emotionally disturbed group at this age.

For a particular cluster to have clinical meaningfulness, it is necessary to demonstrate that those children who form part of the cluster are also similar in other ways. From Table 7.15 it can be seen that children who fell into our "normal" cluster were, as it might be expected, less linked to adverse

Table 7.14. *Characteristics of clusters identified in the combined behaviour problem and control groups at 3 years (N = 183)*

Cluster Number	Percentage of children in cluster	Mean total behaviour score for cluster	Deviant items of behaviour[a]	Clinical description
1	21%	10·8	None	Normal
2	22%	13·7	Night wetting (2·71)	Normal/Night wet
3	24%	20·0	Day wetting (2·82)	Disturbed/widespread sphincter control
			Night wetting (2·80)	
			Soiling (1·98)	
4	10%	21·6	Overactive, restless (1·50)	Disturbed/night wet/ conduct (DNC)
			Tempers (1·35)	
			Difficult to control (1·85)	
			Night wetting (2·35)	
			Poor concentration (1·30)	
			Unhappy mood (1·30)	
			Nail biting (0·85)	
			Relations with siblings (0·80)	
5	23%	16·8	Overactive, restless (1·68)	Disturbed/restless/ food fads (DRF)
			Faddy eating (1·17)	
			Difficult to control (1·31)	
			Poor appetite (1·42)	

[a]Items of problem behaviour for which the mean for the cluster was more than one standard deviation from the mean for the total sample. Actual cluster means are given in brackets.

Table 7.15. *Differences between clusters in the combined behaviour problem and control groups (N = 183) on measures at 3 years*

	Cluster (Figures as percentages, numbers in brackets)					
Measure at 3 years	Normal (N = 40)	Normal/ Nightwet (N = 37)	Disturbed/ Widespread sphincter control (N = 42)	Disturbed/ Nightwet/ Conduct (N = 18)	Disturbed/ restless/ food fads (N = 46)	P^a
Boys	45 (18)	54 (20)	79 (33)	39 (7)	50 (23)	<0·02
Non-manual social class	28 (11)	33 (12)	24 (10)	33 (6)	13 (6)	N.S.
Mother's mental state moderately or severely disturbed	8 (3)	14 (5)	12 (5)	22 (4)	9 (4)	N.S.
Marriage rated poor or very poor	13 (5)	25 (9)	29 (12)	50 (9)	40 (18)	<0·02
Mothers rated as critical of child	5 (2)	16 (6)	26 (11)	50 (9)	27 (12)	<0·002
Mothers rated as low in warmth	3 (1)	19 (7)	24 (10)	44 (8)	40 (18)	<0·001
In families with 3 or more stresses	25 (10)	38 (14)	29 (12)	44 (8)	28 (13)	
Child rated as mild, moderate or severely disturbed	23 (9)	32 (12)	57 (24)	100 (18)	67 (31)	<0·0001
In behaviour problem group	18 (7)	38 (14)	55 (23)	94 (17)	67 (31)	<0·0001

^{a}Significance level of chi-square test, d.f. = 4.

factors, than any of the other groups. Further, as also might have been predicted, children whose sphincter control problem was limited to nocturnal bed wetting were rather similar to normal children in this respect. The DNC and DRF groups were, by contrast, markedly different in the quality of family relationships, with much higher rates of poor parental marriage and mothers rated as highly critical or low in warmth. The "disturbed/widespread general sphincter control problem" group was intermediate between the normal and disturbed groups as far as these background factors were concerned.

Further validation is provided by the degree to which the cluster into which the child fell at three years predicted outcome. At four years 16 out of 18 (89%) of the children in the DNC group remained with problems compared with five out of the 40 (13%) in the normal cluster. At eight years 67% of the DNC group were disturbed compared to 28% of the normal group. The remaining three groups were intermediate in outcome at both four and eight years with very little difference between them.

At this point, therefore, it seems worth drawing the provisional conclusion that cluster analysis of behavioural items at three years seems to produce meaningful groups which need further investigation. Within symptomatic three-year-old children it is possible to distinguish between those who have a specific sphincter problem (night wetting), those who have a general sphincter control problem, those who have a widespread disorder characterized by a range of conduct problems, and those with a somewhat less widespread disorder characterized by appetite disturbance and restlessness or overactivity. The cluster in to which a child falls does have predictive significance for outcome, although three of the groups do not differ in this respect.

The grouping we have identified as valid differs in some respect from those others found in children of this age group. It is however not dissimilar to that described by Wolkind and Everitt (1974). They also identified a cluster of normal children characterized by their lack of symptoms. The second cluster they identified was also low in total symptoms and contained children with bed wetting as well as difficult relationships with others and temper outbursts. This cluster is similar to our normal night wetting group. Feeding and sleeping problems characterized a third cluster which was similar in some respects to our disturbed/restless/food fads group. The remaining groups identified by Wolkind and Everitt, although manifesting a high rate of disturbance were rather dissimilar from those identified in our own cluster analysis.

Our failure to identify a group of young children with emotional problems probably arose from the fact that our questionnaire had a rather limited section relating to fearful and anxious behaviour. Wolkind and Everitt have expanded this section of our questionnaire and were able to achieve delineation of such a group. This, however, raises the issue of whether the pattern of clusters identified owes more to the structure of the questionnaire than to the behaviour shown by the children themselves. Certainly, our ability to identify clusters relating to sphincter disturbances must arise from the fact that we have data from parents as well as teachers. This is in contrast to the work of others who have carried out factor analytic studies (e.g. Kohn and Rosman, 1972; Behar and Stringfield, 1974, and O'Donnell and Tuinan, 1979) on the basis of behavioural information from teachers.

As we have seen, the predictive significance of membership of a particular cluster is considerable in terms of the likelihood of retaining problematic behaviour into the school years. A more detailed description of our follow-up findings is however provided in subsequent chapters.

Summary

In this chapter we have described the prevalence of different individual items of behaviour at three, four and eight years. Some symptoms such as appetite disturbance and difficulty in getting off to sleep remained relatively stable in prevalence. Some, such as day and night wetting and waking during the night declined sharply and others such as a tendency to worry increased. Individual items of behaviour at the three ages were also examined to determine whether the same or different children were affected at different ages by specific symptoms. Finally, a cluster analysis was described which identified five patterns of behaviour occurring at three years: a "normal" group, a "night wetting" group, a "disturbed/widespread sphincter control problem" group, and two other groups characterized by a wider spread of disturbed behaviour. It was demonstrated that these groups had both concurrent and predictive validity. Children in the groups with wider patterns of disturbance had more adverse factors in their background and were more likely to remain problematic over the following five years. In the next chapter we describe a comparison of the outcome at four and eight years of the behaviour problem and control groups.

8 Outcome in Behaviour Problem and Control Children at Four and Eight Years

Behavioural outcome at four years

As already indicated, the same measures of behaviour were used at four years as in the initial phase of the survey, namely the behaviour screening questionnaire (BSQ), the behaviour check-list (BCL), and the clinical rating of behaviour based on the information obtained during the administration of the BSQ. With all these measures there was a high level of continuity from three to four years. At four years, 63% (59 out of 94) children in the behaviour problem group, compared to 11% (10 out of 91) children in the control group scored ten or more on the BSQ — the cut-off point thought best to divide disturbed from non-disturbed children. The other two global measures of behaviour confirmed this trend. Forty-nine per cent of the problem group scored ten or more on the BCL, compared to 7% of the control group. On the clinical rating about 14% of the control group fell into the mild, moderate, or severely disturbed categories at four years, compared with 70% of the behaviour problem group.

To add to the description of the behaviour of the four-year-olds, it may be helpful to insert here some randomly selected illustrative examples of these clinical ratings:

(1) Josephine D., Case No. 211

Josephine D. was rated at three years as having shown a "mild" problem. At four years, on the basis of the following description and with a BSQ score of 5, she was rated as showing no problem.

"She is now rather under-active and spends time just sitting around, but she is usually cheerful and plays happily on her own. She is self-contained and still not close to her mother. She is a rather faddy eater. She tends to be rather aimless in her behaviour. She has infrequent tempers now. Her behaviour is generally independent and occasionally she runs off into the street, but she is not usually naughty."

(2) Keith B., Case No. 339

Keith B. who had been rated as a "moderate" problem at three years, received the same clinical rating at four years when he had a BSQ score of 14. "At his nursery his teachers find him exhausting because they have to shout at him all the time. He is very disruptive and will not share with other children. They regard him as somewhat out of control. At home he tends to get involved in dangerous activities, e.g. he has put his pyjamas on the gas tap, and lights matches. He cannot be left with others because he is so difficult. He is very active and unable to concentrate, always being into things. He sleeps well, but is a faddy eater. He is attention-seeking and doesn't like being left at the nursery by his mother. He is a difficult boy to cuddle, being something of a loner. He tends to be spiteful to animals, to have a vicious temper and to torment his brother and sister and other children of his age. He has threatened to stab other children when he is angry."

(3) Peter K., Case No. 131

Peter K. had had a "marked" problem at three years, and still showed a "marked" problem (BSQ = 19) at four years.
"He is still very difficult and clings to his mother, afraid of being abandoned. It is impossible to control him, and he has severe tempers. He is frequently extremely naughty and drives his mother to the end of her tether. He bosses his mother around, saying things like 'it's your place to do this'. He screams until he gets what he wants and is never happy, always whining and grisly. He has a poor appetite and is very faddy. He is still fighting with his brother, and breaks toys or, for example, drops Lego out of the window. He is very fussy about cleanliness, and food has to be laid out carefully without any marks on the plate. It is important for him not to have a speck on his clothes. He occasionally sleeps with his parents. His concentration is very poor and he never plays with anything for more than a moment or two. He is always attention-seeking, restless, and cannot be left with anyone else."

(4) Jonathan C., Case No. 814

Jonathan C. had been a "moderate" problem at three years, but was now only rated as a "mild" problem (BSQ score = 10).

"He is still a very poor eater, living off ice-cream and chips. He is always on the go, and is very demanding of attention though he is able to play on his own. He torments his sister. He is very frightened of dogs barking. He is mischievous and throws stones. He plays up most of the day, but is never really out of control. He no longer has a toilet training problem. He cries when left at the play-group, but soon gets over his upset. There he tends to be a bit of a bully and fights a lot though he can play with other children."

It is of interest (Table 8.1) that the behaviour problem and control groups continue to differ on so many items and that, in general, the items of behaviour which distinguish the two groups at three years continue to do so at four years. Continuities and discontinuities of behaviour are described in more detail in other chapters, but here it is appropriate just to note that at four years the behaviour problem group had, to a highly significant degree, more appetite difficulties and more sleep problems. They were much more commonly overactive, had poor concentration, and were difficult to control. They were described as more miserable and worried children and they had more specific fears — especially fears of the dark and of thunder. They had worse relationships with their peers and with their sibs.

By contrast, there were a number of areas of behaviour in which the two groups did not differ significantly. The problem group still did not wet the bed by night or their pants by day more, although they did soil themselves to a significantly more marked degree. There was also little difference in the rate of thumb and finger sucking between the two groups.

Behavioural outcome at eight years

There was again a highly significant difference between the two groups in the overall clinical rating of behaviour made on the basis of all available information about the child. On this rating 62% of the problem group remained with a disturbance of at least mild, moderate or severe level, compared to only 22% in the control group. Similarly, examining the scores on the child behaviour questionnaires completed by parents, twice as many problem group children (43% compared to 20%) scored over the cut-off point found to indicate a high risk of behaviour and emotional problems. In those children rated as deviant, an antisocial outcome was found to be somewhat more common than a neurotic outcome on all but one of the comparisons

Table 8.1. *Mean BSQ and BCL scores, percentage of children with specific items of problem behaviour rated as definitely present on the BSQ in the behaviour problem and control groups scoring above the cut off point on the BSQ, and rating clinically as having a problem, at age 4 years*

	Behaviour problem group (N = 94)	Control group (N = 91)	P^a
Mean BSQ score	10·9	5·5	<0·001
Mean BCL score	9·7	6·0	<0·001
Poor appetite	38·3%	15·4%	<0·001
Faddy eating	43·6%	22·0%	<0·001
Difficulty settling at night	25·5%	11·0%	<0·05
Waking at night	19·1%	7·7%	<0·05
Sleeping in parents' bed	20·2%	4·4%	<0·01
Large number of habits	11·7%	14·3%	N.S.
Overactive, restless	40·4%	8·8%	<0·001
Poor concentration	17·0%	2·2%	<0·001
Attention-seeking	23·4%	3·3%	<0·001
Dependency	7·4%	3·3%	N.S.
Difficult to control	39·4%	5·5%	<0·001
Tempers	27·7%	3·3%	<0·001
Unhappy mood	14·9%	4·4%	<0·05
Worries	17·0%	5·5%	<0·05
Fears	24·5%	6·6%	<0·01
Relations with siblings	31·9%	11·0%	<0·001
Relations with peers	11·7%	5·5%	N.S.
Day wetting (at least once a week)	17·0%	7·7%	N.S.
Recent onset day wetting	5·3%	0·0%	N.S.
Night wetting (at least 3 nights a week)	24·5%	13·2%	N.S.
Recent onset night wetting	4·3%	4·4%	N.S.
Soiling (at least once a week)	8·5%	1·1%	<0·05
Recent onset soiling	6·3%	1·1%	N.S.
Scoring ≥ 10 on the BSQ	63%	11%	<0·001
Clinical rating of problem	70%	14%	<0·001

[a]Significance level of chi-square test, d.f. = 1, for percentages or *t*-test for means

Table 8.2. *Behavioural deviance in the behaviour problem and control groups at age 8 years*

Measure of behavioural deviance	Behaviour problem group (N = 94)		Control group (N = 91)		P^a
Rutter parent questionnaire					
Not deviant	57%		81%		
Anti-social and mixed	21%	43%	13%	20%	$0·002^b$
Neurotic	22%		7%		
Rutter teacher questionnaire					
Not deviant	61%		77%		
Anti-social and mixed	25%	39%	13%	24%	$0·055^b$
Neurotic	14%		11%		
Clinical rating of severity					
Not deviant	14%		54%		
Dubious	25%		24%		
Mild	34%		11%		$0·0001^c$
Moderate	25%	62%	11%	22%	
Severe	3%		0%		
Clinical rating of type of deviance					
Not deviant	39%		78%		
Anti-social	38%	61%	14%	22%	$0·0001^b$
Neurotic	23%		8%		
Referral to services					
Any contact with child guidance services	38%		16%		$0·001^b$
Contact specifically about index child	24%		4%		$0·01^b$

^{a}Significance level of chi-square test
^{b}d.f. = 1
^{c}d.f. = 2

made. The fifty fathers also completed behaviour questionnaires on their boys and, in general, there was good agreement between mothers and fathers in this respect ($r = 0·47$).

The scores on the questionnaires completed by teachers confirmed the parental view that the problem group still had more difficulties. Thirty-nine per cent of the problem group children scored over the cut-off point generally thought to indicate a strong likelihood of the presence of significant behaviour or emotional problems, compared to 24% in the control group ($P < 0.05$). If a problem child showed behavioural deviance, it was more likely to be of antisocial than of neurotic type. By eight years, 38% of the families of the problem group had been in contact with child guidance services compared with 16% of the controls; in 24% this contact had been in connection with the index child. Only 4% of the control group families ($P < 0.01$) had attended because of a problem with the index control child. It should be stressed that in most cases, contact with child guidance had been brief and for assessment purposes only.

Obviously, the number of children identified as problematic will depend on the threshold selected to indicate disturbance. Once again, therefore, it may be illuminating to incorporate examples of clinical ratings of different levels of severity. Teachers questionnaire scores of nine or more, and parent questionnaire scores of 13 or more, can be taken as indicative of behavioural deviance.

(1) Peter K., Case No. 131

Peter K. had had a "marked" problem at three and four years. At eight years, with a teacher questionnaire score of five and a parent questionnaire score of 14, he was rated as showing a marked neurotic disorder.

"He is now the eldest of three children, and his father left home when he was five years old. His mother had re-married a few months previously, and the family live on the seventh floor of a tower block. He has had asthma since his father left home. He also has severe migrainous headaches about once a month and on these occasions spends the day in bed. He was very upset when his father left, and worried about his mother, leaving school frequently to see if she was all right. He now goes happily to school, but does not stand up for himself there and is sometimes bullied. He does have friends but will not visit their homes because he does not like to leave his mother. He will only play out on the landing and will not have friends in the flat in case they mess up his toys.

At home he is still very faddy and a poor eater. He never concentrates well and can amuse himself but is nevertheless fidgety and restless. He takes about an hour to go to bed, and will not go to bed at all if his mother is out until she gets back. He has miserable moods which may last several hours. He gets very upset if anything sad happens, for example on the television. He is always worrying about his mother and never likes being separated from her. He is perfectionist about the order in which his toys are kept, the way his bed is made, the way the cutlery is laid out, and how his Weetabix is placed on his plate. If told off, he may have a temper lasting up to an hour. He may rip up his own drawings. He is very attention-seeking of his mother, and has a habit of clearing his throat all the time."

(2) Sandra M., Case No. 012

Sandra M. had been described as having a "mild" problem at three and four years and at eight years, with a parent questionnaire score of 15 and a teacher questionnaire score of 11, was rated as having a mild neurotic disorder.

"Her older brothers and sisters have grown up and left home. There is a problem over attendance at school. She has frequent stomach aches in the morning and very often does not want to go to school. She sometimes cries before school, although she will usually go. She worries over little things there, such as PE and being told off. She does not stand up for herself, and sometimes gets bullied. She is very shy and a poor mixer, and will only play with one girl.

At home her appetite is poor and she is very faddy. She has poor concentration and cannot amuse herself for very long. She is restless and fidgety. She sleeps well, but has frequent miserable moods related usually to worry over some aspect of school. She frequently cries about going to school and is always worried about it. She is very nervous of dogs, cats, and spiders and is said "to do her nut" if she catches sight of any of these in close proximity. She has tempers if frustrated, and occasionally lies. She has stolen money on a couple of occasions and is still slow to settle to sleep."

(3) Jonathan C., Case No. 814

Jonathan C. had been described as having a "moderate" problem at three years and a "mild" problem at four years. At eight years he had a parent questionnaire score of 20 and a teacher questionnaire score of 29. Clinically he was thought to show a moderate conduct disorder.

"His parents are now separated and he is living with his mother and older sister in temporary accommodation. His behaviour has deteriorated since his father left home three years ago.

He finds it hard to adapt to any changes at school and will not do any work there. He tends to beat up other children and has reduced the teacher to tears. He is regarded as out of control there, and his mother is frequently called in by the school. He is thought to be a bully, have little concentration and no close friends.

In his neighbourhood he has a friend who is a 'professional thief'. He is a very faddy eater and has a poor appetite. At home he is able to amuse himself, but he is restless and fidgety, and chews his fingers. He goes out on

Table 8.3. *Percentage of children in the behaviour problem and control groups showing specific items of problem behaviour to a marked degree based on interview with mother at age 8 years*

| | Percentage of children showing item of problem behaviour to a marked degree | | |
	Behaviour problem group	Control group	P^a
Poor appetite	22	9	0·03
Faddy eating	29	12	0·02
Constipation	1	0	N.S.
Poor relations with peers	20	3	0·001
Poor concentration	18	6	0·003
Attention-seeking	16	6	N.S.
Overactive, restless	19	11	N.S.
Fidgetiness	39	21	0·005
Tics	1	0	N.S.
Large number of habits	2	1	N.S.
Poor fine motor coordination	3	0	N.S.
Poor gross motor coordination	3	2	N.S.
Stammering	1	0	N.S.
Poor articulation	3	1	N.S.
Difficulty settling at night	31	9	0·001
Night waking	5	2	N.S.
Sleeping in parents' bed	3	6	N.S.
Difficulty separating from parents	14	6	N.S.
Poor self-help skills	6	2	N.S.
Unhappy mood	15	6	0·01
Worries	38	19	0·009
Obsessions	5	2	N.S.
Fears	0	2	N.S.
Poor relations with siblings	30	18	N.S.
Tempers	21	6	0·001
Difficult to control	18	9	0·001
Soiling	3	3	N.S.
Night wetting	12	6	0·02
Day wetting	0	2	N.S.

[a]Significance level of chi-square test, d.f. = 1

his own and his mother does not know where he is. When he is at home he cries, whines and grizzles a good deal whenever he is frustrated. He never talks about his feelings and has no apparent worries. He still tends to torment his sister and frequently swears and lies. He seems unresponsive to attempts to control him. He is very reckless, for example when he is riding his bike.''

The overall behaviour score results were of course obtained by summing individual behavioural items. It therefore follows that the problem group also showed more specific difficulties, and it is of some interest to note in which areas this tendency was most marked. There were, in fact, differences over a wide range of individual items and this is well illustrated in Table 8.3, in which comparisons are made based on the clinical interview.

It can be seen that the problem group still presented more management difficulties, such as difficulties getting off to sleep at night and settling to sleep. They had significantly more temper tantrums, and were difficult to control, manifesting antisocial behaviour such as attention-seeking, stealing and getting into fights. However, they also showed more neurotic behaviour with unhappy mood and an excess of worries. They showed wetting at night, though not wetting by day, significantly more commonly.

The problem group children showed poorer social relationships. They got on less well with their sibs and had more marked difficulties in forming relationships with other children. They were more likely to be bullied and not to stand up for themselves. They were more fidgety and were thought to be significantly less able to concentrate.

Psychological test results at four years

It will be recalled that at four years the children were all given the English picture vocabulary test, the two sub-scales of the Griffiths mental development scales administered at three years (hand–eye co-ordination and performance), and the expressive scale of the Reynell developmental language scale. In addition, the Wechsler pre-school and primary scale of intelligence (WPPSI) was administered. The behaviour of the child during testing was rated on the same 14 scales as had been the case at three years.

Comparison of mean scores in behaviour problem and control group

There were less marked differences on the EPVT and Griffiths' tests between the groups at age four than at three years. The only significant difference

Table 8.4. *Mean scores for the total group and for boys and girls in the behaviour problem and control groups on developmental and intelligence tests at 4 years*

Test	N	Behaviour problem group Mean	Standard deviation	N	Control group Mean	Standard deviation	P^a
Age in months	94	50·0	1·8	91	50·1	1·8	N.S.
EPVT	91	101.8	13·7	90	104·2	12·1	N.S.
Griffiths Scale D	91	103·8	20·6	90	107·6	18·0	N.S.
Griffiths Scale E	92	101·6	15·8	90	106·3	15·0	0·042
WPPSI Verbal IQ	88	96·1	17·7	88	103·3	15·7	0·004
WPPSI Performance IQ	88	94·7	15·0	89	101·4	15·0	0·003
WPPSI Full-Scale IQ	88	95·2	16·7	88	102·9	15·7	0·002

Test	N	BOYS Mean	Standard deviation	N	BOYS Mean	Standard deviation	P^a
Age in months	52	49.8	1·7	50	50·1	1·8	N.S.
EPVT	51	101·6	12·8	49	104·5	11·9	N.S.
Griffiths Scale D	51	98·1	19·6	50	103·4	15·7	N.S.
Griffiths Scale E	52	100·8	15·0	50	103·6	14·8	N.S.
WPPSI Verbal IQ	49	93·4	15·7	48	101·7	14·9	0·009
WPPSI Performance IQ	49	92·3	14·2	49	99·6	12·8	0·01
WPPSI Full-scale IQ	49	92·3	14·9	48	101·0	14·0	0·004

Test	N	GIRLS Mean	Standard deviation	N	GIRLS Mean	Standard deviation	P^a
Age in months	42	50·2	1·9	41	50·2	2·0	N.S.
EPVT	40	101·9	15·0	41	103·9	12·4	N.S.
Griffiths Scale D	40	111·0	19·8	40	112·9	19·4	N.S.
Griffiths Scale E	40	102·6	16·9	40	109·6	14·8	0·05
WPPSI Verbal IQ	39	99·4	18·9	40	105·2	16·6	N.S.
WPPSI Performance IQ	39	97·6	15·7	40	103·6	17·2	N.S.
WPPSI Full-scale IQ	39	98·9	18·3	40	105·1	17·4	N.S.

^{a}Significance level of *t*-test

found at this age on these tests was that the girls in the behaviour problem group had significantly lower performance IQs than girls in the control group (see Table 8.4). The trend is maintained that children in the control group were developmentally advanced compared to the behaviour problem group but only to the extent of some three or four points on average compared to seven or eight points at three years of age. However, at four years of age the WPPSI was introduced. This test gives verbal and performance IQs based on scores on five subtests in each case. Both the verbal and performance IQs, and consequently the full-scale IQs of the children in the behaviour problem group were significantly lower than those in the control group. This significant difference was restricted to the boys, although the girls in the behaviour problem group were scoring consistently less well than their same sex controls.

Criteria for general and specific delays in development at four years

At this age the following criteria were employed to designate deviance:

(1) Low IQ. This was based on a WPPSI full-scale IQ of less than 85.

(2) General language delay. The child's measured language age on the expressive language scale of the Reynell development language scale was compared to its chronological age. If the language age was six months or more behind chronological age, the child was designated as showing mild general language delay or, if more than twelve months behind, as showing severe general language delay.

(3) Specific language delay. A predicted language age was obtained from the child's chronological age and WPPSI full-scale IQ, by the use of separate regression equations. Each child's observed language age on the RDLS was then compared to the predicted language age. If the observed language age was more than six months below predicted language age, the child was designated as showing mild specific language delay, or, if more than twelve months below, as showing severe specific language delay.

Comparison of rates of children in control and problem groups with significantly delayed development at four years

As at three years, there was a tendency for higher rates of all types of delay, both specific and general, to occur in the problem group. In the total group of boys and girls the problem group had a significantly higher proportion of children with low IQ, as well as higher rates of both specific and general language delay. The same trend was evident when the sexes were examined

Table 8.5. *Percentage of the total group and of boys and girls in the behaviour problem and control groups showing various developmental delays at 4 years*

				Percentage with developmental delay					
Developmental delay	Behaviour problem group (N = 94)	Control group (N = 91)	P^a	Behaviour problem group BOYS (N = 52)	Control group BOYS (N = 50)	P^a	Behaviour problem group GIRLS (N = 42)	Control group GIRLS (N = 41)	P^a
Mild specific language delay	36·2	23·1	N.S.	44·2	28·0	N.S.	26·2	17·1	N.S.
Severe specific language delay	26·6	17·6	N.S.	28·8	18·0	N.S.	23·8	17·1	N.S.
Mild general language delay	39·4	24·2	0·05	44·2	28·0	N.S.	33·3	19·5	N.S.
Severe general language delay	31·9	16·5	0·05	36·5	16·0	0·05	26·2	17·1	N.S.
Low WPPSI Full-Scale IQ	33·0	12·5	0·01	32·7	14·6	N.S.	33·3	10·0	0·05

^{a}Significance level of chi-square test, d.f. = 1

separately, although only in the case of severe general language delay in boys and low IQ in girls did the differences achieve statistical significance, (see Table 8.5).

Psychological test results at eight years

At this age the children were given a shortened form of the Wechsler intelligence scale, so that it was possible to calculate a full-scale IQ as well as a verbal and performance IQ. In addition, the Neale analysis of reading test was administered, from the results of which it is possible to compute scores related to both reading accuracy and comprehension. Finally the children were given the Schonell spelling test.

Comparison of mean scores in behaviour problem and control group at eight years

The behaviour problem group scored on average less well on all items of the WISC, and this difference was significant as far as the full-scale and verbal IQ mean scores were concerned. The same trend appeared when comparisons were made separately for boys and girls, although in neither case were statistically significant differences obtained, except in the case of the boys' full-scale IQ.

The scores on the reading test were calculated separately for reading accuracy (based on a count of reading errors) and reading comprehension (obtained by asking the child questions on the prose texts they had just read). For each measure of reading two scores were obtained. The first (called the CA-related score) was obtained by subtracting the child's chronological age from his measured reading age. The result is expressed in months of reading age above or below that expected from chronological age. The second (IQ-related score) is that obtained by subtracting the child's predicted reading age, calculated from a knowledge of the child's IQ as well as his chronological age from his measured reading age. Once again the technique of multiple regression was used to obtain the predicted reading age. From Table 8.6 it can be seen that the mean score of the problem and control groups differs most in the CA-related scores of reading and, particularly markedly, spelling rather than in the IQ-related scores, though the same trend is apparent throughout.

We were again concerned to examine whether disturbed behaviour during the testing situation might be important in producing lower scores in the behaviour problem group. Test behaviour was assessed at eight years on the following 18 scales: rapport, disinhibition, emotional responsiveness, mood, anxiety, fidgetiness, gross motor activity, tics, clarity of speech,

Table 8.6. *Mean scores for the total group and for boys and girls in the behaviour problem and control groups on attainment and intelligence tests at 8 years*

Test	N	Behaviour problem group Mean	Standard deviation	N	Control group Mean	Standard deviation	P^a
Age in months	94	96·3	2.7	91	95·9	1·7	N.S.
WISC verbal IQ	93	109·1	20·5	91	113·9	17·1	N.S.
WISC performance IQ	93	105·9	15·9	91	110·4	12·3	0·035
WISC full-scale IQ	93	106·3	13·1	91	110·1	10·4	0·031
Neale comprehension IQ-related RA	93	−1·2	10·9	91	−0·1	12·0	N.S.
Neale accuracy IQ-related RA	93	−3·2	11·8	91	0·1	11·6	N.S.
Neale comprehension CA-related RA	93	0·0	16·3	91	4·7	16·0	0·049
Neale accuracy CA-related RA	93	1·5	16·0	91	7·8	14·6	0·006
Schonell CA-related spelling age	88	−5·7	18·6	87	1·9	15·7	0·004

| | | BOYS | | | BOYS | | |
Test	N	Mean	Standard deviation	N	Mean	Standard deviation	P^a
Age in months	52	96·2	2·5	50	95·9	1·6	N.S.
WISC verbal IQ	52	109·1	20·3	50	115·6	18·0	N.S.
WISC performance IQ	52	106·1	16·9	50	111·8	13·5	N.S.
WISC full-scale IQ	52	106·4	13·7	50	111·4	11·1	0·047
Neale comprehension IQ-related RA	52	−3·2	10·1	50	−2·3	10·8	N.S.
Neale accuracy IQ-related RA	52	−8·0	10·4	50	−3·1	10·7	0·021
Neale comprehension CA-related RA	52	−2·0	16·2	50	3·8	15·6	N.S.
Neale accuracy CA-related RA	52	−3·3	14·4	50	5·7	14·2	0·002
Schonell CA-related spelling age	50	−11·4	17·8	48	−0·6	16·4	0·002

		GIRLS			GIRLS		
Age in months	42	96·5	2·9	41	95·9	1·8	N.S.
WISC verbal IQ	41	109·0	21·1	41	111·7	15·9	N.S.
WISC performance IQ	41	105·7	14·8	41	108·7	10·6	N.S.
WISC full-scale IQ	41	106·2	12·4	41	108·5	9·3	N.S.
Neale comprehension IQ-related RA	41	1·4	11·4	41	2·5	13·0	N.S.
Neale accuracy IQ-related RA	41	2·9	10·7	41	3·9	11·5	N.S.

	Behaviour problem group			Control group			
Test	N	Mean	Standard deviation	N	Mean	Standard deviation	P^a
Neale comprehension CA-related RA	41	2·4	16·4	41	5·7	16·6	N.S.
Neale accuracy CA-related RA	41	7·6	16·1	41	10·3	14·8	N.S.
Schonell CA-related spelling age	38	1·8	17·1	39	5·0	14·2	N.S.

[a]Significance level of *t*-test

frequency of spontaneous remarks, conversational coherence, maturity, effort to control testing, coordination of gross motor movements, coordination of fine motor movements, concentration, distractability and attractiveness of appearance. At this age it did appear as a result of the statistical technique carried out (the two-way analysis of variance) as if the demonstration of disturbed or immature behaviour in the test was related more closely to a poor score in the behaviour problem group rather than in the control group. This effect was demonstrated in six out of the 18 test behaviours examined. For example, the mean IQ of the control group children who were thought to be showing age-appropriate behavioural "maturity" was 110·5; for the "immature" it was 112·6. However, in the behaviour problem group the "mature" children scored 108·0 and the "immature" a mean of 99·6. It will be seen, however, that in this case there were sizeable differences even after the effect of "maturity" was taken into account, and the same was true for the other variables examined. It seems, therefore, that behaviour during testing does relate to, and perhaps affect, performance in testing, but this in itself is not sufficient to account for the differences found between the two groups.

Criteria for general and specific delays in development at eight years

(1) Low IQ. This was based on a short-form WISC full-scale IQ of less than 90 — this may seem a high criterion, but this was necessary in order to obtain an appropriately sized group.

(2) Reading backwardness. This was a measure of the child's measured reading and comprehension age when compared with chronological age. If

either of these was 12 months or more behind chronological age the child was designated as showing mild reading backwardness, and if 18 months or more behind, as showing severe reading backwardness.

(3) Specific reading retardation. If the observed reading age for either comprehension or accuracy was more than 12 months below predicted reading age (based on the result of a regression analysis of reading age on chronological age and full-scale IQ), the child was designated as showing mild specific reading retardation. If the child was more than 18 months below this predicted reading age he was designated as showing severe specific reading retardation.

Comparison of rates of children in control and problem groups with significantly delayed development at eight years

There are marked differences between the behaviour problem and control groups in the rates of mild and severe reading backwardness, but this is not the case in specific reading backwardness when IQ is taken into account. There is also a significantly greater number of children in the behaviour problem group with low IQ at this age. Also at this age, clear-cut sex differences begin to emerge. The problem group of boys have much higher rates of reading backwardness and low IQ than do control boys. This trend is much less apparent as far as the girls are concerned (see Table 8.7).

Outcome and the family when the child was eight-years-old

(a) Family background

The families were geographically more stable than we had expected, although, as already mentioned, over half of them had moved at least once since the previous interview. However, about 80% were still living in Waltham Forest, of whom a few had moved out of the Borough and then back again. Of the rest, most were living in Greater London or Essex, and only 9% in other parts of the country. Eighty-six per cent of the problem group and the same percentage of the control group were still living with their two natural parents. Most of the remainder were living with their mothers alone and half of these were now single parents. The average number of children per family in the total group of problem and control groups was 2·7, with 7% only children. Thirty per cent of our children had two brothers or sisters, and 22% had three or more sibs, very large families being rather uncommon.

Table 8.7. *Percentage of the total group and of boys and girls in the behaviour problem and control groups showing educational retardation and low IQ at 8 years*

Educational retardation	Percentage with educational retardation								
	Behaviour problem group (N = 94)	Control group (N = 91)	P^a	Behaviour problem group BOYS (N = 52)	Control group BOYS (N = 50)	P^a	Behaviour problem group GIRLS (N = 42)	Control group GIRLS (N = 41)	P^a
Mild specific reading retardation	24·7	22·0	N.S.	38·5	28·0	N.S.	7·3	14·6	N.S.
Severe specific reading retardation	10·8	6·6	N.S.	19·2	8·0	N.S.	0·0	4·9	N.S.
Mild reading backwardness	29·0	14·3	<0·05	36·5	14·0	<0·05	19·5	14·6	N.S.
Severe reading backwardness	15·1	3·3	<0·05	19·2	2·0	<0·05	9·8	4·9	N.S.
Low WISC full-scale IQ	10·8	2·2	<0·05	11·5	0·0	<0·05	9·8	4·9	N.S.

[a]Significance level of chi-square test, d.f. = 1

The two groups did not differ significantly in family size, although there were somewhat more problem children living in families with four or more children. The birth order of the children was still not different in the two groups.

The two groups had been matched initially for social class when the children were three years old and there was no indication that the problem group had declined relatively in occupational status over the five-year period. Twenty-four per cent of the fathers were now in non-manual and 65% in manual occupations. Almost exactly the same proportion (about 45%) of the women in the two groups were working at least part-time — a higher proportion than when the children were younger. In general no special caretaking arrangements were thought necessary for the children but when this was required, in most cases the father was the person responsible. Occasionally neighbours, friends, relatives or other children helped out, but in no case was paid help employed for this purpose.

Most women who worked gave the earning of money as an important reason for doing so (78%). Only 20% worked because it provided company for them and a somewhat higher proportion (36%) gave as a reason that they wanted to get out of the house. Most fathers approved of their wives working — only 1% of fathers was said to dislike their wives going out to work, and a further 10% were thought to be dubious about it. Amongst those women not working, about half did not wish to do so, and only a third definitely wanted to. The reason most often given for not working, amongst those wishing to do so, was a caretaking problem with younger children. Only a very small number did not work because their husbands disapproved or because they could not find a suitable job.

There were also no striking differences between the two groups in their housing circumstances. They did not differ in the type of accommodation in which they lived (house, flat, maisonette, etc.), nor in the form of possession (council or owner-occupation). The groups were very similar in their domestic facilities, but the problem group were somewhat less likely to have access to a garden. Twenty-seven per cent, against 13%, did not enjoy access to a garden ($P < 0.06$). Virtually all the families owned a television set. On parental report, about 16% of the children watched three or more hours television during the week, but 59% watched more than three hours on Saturdays and 34% watched for at least this period on Sundays. There was no difference between the two groups in the amount of television they watched. We have no information on the types of programme the children observed.

(b) Contact with family and friends

In both groups, contact with grandparents remained quite frequent and the groups did not differ in this respect. Thus 59% of both groups had seen the paternal grandmother in the month prior to interview and about two-thirds of both groups had visited or been visited by the maternal grandmother during this period.

The children's range of contacts was, in general, quite wide, but there were differences between the groups. The group that had shown behaviour problems at three years more commonly had not seen or had any friends round over the previous month (15%, compared to 4% in the control group), and they also had a narrower range of acquaintances — 73% of the controls having three or more friends on visiting terms, compared to only 50% of the behaviour problem group. The groups did not appear to differ in the amount of encouragement their parents gave them to see friends, but the behaviour problem group had more difficulties in their relationship with other children — 20% of them being rated as having marked difficulties in this respect, compared to 3% of controls.

(c) Stress on the family

As on the previous occasions, the respondents were asked about acute and chronic stresses which might have impinged on their lives in a number of different areas, such as deaths or serious illnesses among family or close friends, financial worries, serious housing difficulties, etc. Again, the problem group seemed to have suffered more of these events, both recently and over the previous four years. Seventeen per cent of the problem group families had had three or more acute stresses over the previous four years, compared to 2% in the control group ($P < 0.05$) and a total score of four or more stresses (acute and chronic) was rated for 29% of the problem group, compared to 7% of the control group ($P < 0.03$). Despite their similar occupational status, therefore, the two groups continued to differ in the degree of adversity of their external social circumstances.

(d) The family and schooling

This was the first occasion on which we were able to obtain information about the parental attitudes to education and the child's schooling. Few of the parents had had the benefit of further education themselves, indeed only about one in seven of the fathers and about one in five of the mothers had experienced any further education beyond the age of fifteen years. One of the fathers and none of the mothers had had a university education.

Nevertheless, the interest taken in the child's education was considerable and, bearing in mind the number of variables examined, there were rather few differences between the two groups. Fifty-five per cent of the mothers in the total group had talked to the child's teacher six or more times since the child had begun school about three years previously. Only 2% of mothers, but 30% of fathers had seen the teacher on only one occasion or not at all. Seventy per cent of mothers and about half the fathers reported that they helped the child with reading and/or number work, and about a third of the mothers read together regularly with their children. Interestingly, just under a third of the mothers of these eight-year-olds thought their children should have homework or more homework to do, and significantly more of the problem group mothers (15% against 5%) had actually asked the teacher for homework. Parental aspirations for their children were significantly lower in the problem than in the control group with 45% wanting their children to stay on beyond compulsory leaving age, compared to 60% in the control group. These findings may be a reflection of the fact that the problem group children were certainly having more difficulties in school. Three of them were already at special schools and a significantly higher number (a quarter compared to a tenth) were receiving special help in ordinary schools. A significantly higher proportion of the problem group parents were definitely worried about their children's educational progress.

The children's performance on formal testing by the project psychologist (J.S.) is discussed earlier in this chapter.

The educational difficulties experienced by the problem group and described above were accompanied by a higher rate of behavioural difficulties in the classroom as reported by parents. The problem group children were more often thought by their parents to be showing poor concentration and to be a disruptive influence in the classroom and, as mentioned above, they also had more difficulties with their peers outside the classroom. There were less marked differences between the groups on data provided by the teachers.

(e) Family relationships

As in previous years, the parents (or, more usually, the mother alone) were interviewed regarding various aspects of their marital relationship and the attitudes towards their children, and again the information obtained revealed marked continuing differences between the two groups. The marital relationship rating, based on the amount of mutual affection, satisfaction, tension and quarrelling, etc., was rated as poor or very poor in 42% of the problem group and 17% of the control group ($P < 0.003$).

The problem group marriages were less satisfactory in more specific ways. Although the amount of help given with the children by fathers in the two groups did not differ, there was significantly more dissatisfaction by mothers with father's role in the problem group. Problem group parents talked over problems together less and the mothers in this group confided less in their husbands. Decisions were reported to be made significantly less often by mutual agreement. Nevertheless, there was a definite tendency in both groups, perhaps more marked in the control group, for the informants to see the marital relationship as having improved over the years since the previous interview. Overall, 32% felt their relationship had improved compared to only 9% who perceived a deterioration.

Similar differences were noted in parental attitudes towards the children. Both problem group mothers and fathers found it significantly more difficult to show affection and the interviewers rated them as showing less demonstrated warmth towards their children. They were also significantly more critical of their children at interview and the mothers, though not the fathers, described themselves as being more irritable towards their children. Forty per cent of the problem group mothers reported at least one outburst of temper a day towards their child, compared to 22% in the control group. Feelings of loss of control and frequency of smacking did not, however, differ between the two groups at this age.

(f) Physical and mental health of the parents

With increase in age, the number of physical problems in the parents inevitably increased too, and a surprisingly high proportion of the mothers in particular had at least a mild physical problem. Twenty-three per cent of the control group and a significantly higher rate (47%) of the behaviour problem group mothers had had at least some sort of physical disorder over the previous year. The differences were also marked in the rates of psychiatric problems experienced by the mothers in the two groups. Forty-nine per cent of the problem group mothers had had at least a mild psychiatric problem and in 26% this was of at least moderate severity. Only 10% of the control group mothers had had a psychiatric problem at a moderate level of severity. By contrast, fathers in the two groups differed in their rate of psychiatric disorder hardly at all. Only 9% of the problem group fathers and 3% of the control fathers had had a moderate or severe psychiatric disability over the previous year. This finding was to some degree confirmed by information obtained from fathers of 49 boys (23 behaviour problems and 26 control group) who were seen separately. Although because of the relatively small numbers involved the differences did not reach statistical significance, 15% of the control group fathers and 22% of the behaviour problem fathers had at least a mild disturbance, compared to 27% and 44% of the mothers of these children. In so far, therefore, as childhood disturbance interrelates with parental problems in three to eight-year-old children, there appears to be a much closer link with maternal than with paternal psychiatric disorder.

(g) Physical health of the children: outcome

The children were not physically examined at this stage of the study and our information regarding their physical state is derived entirely from parental report. Most of the children seemed in good general health and, although there was a tendency for the children in the problem group to have more indication of physical disorders, in few cases did this difference reach a statistically significant level. In the total group, 2% of the children had had asthma over the previous year, 1% had had epilepsy or were on anti-convulsants, 2% had a visual and 4% had a hearing problem. There was a significant tendency for behaviour problem group children to have a higher rate of other physical disabilities and they were also more likely (though not significantly so) both to be admitted to hospital and to have had an accident requiring medical attention over the previous year.

Summary

This chapter presents an overview of the findings when the children were followed up at four and eight years of age. There continued to be substantial differences in the behaviour of the two groups, with the behaviour problem group showing a continued high level of disturbance at home and school both at four and eight years. The control group mean scores on tests of development, intelligence and educational attainment were consistently higher than the problem group. The proportion of children with both specific and general delays in development remained higher in the problem group and, at eight years, this was particularly noticeable in the boys.

The group of disturbed children had to cope with more external stress during the four-year period in question. In addition, the rates of psychological disturbance in parents, especially mothers, remained higher in the problem group. Parents of problem group children showed more difficulties in their own marital relationships and had also had more physical ill-health.

9 Factors Associated with Outcome — an Overview

In the previous chapter we reported our finding that there was a highly significant difference in behavioural outcome between the problem and control groups. This difference was present in comparisons based on teachers', as well as parents', accounts. Comparison was also made in the previous chapter between problem and control groups on a variety of other factors.

It was, of course, also possible to examine the influence of these factors on outcome in each of the groups separately. Thus, in the group which had been problematic at three years, using the clinical rating of disturbance at eight years as perhaps the best measure of outcome, of the 94 children who were seen at both three and eight years, 58 (62%) still showed mild, moderate or severe disorders, and 36 (38%) showed none, or only dubious problems, at eight years. What were the factors that distinguished these two groups? Was there any way of predicting which would be more likely to have persistent problems and which would remit? Similarly, of the 91 children in the control group at three years, by eight years 20 children (22%) had developed disorders. By examining factors related to the production of disturbance, is it possible to identify factors which put three-year-old children at risk for the development of disorders? In this chapter we shall first examine those factors leading to persistence of disorders in the problem group, and then go on to examine which factors lead to the production of disorders in the non-problem group. In subsequent chapters we will examine in more detail those factors that seemed most closely related to persistence of disorders to determine how they might have exerted their effect.

Factors within the child predicting outcome

(a) Sex

The sex of the child was a significant predictor of outcome. Seventy-three per cent of the boys in the problem group remained disturbed, compared to only 48% of the girls in this group. Disturbed three-year-old boys were significantly more likely to persist as disturbed, at least to the age of eight years, than were disturbed three-year-old girls ($P < 0.02$). This finding, which is related to the fact that the sex ratio in rates of disturbance changed between three and eight years, is discussed in more detail in the next chapter.

(b) Severity of disorder and individual items of behaviour

How far does the severity of disturbance and the pattern of symptomatology shown by children at three years enable one to predict whether the disorder shown by the child will persist or remit? From Table 9.1 we can see that severity of disorder is a predictor of outcome.

Of those children who had moderate or severe disorders at three years, roughly three-quarters (74%) continued to show problems at eight years. Of those children with mild disorders about half (49%) persisted. By contrast,

Table 9.1. *Relationship between individual problem behaviours at 3 years and clinical rating of disturbance at 8 years in the behaviour problem group (N = 94)*

Individual problem behaviours at 3 years	Percentage of children clinically rated as disturbed in the behaviour problem group at age 8 years (Numbers in brackets)		P^a
	Present	Absent	
Poor appetite	60 (25/42)	64 (33/52)	N.S.
Night waking	67 (18/27)	60 (40/67)	N.S.
Tempers	67 (14/21)	60 (44/73)	N.S.
Difficult to manage	70 (35/50)	52 (23/44)	N.S.
Worries	50 (3/6)	63 (55/88)	Insufficient numbers
Overactive, restless	70 (37/53)	51 (21/41)	N.S.
Poor relations with siblings	68 (19/28)	60 (31/52)	N.S.
Poor relations with peers	78 (18/23)	57 (38/67)	N.S.
Soiling	72 (18/25)	58 (40/69)	N.S.
Night wetting	70 (32/46)	54 (26/48)	N.S.
Clinical rating of moderate or severe disturbance	74 (33/45)	49 (24/49)	<0.025

[a]Significance level of chi-square test, d.f. = 1

the presence of individual items of behaviour did not predict outcome. The problematic behaviour that seemed most related to adverse outcome was "poor relationships with other children". Seventy-eight per cent of children with this particular type of problem persisted in difficult behaviour from three to eight years, compared with 57% of those who did not, but the difference was not statistically significant. In general, therefore, it seems that the extent of disturbance at three years is a better general predictor of outcome than any particular symptom.

By the time these problematic children reached four years old (see Table 9.2) the possibility of prediction from symptomatology had become a little better. It is important to remember that here we are referring only to four-year-old children who have already been problematic for at least a year. In such children, not only is severity of disorder highly related to outcome, but certain symptoms, in particular a high level of activity and being generally difficult to manage, also predict an adverse course. In addition, nearly all the children who were soiling at four years were still disturbed at eight years, but the numbers of children involved here were rather small. In

Table 9.2. *Relationship between individual problem behaviours at 4 years and clinical rating of disturbance at 8 years in the behaviour problem group (N = 94)*

Individual problem behaviours at 4 years	Percentage of children clinically rated as disturbed in the behaviour problem group at age 8 years (Numbers in brackets)		
	Present	Absent	P^a
Poor appetite	69 (25/36)	57 (33/58)	N.S.
Night waking	61 (11/18)	62 (47/76)	N.S.
Tempers	69 (18/26)	59 (40/68)	N.S.
Difficult to manage	81 (30/37)	49 (28/57)	<0·004
Worries	56 (9/16)	63 (49/78)	N.S.
Overactive, restless	87 (33/38)	45 (25/56)	<0·0001
Poor relations with siblings	70 (21/30)	58 (31/53)	N.S.
Poor relations with peers	64 (7/11)	61 (51/83)	N.S.
Soiling	87 (7/8)	59 (51/86)	N.S.
Night wetting	78 (18/23)	56 (40/71)	N.S.
Clinical rating of moderate or severe disturbance	84 (52/62)	50 (16/32)	<0·0025

^{a}Significance level of chi-square test, d.f. = 1

Chapter 11 we shall see how specific problems at three and four years relate to different types of outcome.

(c) Family relationships

As we have already seen, disturbed family relationships were much more commonly found in families with disturbed three-year-olds than in families when the child was not posing problems. We now consider in a preliminary way, whether the presence of such disturbed relationships was a good indicator of outcome (see Table 9.3).

We can immediately see from Table 9.3 that they are not. For example, of those disturbed children whose mothers were critical of them at three years, 62% persisted in showing problems to eight years. Sixty-one per cent of those whose mothers were not critical persisted. This finding held in relation to maternal warmth and depression, as well as in the quality of the parental

Table 9.3. *Relationship between family factors at 3 and 8 years and clinical rating of disturbance at 8 years in the behaviour problem group (N = 94)*

| Family factor | Percentage of children clinically rated as disturbed in the behaviour problem group at age 8 years (Numbers in brackets) | | P^a |
	Present	Absent	
Mother highly critical of child at 3 years	62 (20/32)	61 (38/62)	N.S.
Mother highly critical of child at 8 years	85 (35/41)	42 (22/52)	<0·0001
Mother low in warmth to child at 3 years	51 (18/35)	68 (40/59)	N.S.
Mother low in warmth to child at 8 years	91 (20/22)	52 (37/71)	<0·003
Mother depressed at 3 years	70 (26/37)	56 (32/57)	N.S.
Mother depressed at 8 years	70 (30/43)	54 (27/50)	N.S.
Poor marriage at 3 years	65 (24/37)	60 (33/55)	N.S.
Poor marriage at 8 years	56 (20/36)	59 (23/49)	N.S.
Index of family adversity high at 3 years	63 (36/57)	60 (21/35)	N.S.
Index of family adversity high at 8 years	65 (33/51)	47 (16/34)	N.S.

[a]Significance level of chi-square test, d.f. = 1

marriage. It held, too, when the child's likelihood of remaining disturbed was related to an index of family adversity (IFA) derived from summating scores on quality of marriage, maternal mental health, and the level of external stress operating on the family. The family was regarded as high on this index if two or more of these factors were present.

By contrast, the presence or absence of family disturbance at eight years was associated with persistence of disturbance. Thus nearly all the children whose mothers showed little warmth towards them at eight years persisted with their problems. Family disturbance is therefore much more likely to relate to contemporaneous presence of the problem than it is to predict outcome. This suggests that outcome is as much influenced adversely by factors not related to family disturbance, such as adverse temperamental characteristics, as it is to adverse factors within the family. In Chapter 12 we consider further continuity and discontinuity in adverse family relationships, and how they relate to outcome in the child.

(d) Social and other stress factors

In Table 9.4 we present data regarding the relationship between outcome and a variety of factors which, it has been claimed, tend to affect the outcome of disturbance adversely. We looked to see whether working class disturbed children did worse than those from middle class families, and found they did not. We wondered whether the fact that a mother was employed at the time the child was three or four years old might act to the benefit or disadvantage of the child — there were no differences. Disturbed children who attended pre-school facilities at three and four years did no worse or better than those who did not. Finally, it was unimportant to outcome whether the family lived in council housing or had a high level of external stressful factors operating upon it. There were, of course, small differences found when all these comparisons were made, but they were inconsistent and therefore more likely to be due to chance than anything else.

The fact that these social and related factors did not predict outcome when various groups of children were compared does not mean that it is a matter of indifference to the fate of a disturbed pre-school child whether, for example, it is sent to a pre-school facility or whether its mother works or not. Some children will benefit enormously from the opportunities for independence a play group provides whereas others, perhaps suffering further rejection as a result of their disturbed or immature behaviour at the play group may be harmed by the experience. It must be assumed from the fact that the group outcomes do not differ, that positive and negative effects balance up, and that therefore broad generalizations about the value of, for example, the

Table 9.4. *Relationship between social factors at 3, 4 and 8 years and clinical rating of disturbance at 8 years in the behaviour problem group (N = 94)*

| Social factor | Percentage of children clinically rated as disturbed in the behaviour problem group at age 8 years (Numbers in brackets) | | P^a |
	Present	Absent	
Manual social class	62 (44/71)	59 (13/22)	N.S.
Mother working when child 3 years	72 (18/25)	58 (40/69)	N.S.
Mother working when child 4 years	58 (19/33)	64 (39/61)	N.S.
Child attending pre-school facility at 3 years	65 (22/34)	60 (36/60)	N.S.
Child attending pre-school facility at 4 years	64 (39/61)	57 (16/28)	N.S.
Family in council housing at 3 years	65 (28/43)	59 (30/51)	N.S.
Family in council housing at 8 years	70 (32/46)	54 (26/48)	N.S.
Family have high stress score at 3 years	68 (36/53)	54 (22/41)	N.S.
Family have high stress score at 8 years	64 (37/58)	58 (21/36)	N.S.

^{a}Significance level of chi-square test, d.f. = 1

benefits or hazards of play group experience for disturbed three-year-olds cannot be justified. This matter is discussed in more detail in Chapter 14.

Production of disorders

We now turn to consider factors related to the production of disturbance in those 91 control children who were not showing significant signs of disturbance at the age of three years. This aspect of the statistical analysis is made more difficult by the fact that relatively few, only 22%, of these 91 children developed disorders by the time they were eight years old, so that unless differences between those children who became disturbed and those who did not were really very large, they were unlikely to reach a statistically significant level.

Table 9.5. *Relationship between individual problem behaviours at 3 years and clinical rating of disturbance at 8 years in the control group (N = 91)*

Individual problem behaviours at 3 years	Percentage of children clinically rated as disturbed in the control group at age 8 years (Numbers in brackets)		
	Present	Absent	P^a
Poor appetite	15 (2/13)	23 (18/78)	N.S.
Night waking	20 (2/10)	22 (18/81)	N.S.
Tempers	50 (1/2)	21 (19/89)	Insufficient numbers
Difficult to manage	100 (2/2)	20 (18/89)	Insufficient numbers
Worries	0 (0/2)	23 (20/89)	Insufficient numbers
Overactive, restless	50 (4/8)	19 (16/83)	N.S.
Poor relations with siblings	50 (3/6)	17 (11/65)	Insufficient numbers
Poor relations with peers	0 (0/1)	23 (20/88)	Insufficient numbers
Soiling	29 (4/14)	21 (16/77)	N.S.
Night wetting	23 (7/30)	21 (13/61)	N.S.

[a]Significance level of chi-square test, d.f. = 1

(a) Individual items of behaviour

In Table 9.5 difficulties of interpretation arising from the small numbers can be immediately seen. In order to maintain consistency we have presented data in the same form as in those previous tables dealing with the outcome of disturbed children but, where there were six or fewer children in any one group, we have not presented the results of statistical analyses. Even when the numbers were sufficiently high to make statistical analysis meaningful, the presence of individual items of behaviour at three years did not relate to outcome. It seems possible, however, that the high level of activity in a non-disturbed child at three years has a poor prognostic implication. By definition, none of those children described in this section had definite behaviour or emotional problems at three years, but we shall see in subsequent chapters how, nevertheless, outcome was worse in those children who had even minor indications of disorder or whose behaviour put them just below the threshold for disturbance, when compared with those who

Table 9.6. *Relationship between individual problem behaviours at 4 years and clinical rating of disturbance at 8 years in the control group (N = 91)*

Individual problem behaviours at 4 years	Percentage of children clinically rated as disturbed in the control group at age 8 years (Numbers in brackets)		P^a
	Present	Absent	
Poor appetite	36 (5/14)	20 (15/77)	N.S.
Night waking	57 (4/17)	19 (16/84)	N.S.
Tempers	100 (3/3)	19 (17/88)	Insufficient numbers
Difficult to manage	80 (4/5)	19 (16/86)	Insufficient numbers
Worries	20 (1/5)	22 (19/86)	Insufficient numbers
Overactive, restless	75 (6/8)	17 (14/83)	<0·0008
Poor relations with siblings	50 (5/10)	16 (11/68)	<0·04
Poor relations with peers	20 (1/5)	21 (18/84)	Insufficient numbers
Soiling	0 (0/1)	22 (20/90)	Insufficient numbers
Night wetting	25 (3/12)	22 (17/79)	N.S.

^{a}Significance level of chi-square test, d.f. = 1

had no evidence at all for disturbance or very low scores indeed on the behaviour screening questionnaire.

By four years, the predictive value of individual symptoms had improved somewhat (see Table 9.6), and it became clear that a higher level of activity was indeed related to poor outcome. Bad relationships with other brothers and sisters also appeared to reflect the likelihood of a poor outcome. In Chapter 11 the particular significance of a high level of activity or restlessness in the early years in terms of diagnostic outcome is considered further.

(b) Family factors

It is of interest that family factors appear to be of greater significance in the production of disorders from three to eight years than they are in the maintenance of problems once they are established. Thus one can see, from Table 9.7, that about half the non-disturbed three-year-olds whose parents

Table 9.7. *Relationship between family factors at 3 and 8 years and clinical rating of disturbance at 8 years in the control group (N = 91)*

Family factor	Percentage of children clinically rated as disturbed in the control group at age 8 years (Numbers in brackets)		P^a
	Present	Absent	
Mother highly critical of child at 3 years	50 (4/8)	20 (16/82)	N.S.
Mother highly critical of child at 8 years	69 (11/16)	11 (8/73)	<0·0001
Mother low in warmth to child at 3 years	44 (4/9)	20 (16/81)	N.S.
Mother low in warmth to child at 8 years	36 (4/11)	19 (15/78)	N.S.
Mother depressed at 3 years	33 (8/24)	18 (12/67)	N.S.
Mother depressed at 8 years	46 (12/26)	11 (7/63)	<0·0007
Poor marriage at 3 years	47 (8/17)	16 (12/73)	<0·016
Poor marriage at 8 years	43 (6/14)	17 (12/71)	N.S.
Index of family adversity high at 3 years	39 (10/26)	16 (10/63)	<0·041
Index of family adversity high at 8 years	48 (12/25)	10 (6/60)	<0·0003

*a*Significance level of chi-square test, d.f. = 1

had a poor marriage developed a problem over the next five years, whereas only about one in six of non-disturbed children whose parents had a satisfactory marriage became disturbed. The same trend was evident in the case of children whose mothers were depressed at the earlier age, though here the differences were not statistically significant. Family environment at three years which was generally adverse also resulted in a poor outcome for the child more often than one would expect by chance. The importance of family factors in the production of disorders is unsurprising. It supports the views of those who hold family relationship problems as carrying the key to the development of much behaviour and emotional disturbance in early childhood. It represents one of the few pieces of evidence which indicate firmly, not merely that psychological disorders in children and family tensions between parents are associated, but that family tension can lead to the development of disorder in children who have not previously shown it. In later chapters we shall elaborate on this finding, in terms of the responsiveness of children's behaviour to continuity and discontinuity in family factors.

Table 9.8. *Relationship between social factors at 3, 4 and 8 years and clinical rating of disturbance at 8 years in the control group (N = 91)*

Social factor	Percentage of children clinically rated as disturbed in the control group at age 8 years (Numbers in brackets)		P^a
	Present	Absent	
Manual social class	25 (17/67)	13 (3/23)	N.S.
Mother working when child 3 years	21 (5/24)	22 (14/65)	N.S.
Mother working when child 4 years	23 (7/31)	22 (13/59)	N.S.
Child attending pre-school facility at 3 years	24 (5/21)	21 (15/70)	N.S.
Child attending pre-school facility at 4 years	20 (12/59)	27 (8/30)	N.S.
Family in council housing at 3 years	34 (11/32)	15 (9/59)	N.S.
Family in council housing at 8 years	26 (10/38)	19 (10/53)	N.S.
Family have high stress score at 3 years	28 (13/47)	16 (7/44)	N.S.
Family have high stress score at 8 years	32 (12/38)	14 (7/52)	N.S.

[a]Significance level of chi-square test, d.f. = 1

In this section (see Table 9.8) we consider the impact of possible stressful factors outside the family in the production of disorders. Social class does not relate significantly to outcome, and there is absolutely no evidence that it makes any difference to the development of disturbance whether the mother goes out to work or not, or whether the child attends a play group or other pre-school facility. Again, the reasons for this lack of predictive power in the presence or absence of maternal employment and play group attendance are likely to lie in counter-balancing effects. To some children, a mother who goes out to work is likely to be beneficial because of the improvement in her general level of satisfaction and contentment. For others, inadequate substitute care or a mother who is under greater tension at work than she can cope with, may adversely reflect on the child's behavioural development. For yet other children, perhaps the majority, their resilience is quite sufficient to allow them to cope adequately with a variety of experiences. Again, these issues are discussed further in Chapter 14.

Although the fact that the family lived in council housing rather than owner-occupied accommodation, and the presence of a number of external stress factors, did not relate significantly to outcome, there were definite trends to suggest that non-disturbed children whose families were under stress and/or in council housing tended to do worse. It seems likely from the results that unless these external stresses resulted in family disturbance, the child was likely to be sufficiently protected from them so as not to develop serious behaviour problems.

Implications for screening for behaviour disturbance

Finally, in this chapter we consider the implications of our findings on continuity and discontinuity of behaviour problems for screening programmes. It is generally agreed, and this agreement is reflected in such policy documents as the Court Report (DHSS, 1976) that health surveillance should include the assessment of a child's behaviour and social relationships. We have demonstrated (see Chapter 3) that the behaviour check-list (BCL) would be a quick, easily administered method to use which would pick up most children with significant behaviour problems, and that the BSQ (behaviour screening questionnaire), though more time-consuming, and therefore more inappropriate to use in regular practice, is a more efficient method. We imagine that, if a child was identified as possibly disturbed at three or four years, further enquiry should be made to clarify the extent and nature of the problems so as to ensure that appropriate measures could be taken to intervene.

Our data can also be used to consider how far it might be possible to prevent problems arising in school by detection and treatment before children go into school.

Tables 9.9 and 9.10 contain information derived from our representative group (see Chapter 6). From these tables it can be seen that although when compared with non-problematic three-year-olds, a much higher proportion of children who are problematic at three years are still showing difficulties at eight years, the possibilities for prevention by early detection and treatment are nevertheless limited. Thus, of 25 eight-year-old children in the general

Table 9.9. *Relationship between BSQ score at age 3 years and clinical rating of disturbance at age 8 years in the representative group (N = 98)*

| BSQ at 3 years | Clinical rating at 8 years (Percentages in brackets) | | |
	Disturbed	Non-disturbed	Total
Disturbed (BSQ score 10+)	9 (9)	7 (7)	16 (16)
Non-disturbed (BSQ score < 10)	16 (16)	66 (68)	82 (84)
Total	25 (25)	73 (75)	98

$$\text{False alarm rate} = \frac{7}{16} = 43 \cdot 8\%$$

$$\text{Hit rate} = \frac{9}{25} = 36\%$$

Table 9.10. *Relationship between BSQ score at age 4 years and clinical rating of disturbance at age 8 years in the representative group (N = 98)*

| BSQ at 4 years | Clinical rating at 8 years | | |
	Disturbed	Non-disturbed	Total
Disturbed (BSQ score 10+)	15	9	24
Non-disturbed (BSQ score < 10)	10	64	74
Total	25	73	98

$$\text{False alarm rate} = \frac{9}{24} = 37 \cdot 5\%$$

$$\text{Hit rate} = \frac{15}{25} = 60\%$$

population, we estimate that nine (36%) would have been detected at three years and sixteen (64%) would not. By four years the situation has improved somewhat, in that 15 out of 25 (60%) children disturbed at eight years would have been problematic at four years. As indicated however in Table 9.10, the proportion of false negatives (the "false alarm rate") would be high at 37·5%. This means that if screening and effective treatment were undertaken at three years, only 36% of children disturbed at eight years would no longer be expected to be problematic. Even this assumption implies a totally effective form of treatment and, in the light of present knowledge, it would be rash to assume that anything like this level of therapeutic success could be achieved.

Summary

In this chapter we have taken a preliminary look at those factors related to persistence of problems in disturbed three-year-olds, and those related to the production of problems in non-disturbed children of the same age. Amongst the disturbed children, boys were more likely to remain disturbed than girls. Those with moderate and severe disorders were more likely to stay problematic than those with mild problems. Restlessness and high activity in disturbed children was a sign of poor outcome. By contrast, adverse family relationships at three years and possible stress factors, such as maternal employment or attendance at a playgroup, did not predict whether the child persisted as disturbed or not.

Children who were not disturbed at three years were most likely to become so if they were problematic in behaviour even to a minor degree, if they were restless and active, and if their family relationships were disharmonious. Again, maternal employment/unemployment and attendance at a pre-school facility were unrelated to outcome.

Despite the high level of continuity of disturbance from the pre-school to school-age years, our findings do not suggest that screening in the pre-school years would be adequate to detect many children disturbed at eight years. Consequently, continual monitoring by parents and teachers is necessary if disturbed children in need of help are to be identified and appropriate measures taken.

In the subsequent chapters we consider in more detail those factors leading to differences in outcome between boys and girls, as well as diagnostic continuity, the prediction of educational difficulties, and the relative stability of adverse family factors.

10 Sex Differences in Outcome

Introduction

There are well-established differences between boys and girls in the middle period of childhood in the degree to which they show a range of behavioural and emotional problems. Boys outnumber girls by about two to one in rates of referral to child guidance clinics and child psychiatric departments. This difference in referral rate is mirrored by differences in rates found in studies of the general population. Delinquency of various types has been found to be as much as five to ten times as common in boys as in girls. Many varieties of developmental disorder — hyperactivity, developmental speech disorders and childhood autism are three or four times more common in boys. For other types of symptom such as enuresis and encopresis, the male preponderance is less marked, perhaps in the order of 1·5:1, but is nevertheless well-established.

Conditions in which the sexes are equally represented or where there is a female preponderance are less common. Emotional disorders occurring in the mid-school period are about equally common in boys and girls, though as children enter into early and mid-adolesence such problems begin to present more frequently in girls (Rutter *et al.*, 1976) and by late adolescence and young adulthood there is a definite excess of females involved. Anorexia nervosa is about ten times more common in young women and there is an equally strong female preponderance when the condition begins in earlier in adolescence. The reasons for these clear-cut differences are rather obscure. Genetic determination of sex differences in psychological development may account for some of the variations and indeed there is evidence for the importance of sex hormones in the origin of some aggressive behaviour (Shaffer *et al.*, 1980). Genetic factors may also be responsible for the rather small sex differences in the manifestation of temperamental characteristics (Thomas *et al.*, 1963). These are unlikely to be a sufficient explanation for all the differences found and various additional possibilities have been explored.

Consistent differences have been found in child-rearing practices. Parents tend to be more punitive and harsh in their treatment of misbehaviour in boys and they put more emphasis on the development of compliant and gentle behaviour in their upbringing of girls (Maccoby and Jacklin, 1980). Once children enter school boys and girls may also be exposed to different attitudes on the part of teachers. Thus Serbin *et al.* (1973) found that girls but not boys were reinforced in their behaviour if they remained in close physical proximity to their teacher. Teachers were more likely to lay emphasis in their dealings with girls on academic attainment and failure whereas in boys their interactions were more likely to involve class-room misbehaviour.

Thus differences in patterns of child-rearing behaviour shown by teachers as well as parents, may give rise to variations in rates of deviant psychological development. But it is also important to remember that even where such differences in manifestation rate do not exist as is the case with emotional disorders, the reason why boys and girls develop their problems may not be the same. Rutter (1970), and Hetherington *et al.*, (1977) have shown that although the rates of disturbance in boys and girls may be rather similar, boys seem to be more responsive to stress situations than girls. Illness of the parents or break-up of the parental marriage seems to affect boys and girls for different reasons, and this, of course, has implications both in prevention and clinical management.

Our study offered an opportunity to advance knowledge by examining the different longitudinal course of behaviour problems, cognitive delays and family circumstances in boys and girls, and in the present chapter we discuss our findings with this in mind.

Sex differences in outcome — general picture

Table 10.1 shows the outcome at eight years for boys and girls in the problem and control groups on the three main outcome measures namely clinical rating and Rutter Parent and Teacher Questionnaires. There is a tendency for boys in the control group to show more deviance than the girls, with 26% of the former and 17% of the latter developing disorders between three and eight years. In the problem group there are significant differences between the sexes on two of the outcome measures: twice as many boys as girls are rated as deviant on the teacher questionnaire and on the clinical rating three quarters of the boys compared with just under half the girls still have problems. Thus the recovery rate in girls was almost exactly double that in boys (52·4% v. 26·9%).

Using the rates of recovery from and development of problems based on the clinical ratings in the problem and control groups it is possible to estimate

Table 10.1 *Sex differences at 8 years in rates of deviance in problem and control groups*

| | Problem group | | |
	Boys N = 50–51	Girls N = 41–42	P
Deviant at 8 years:			
Clinical rating	73%	48%	0·01
Rutter parent questionnaire	45%	39%	N.S.
Rutter teacher questionnaire	50%	24%	0·01

| | Control group | | |
	Boys N = 49–50	Girls N = 39–41	P
Deviant at 8 years:			
Clinical rating	26%	17%	N.S.
Rutter parent questionnaire	20%	18%	N.S.
Rutter teacher questionnaire	29%	15%	N.S.

the expected rates of disturbance at eight years in hypothetical samples of boys and girls (Table 10.2). The resulting estimated rates of problem behaviour in 34% of boys and 20% of girls at eight years is in agreement with the actual findings for the representative sample in which the rates of disturbance were 31% in the boys and 19% in the girls.

At three years the rates of problems, based on the clinical ratings was 17·7% in boys and 11·4% in girls; at eight years the rates were 34% and 20% respectively (Table 10.3). Thus on our criteria there has been an increase in rates of disorder in both sexes with a slightly higher proportional increase in boys. Between three and eight years the gap has widened from 6·3% to 13·8%.

The sex ratio of our disturbed children at three years showed only a slight excess of boys, the sex ratio being 1·5:1. As the children moved into middle childhood, there was a slight increase in the male preponderance with a sex ratio at eight years of 1·7:1. This rather small size in relative increase masks, however, the rather more remarkable differences between the sexes in outcome.

The rate of *new* disorders (i.e. disorders arising between three and eight) was 21% and 15% in boys and girls respectively — a ratio of approximately

Table 10.2. *Prevalence of behaviour problems at 8 years in hypothetical samples of boys and girls estimated from the rates of persistence and development of problems found in the behaviour problem and control groups respectively*

	Observed prevalence at 3 years	Estimated number of children with behaviour problems at age 3 years	Observed changes between 3 and 8 years	Estimated number of children with behaviour problems at age 8 years	
Boys—1000	(Behaviour problems) 17·7%	177	(Recovery rate) 26·9%	Behaviour problems 129	343 (34%)
				No behaviour problems 48	
	(No behaviour problems) 82·3%	823	(Production rate) 26·0%	Behaviour problems 214	657 (66%)
				No behaviour problems 609	
Girls—1000	(Behaviour problems) 11·4%	114	(Recovery rate) 52·4%	Behaviour problems 54	205 (20%)
				No behaviour problems 60	
	(No behaviour problems) 88·6%	886	(Production rate) 17·0%	Behaviour problems 151	795 (80%)
				No behaviour problems 735	

Table 10.3. *Estimated rates of disturbance in boys and girls at 3 and 8*
          years

	Boys	Girls	Difference in rates	Ratio of rates
Prevalence rate of behaviour problems at age 3 years	17·7%	11·4%	6·3%	1·5:1
Prevalence rate of behaviour problems at age 8 years	34·3%	20·5%	13·8%	1·7:1
by persistence of problems from 3 years	12·9%	5·4%	7·5%	2·4:1
by production of problems since 3 years	21·4%	15·1%	6·3%	1·4:1

1·4:1. The greatest contribution to the high rate of disorders at eight years (34·3% in boys, 20·5% in girls) came in both sexes from the production of new disorders (see Table 10.3) but in boys a distinctly higher proportion of the contribution, 12·9% as against 5·4% came from the persistence of disorders present at three years (a ratio of 2·4:1). Increased persistence in boys therefore goes over half the way to explain why, as children get older, there is an increase in divergence in rates between the sexes.

Why should problems persist more in boys than in girls? Is it that boys and girls in the problem group from the start had different characteristics and boys showed more of those characteristics predictive of continuing disorder? Are different factors related to outcome in boys and girls, or are boys merely more vulnerable to the same adverse factors. To attempt to examine these questions we need to compare factors associated with outcome both between boys and girls and within the two sexes separately.

Differences between boys and girls in the general population

As indicated in Chapter 3, in the total 705 sample at three years boys showed a certain number of problems more often than girls, and they also tended to be rated as showing problems in more severe form, although many of the differences were non-significant. Boys were significantly more restless, had more sphincter problems and showed more general developmental delay and more language problems.

In the reconstituted representative sample of 98 children described in

Chapter 6 differences between boys and girls were similar but, because of the smaller sample size, the number of significant results was fewer. At three years boys were, however, significantly more likely to wet themselves by day and night and they scored lower on developmental scales. Girls were reported to have more appetite problems. At four years boys had lower scores on the Griffiths mental development D and E scales (Table 10.4).

Table 10.4. *Sex differences at 3 and 4 years in the representative group (N = 98)*

	Boys (N = 51)	Girls (N = 47)	P^a
Characteristics at 3 years			
Overactive, restless	24%	11%	N.S.
Poor appetite	10%	30%	0·02
Day wetting	37%	15%	0·02
Night wetting	45%	21%	0·02
Fears	6%	15%	N.S.
Mean Vineland raw score	11·2	12·2	0·02
Characteristics at 4 years			
Overactive, restless	18%	9%	N.S.
Difficult to control	16%	4%	N.S.
Fears	10%	15%	N.S.
Mean Griffiths scale D	101·9	112·9	0·01
Mean Griffiths scale E	102·1	109·0	0·05

[a]Significance level of chi-square test, d.f. = 1, for percentages and of *t*-test for means

Differences between boys and girls in the problem group

It was next necessary to determine whether the same differences between boys and girls existed in our problem group at three years as existed in our total random sample and our representative group. Differences in outcome might be due either to differences in onset between boys and girls generally, or they might be due only to the fact that disturbed boys differed from disturbed girls. We therefore determined whether there were important differences between boys and girls in the problem group. In fact, apart from sphincter problems at three years there were no significant differences

Table 10.5. *Sex differences at 3 and 4 years in the behaviour problem group (N = 94)*

	Boys (N = 52)	Girls (N = 42)	P^a
Characteristics at 3 years			
Overactive, restless	59%	55%	N.S.
Day wetting	47%	14%	0·05
Night wetting	61%	36%	0·05
Soiling	33%	19%	N.S.
Clinical rating of moderate or marked problem	57%	48%	N.S.
Characteristics at 4 years			
Difficult to control	54%	21%	0·01
Poor concentration	25%	7%	0·05

[a]Significance level of chi-square test, d.f. = 1

between boys and girls in this group in individual items of behaviour. Boys had slightly more marked problems but the difference was not significant. By four years boys in the problem group were significantly more likely to be described as difficult to control and to have poor concentration. Concentration and ease of control improved in girls between three and four years, but not in boys. Overall the children were described as less restless at four years than at three and this improvement in restlessness tended to be less marked in boys than in girls (Table 10.5).

Boys in the problem group, as already reported in Chapter 4 did have significantly lower test scores at three years on the tests of general development. Thus, on the Griffith mental development scale D, their mean quotient was 101·7 compared to 109·7 in girls. On scale E of the same test, the mean score for boys was 101·6 and for girls 108·7. In the problem group therefore boys did differ from girls in much the same way as in the representative group. Were these the differences that related to outcome?

It turned out that the same types of behaviour which were more common in boys than in girls in the representative group also related differentially to outcome in the problem group of boys (see Table 10·6). Thus, the most prominent symptoms in problem boys which related to adverse outcome were restlessness, poor relationships with siblings and being difficult to manage. In girls, difficulty in management and restlessness were not so related, and not getting on well with siblings did not seem to predict adversely — indeed as far as this last item of behaviour was concerned, the reverse seemed to be the case.

Table 10.6. *Association between characteristics at 3 years and subsequent persistence of behaviour problems separately for boys and girls in the behaviour problem group (N = 94)*

Characteristic at 3 years	Percentage of children showing characteristic at 3 years		P^a
	Problems persisted from 3 to 8 years	Problems recovered between 3 and 8 years	
BOYS	N = 38	N = 14	
Poor relations with siblings	42	8	0·07
Difficult to control	60	29	0·08
Overactive, restless	68	29	0·02
Clinical rating of severity of problem			
None or dubious problem	3	21	0·05[b]
Mild problem	32	50	
Marked/severe problem	66	28	
GIRLS	N = 20	N = 22	
Poor relations with siblings	29	44	0·09
Difficult to control	60	50	N.S.
Overactive, restless	55	55	N.S.
Clinical rating of severity of problem			
None or dubious problem	15	0	0·06[b]
Mild problem	30	59	
Marked/severe problem	55	41	

[a]Significance level of chi-square test, d.f. = 1
[b]d.f. = 2

Severity of the problem as assessed by clinical rating was related to adverse outcome in both boys and girls, but there was a difference in the sexes in the significance of the number of items of deviant behaviour present (see Table 10.7). Boys who recovered tended to have symptoms only just above the cut-off point in number or disturbance compared to those who did not recover, whereas in girls there was a wider spread and indeed there was no difference in the number of symptoms shown by girls who persisted and recovered. In neither sex did the quality of emotional environment at three years relate to outcome at eight years, but in girls (though not in boys) there was a non-significant tendency for improved emotional environment between three and eight years to be related to recovery.

Table 10.7. *Association between BSQ score at age 3 years and subsequent recovery from behaviour problems separately for boys and girls in the behaviour problem group (N = 94)*

	Cumulative percentages for children recovering from behaviour problems between 3 and 8 years									
	BSQ scores at 3 years									
	10	11	12	13	14	15	16	17	18	19
Boys recovering	36	79	86	93	93	100				
Girls recovering	9	32	50	64	77	86	91	96	96	100

Developmental factors were also related to a poor outcome in boys but made no difference to girls. Boys who had lower scores on the Griffiths D and E scales were more likely to have persisting problems (see Table 10.8). In boys whose problems persisted their scores on the EPVT were lower than in those where the problems recovered; and to a significant degree this was

Table 10.8. *Comparison of the mean scores on developmental tests at 3 years of children recovering from and persisting with behaviour problems separately for boys and girls in the behaviour problem group (N = 94)*

Outcome of behaviour problem at age 8 years		Mean scores on developmental tests at age 3 years		
	N	EPVT Standard score	Griffiths scale D	Griffiths scale E
1. Boys persisting	38	94·8	97·2	97·7
2. Boys recovering	14	101·9	113·9	112·0
3. Girls persisting	20	102·7	113·2	108·2
4. Girls recovering	20	97·8	106·7	109·0
1 v. 2		N.S.[a]	0·01	0·05
1 v. 3		0·01	0·001	0·05
1 v. 4		N.S.	N.S.	0·05
2 v. 3		N.S.	N.S.	N.S.
2 v. 4		N.S.	N.S.	N.S.
3 v. 4		N.S.	N.S.	N.S.

[a]Significance levels for differences between pairs of means determined by the use of Duncan's multiple range test following a one way ANOVA

also true with the Griffiths D and E scales. There was no difference in scores on these tests in the girls in relation to whether their problems persisted or recovered, and indeed there was a non-significant tendency for brighter three-year-old girls to persist in having problems. Boys with persisting problems had significantly lower scores on developmental tests than girls with persisting problems.

In conclusion, then, we have found that boys whose problems persist to eight years show features in the pre-school period which distinguish them both from boys whose problems disappear and from girls whose problems persist. They are more often described as being difficult to manage and as overactive or restless, they have less good sibling relations and their developmental scores are lower. When boys and girls with persisting problems are compared, boys have more symptoms and lower developmental scores; girls tend to have better sibling relationships and higher developmental scores.

Restlessness was more common in boys than girls in the representative group but not in the problem group. A low developmental score was more characteristic of boys in both representative and problem groups. This suggests various possible explanations for the poor outcome in boys. The link with lower developmental scores suggests that in boys either constitutional factors producing general immaturity enhance sensitivity to stress, or that some factors such as an early adverse emotional environment are selectively harmful to boys because they interact with factors such as poor quality of stimulation which also lead to poor early developmental status. The fact that early restlessness in boys, not girls, leads to a poorer outcome can also be explained in different ways. The course of restlessness in boys could be different in that it might be determined by constitutional or organic factors to a greater degree or it might differ qualitatively in the way it is manifested. Restless boys might also encounter different responses both at school and at home from the sort of responses encountered by restless girls. These responses, if they were unduly restrictive or punitive might result in negative interactions between parents, teachers and children which in themselves were likely to lead to greater persistence of problems. Parents and teachers might well reinforce or reward overactivity in boys by giving undue attention. If overactive and restless behaviour becomes the only way in which a boy can gain attention, it is more likely to recur. There is evidence to suggest that rewarding inappropriate behaviour in boys by parents and teachers does indeed occur. Such evidence does not exist in girls and it could well be that different responsiveness to restless boys and girls by parents and teachers is of importance in the different outcome in the two sexes. Reactions of other children may also be of relevance. The restless, physically active boy who is also somewhat reckless and impulsive may well develop a higher status in a peer group because of his physical aptitudes. Again this could lead to reinforcement of behaviour which might eventually come to be regarded as inappropriate and objectionable by parents and teachers. Girls are much less likely to be influenced by their friends in this way. A similar mechanism is thought to account for sex differences found in the influence of early puberty on personality development in boys and girls (Mussen and Bouterline-Young, 1964).

The factors associated with persisting disturbance in girls are, therefore, much less clear-cut than those in boys. If anything, more intelligent problematic girls seem more likely to persist in their difficulties. This finding though not a statistically significant one, is nevertheless rather consistent and does require some discussion. One possible, though highly conjectural explanation, is that the more developmentally mature girl may also have a greater tendency to identify with her depressed mother than the less mature girl. The capacity to identify increases with age over the time span we are considering, and it could be that the brighter girls in our study were also demonstrating a more mature capacity in their response to maternal distress. Others (Rutter, 1970) have suggested genetic mechanisms may be partly responsible for the development of emotional disturbances in older girls, but we have no evidence to test this possibility. We must conclude that, in contrast to the situation with boys at this age, the mechanisms whereby some girls persist or develop disorders and others fail to do so, remain obscure.

Differences between boys and girls in the development of problems in the control group

We have noted that one and a half times as many boys as girls develop problems in the control group between three and eight years of age. To see whether similar factors were involved in this as in persisting problems we again looked at differences within and between the sexes.

Once again, boys who were rated as having developed a problem in the control group had lower scores on the Griffiths E scale (see Table 10.9) than those who did not develop a problem. Children in the control group all scored, it will be remembered, less than 10 on the behaviour screening questionnaire at three years. A small proportion of them were rated clinically as showing a mild problem on the basis of a description of their behaviour. A significantly higher proportion of control boys clinically rated as showing a mild problem at three years seemed to develop a problem by the time they were eight years old (see Table 10.10). Control boys who developed problems were rather more likely to have a father in a

Table 10.9. *Comparison of the mean scores on developmental tests at 3 years of children developing or not developing a behaviour problem separately for boys and girls in the control group (N = 91)*

Outcome in terms of behaviour problems at 8 years	N	Mean scores on developmental tests at age 3 years		
		EPVT Standard score	Griffiths scale D	Griffiths scale E
1. Boys still no problem	37	102·4	108·3	109·2
2. Boys problem developed	13	105·0	111·5	101·1
3. Girls still no problem	34	104·7	113·4	108·1
4. Girls problem developed	7	98·1	117·4	110·4
1 v. 2		N.S.[a]	N.S.	0·07
1 v. 3		N.S.	N.S.	N.S.
1 v. 4		N.S.	N.S.	N.S.
2 v. 3		N.S.	N.S.	N.S.
2 v. 4		N.S.	N.S.	0·07
3 v. 4		N.S.	N.S.	N.S.

[a]Significance levels for differences between pairs of means determined by the use of Duncan's multiple range test following one way ANOVA

manual occupation. They were more restless and showed more management problems at three years, but not to a significant degree. Girls who developed a problem were also more likely to have had a clinical rating of a problem at three years. They were not more restless but did have poorer relationships with their siblings, though not to a significant degree.

Both boys and girls who developed a problem were more likely to have had a poor emotional environment currently at eight years, but they were not significantly more likely to have been living in such an environment at three years though there was a definite trend in this direction. With small numbers of problems at eight years and low rates of behavioural symptoms at three and four years, it is likely that the predictive value of certain types of behaviour has been underestimated in this analysis. There were, however, some consistent non-significant differences. Thus, for example, as we have

Table 10.10. *Association between characteristics at 3 and 8 years and the development of behaviour problems separately for boys and girls in the control group (N = 91)*

	Percentage of children showing characteristics		
Characteristics	Problem developed between 3 and 8 years	No problem developed between 3 and 8 years	P^a
BOYS	N = 13	N = 37	
Poor relations with siblings at 3 years	11·2	3·2	N.S.
Difficult to control at 3 years	15·4	0·0	N.S.
Overactive, restless at 3 years	30·8	8·1	N.S.
Clinical rating of mild problem at 3 years	30·8	2·7	0·01
Manual social class at 3 years	92·3	62·2	0·09
Index of family adversity at 8 years high	72·7	28·6	0·05
GIRLS	N = 7	N = 34	
Poor relations with siblings at 3 years	40·0	7·7	N.S.
Difficult to control at 3 years	0·0	0·0	N.S.
Overactive, restless at 3 years	0·0	2·9	N.S.
Clinical rating of mild problem at 3 years	42·9	2·9	0·01
Manual social class at 3 years	71·4	81·8	N.S.
Index of family adversity at 8 years high	57·1	9·4	0·02

[a]Significance level of chi square test, d.f. = 1.

stated, girls with poor sibling relations and with undue fears, and boys with management problems and restlessness were more likely to develop problems. Overall, however, it is striking how few significant associations or even clear-cut trends there were between variables at three and four years and outcome at eight years in the control group.

In the group of children developing problems over the five-year period from three to eight years, there were again more boys than girls though the ratio 1·4:1 was not strikingly different (see Table 10.3). It appears that both boys and girls are sensitive to current disharmony in family relationships, and that the longer this has persisted the more likely they both are to develop problems. Further, in both boys and girls, mild signs of disturbance at three years can presage the development of greater difficulties later on. Duller boys are perhaps slightly more likely to develop problems than dull girls, but here the differences between the sexes are unremarkable. It is clear from other work (Rutter *et al.*, 1970) that, as boys get older, certainly by the time they are ten or eleven years old, learning problems have developed in them much more frequently than is the case with girls. It could be that in our own society it is over this middle period of childhood from eight to ten years that learning failure commonly leads to the development of behaviour problems.

Summary

Behaviour problems in three-year-old boys tend to *persist* to a significantly greater extent than they do in girls and this is one important factor explaining sex differences in rates of disturbance in middle childhood. Further, there are probably different reasons why problems persist in boys and girls. Boys whose problems persist are more likely to be restless and slow in their development, and this is not the case when girls whose problems persist are compared with those who remit. In the *development* of problems from three to eight years, there are much smaller sex differences, and also fewer differences between boys and girls in underlying factors responsible. In both sexes the presence of current family tension and the previous manifestation of mild behaviour difficulties are of significance.

In the next Chapter, we consider ways in which the *types* of disorder shown by boys and girls at eight years differ and discuss whether such differences can be related to sex differences in the pre-school period.

11 Early Factors Leading to Conduct and Emotional Disorders

Introduction

We have seen some of the difficulties which arise in attempting to apply a classification of disorders in three-year-old children and the way in which these can be partially overcome by using cluster analysis. By eight years, differentiation of disorders is an easier matter. Studies of children a little older (Rutter, 1965) make it clear that the great majority of problems in this age group can be classed as either conduct (antisocial) or emotional (neurotic) disorders. The two are distinct in their manifestation, their causation, their association with family and educational factors, their natural history and their responses to treatment. According to present knowledge, conduct or antisocial disorders are characterized by aggressive behaviour, truancy, stealing and other antisocial symptoms, occur much more commonly in boys and are produced partly by inconsistencies and over-punitiveness in parental management. They are linked to a high incidence of broken homes and parental rejection, as well as to educational failure. In their severe form they tend to persist and to respond poorly to psychotherapy. By contrast, emotional (neurotic) disorders characterized by anxiety, inhibitions, undue fears, and depression occur equally commonly in boys and girls during the middle period of childhood. They are produced partly by over-protective parental attitudes and practices, and are linked to high rates of maternal depression. They tend to have a somewhat better outlook and to be responsive to various forms of psychotherapy. These descriptions of these two types of disorder make them sound perhaps rather more clearly differentiated than they are in practice. There is in fact a fair amount of overlap, for example, in their manifestation and response to treatment, but the distinction is nevertheless a valid and useful one. Examples of both conduct and neurotic disorders in the children in our study are given in Chapter 8.

In view of the wide prevalence of both these types of problem and the differences that exist between them in the areas we have described, we were naturally interested to know about their antecedents. What could we discover from our data regarding the roots of these problems?.

The overall picture

We first looked at the rates of each of these types of disorder in our representative, problem, and control groups (see Table 11.1). In the representative group there were roughly equal numbers of children with antisocial (13) and neurotic (12) problems. The proportion of boys and girls in the neurotic group was roughly equal, but there were five times more boys in the antisocial group. Among our group of children who had problems at three years, distinctly more antisocial (35) than neurotic (21) types of difficulties had developed. In this group, the sexes were equally affected by neurotic problems, but there were over three times the number of antisocial boys compared to girls. In the control group the numbers of disturbed children were of course smaller, but again there were more antisocial (13) than neurotic (7) problems, and the same sex differences and similarities were found as in the other groups. This overall picture of an excess of

Table 11.1. *Differences between the sexes in the clinical rating of type of disturbance shown at 8 years in the representative, behaviour problem and control groups*

Group	Sex	N	No problem		Antisocial problem		Neurotic problem		P^a
Representative group	Boys	51	70%	(35)	22%	(11)	10%	(5)	
	Girls	47	81%	(38)	4%	(2)	15%	(7)	0·04
Behaviour Problem[b] group	Boys	51	28%	(14)	53%	(27)	20%	(10)	
	Girls	41	54%	(22)	20%	(8)	27%	(11)	0·004
Control group	Boys	50	74%	(37)	22%	(11)	4%	(2)	
	Girls	41	83%	(34)	5%	(2)	12%	(5)	0·03

Header spanning: Percentage of children in group showing type of disturbance (numbers in brackets)

[a]Significance level of chi-square test, d.f. = 2
[b]Two children from the behaviour problem group were clinically rated as showing neither of these two types of disturbance

antisocial behaviour in boys is in accord with findings in older children. (Rutter *et al.*, 1970, 1975).

Development of antisocial and neurotic problems

In order to investigate the possible causation of antisocial and neurotic problems we decided to look first at the factors at three and four years which characterized children with these different types of problem when they were eight years old. In this respect it seemed sensible to concentrate first on those factors which had already been identified in other studies as linked in some way — the types of symptom shown, and family relationships, parental mental health and cognitive characteristics. Although there were more children with antisocial and neurotic problems at eight years in the problem group, and consequently statistical analysis of children in this group would have been easier, comparison of these children with each other could only give an incomplete picture. It could only provide information on earlier patterns of those eight-year-old disturbed children who were already showing problems at three years of age, and, as we have already indicated, these only formed less than half of the total group disturbed at eight years. Similarly, study of those control group children with antisocial and neurotic problems at eight years, could only provide information on such children who were not disturbed at three years. By contrast, the representative group provided us with a body of children drawn from the general population with rates of disturbance at three years typical of that population; consequently it was the antecedents of the antisocial and neurotic children in this group that it was most appropriate to study.

From Tables 11.2 and 11.3 it can be seen that, in this representative group of eight-year-olds with neurotic and antisocial problems, both types of difficulty were significantly associated with a high rate of earlier disturbance whether assessed by the clinical rating or by the behaviour screening questionnaire (BSQ) score at three years. There were highly significant differences on both these measures when comparisons were made with a representative group of children with no disorder at eight years. Further, the rates of earlier problems were very similar in the two differently disturbed groups. There was no indication, for example, that antisocial eight-year-olds had been more disturbed than neurotic children in the past.

When individual symptoms at the earlier age were considered, the most striking differences were found in the presence of restlessness (present in the earlier background of antisocial children) and fearfulness (present in the earlier background of children with neurotic problems). A large number of other comparisons between the groups with respect to different symptoms

Table 11.2. *Characteristics at 3, 4 and 8 years associated with antisocial disorder at 8 years of age in the representative group (N = 98)*

Characteristics		Percentage of children in group showing characteristics at 3, 4 and 8 years Clinical rating at 8 years		
		Anti-social disorder (N = 13)	No disorder (N = 73)	P^a
At 3 years				
Sleeping in parents' bed		31	5	0·02
Overactive, restless		46	11	0·006
Clinical rating mild, moderate or marked problem		54	14	0·009
Mean score on BSQ		8·7	6·1	0·007
Mother depressed		54	14	0·003
Adverse emotional environment				
Index score:	0	0	32	$0·08^b$
	1	42	39	
	2	25	15	
	3+	33	14	
At 4 years				
Mother depressed		62	15	0·001
At 8 years				
Adverse emotional environment				
Index score:	0	0	36	0·0001
	1	10	37	
	2	20	20	
	3+	70	7	

[a]Significance level of chi-square test, d.f. = 1, for percentages and t-test for means
[b]d.f. = 3

were made but only one was positive — eight-year-old children with anti-social problems had slept more often in their parents' bed at three years than children without such problems. There was also some evidence that dis-harmonious family relationships were important in the development of both types of problem. To examine this issue further we devised an expanded version of the index of family adversity. This emotional environment index

Table 11.3. *Characteristics at 3 and 4 years associated with neurotic disorder at 8 years of age in the representative sample (N = 98)*

Characteristics	Percentage of children in group showing characteristics at 3 or 4 years Clinical rating at 8 years		
	Neurotic disorder (N = 12)	No disorder (N = 73)	P^a
At 3 years			
Fears	33	8	0·05
Tempers	17	2	0·07
Clinical rating of marked/ severe problem	25	3	0·02
Mean score on BSQ	9·8	6·1	0·02
Mother depressed	58	14	0·01
At 4 years			
Severe specific language delay	50	19	0·05
Severe general developmental delay	50	19	0·05

[a]Significance level of chi-square test, d.f. = 1, for percentages and of t-test for means

(EEI) (a composite score derived from the presence of the following: two or more external stresses, high maternal criticism, low maternal warmth, poor marital relationship, and mother's poor mental health) was higher (though not significantly so) in both neurotic and antisocial groups when comparisons were made between the children when three years old. The only significant finding when these factors were examined separately was in the rate of mother's mental health problems when the child was three years old. In both antisocial and neurotic eight-year-olds, there was a clear indication that women who were depressed and anxious when their children were three years old, tended to have more disturbed children later on, and this effect appeared more marked than any other measure of family disharmony and distorted relationships.

By contrast, the measures of cognitive development at three years which we examined did not distinguish the groups, At this age, we looked at one index of visuo-spatial ability (the Griffiths mental development scale D) and two measures of language development (the English picture vocabulary test and the Reynell development language test), but in none of these did the mean scores differ between the normal, neurotic and antisocial eight-year-olds. There was, however, a near significant tendency for antisocial children to be behind-hand on the test of picture-naming (the English picture vocabulary test).

A very similar picture emerged when the characteristics at four years of those children destined to show neurotic and antisocial disorders at eight years were examined (see Table 11.3). Once again both groups of disturbed eight-year-olds had shown significantly higher rates of problematic behaviour at the earlier age. Once again, the adverse emotional environmental index revealed a generally higher score in the deviant groups with a considerable and significant difference as far as maternal depression and anxiety were concerned.

Finally, again the mean scores on the various cognitive measures were no different. It was interesting to note in this respect, however, that the rate of both severe general delay and severe specific language delay defined in Chapter 4 were higher in the neurotic group. It might have been predicted from the Isle of Wight data that the association would have been closer in the antisocial group, but this was not the case. Links between types of disorder and educational outcome are discussed further in Chapter 13.

At eight years the behaviour scores of both the neurotic and antisocial children in the representative group were, by definition, higher than those in the no-problem group, but to complete the developmental picture it is of interest to note differences in background factors at this age. By this age, there is a massive difference between the antisocial and no-problem groups in the adverse emotional environment index. A world of caution is, however, necessary here. The index contains measures of maternal criticism, hostility and warmth. When a mother is reporting antisocial behaviour she is very likely to be critical and lacking in warmth, and, although the interviewers were careful not to rate as critical, mothers who described difficult behaviour in a non-critical way, it is clearly difficult to avoid rating contamination. Once again, however, it is notable that maternal depression was distinctly higher in the deviant group and that the cognitive characteristics of the disturbed eight-year-olds in this representative group were not significantly different from those of the non-disturbed.

Investigations of antisocial problems in boys and girls

It seems therefore, that as a group, antisocial eight-year-olds have been more disturbed and more restless in the past, and that more often their mothers have been depressed. They have perhaps shown a slight tendency to developmental delay, but this has not been marked. Neurotic eight-year-olds have been both more disturbed and more fearful in the past. Their mothers have been more depressed, and they too have shown slight but not very consistent delays in the past. We wondered, in view of the sex differences described in the previous chapter, whether these findings might be clarified by examining whether the same or different factors would be revealed if boys and girls were looked at separately. Unfortunately, the numbers of children available for statistical analysis in the representative group were not large enough to allow this. In particular, there were only two girls with antisocial problems in the representative group. We therefore turned our attention to the eight-year-old boys and girls who showed antisocial and neurotic deviance in the problem group. This is a less satisfactory approach because it only provides information on those disturbed eight-year-olds who also had problems at three years and, as we have indicated, these account only for a proportion of the total group. However, we thought it worthwhile to report our findings in these groups selected on this basis.

The findings were reasonably clear-cut. Both boys and girls who were antisocial at eight years had been unusually active and restless at three years old. They had also been less fearful than children without any problems at all at eight years.

Both boys and girls who showed neurotic behaviour at eight years had been more fearful at three years than either children who developed antisocial problems at eight years or those who were asymptomatic by that age. By contrast, there were clear-cut consistent differences between the sexes in earlier cognitive development. Both antisocial and neurotic eight-year-old boys showed lower mean scores in developmental tests at three and four years. There was a non-significant tendency for girls that developed both antisocial and neurotic problems to have been brighter. Indeed in neurotic girls this tendency did reach a statistically significant level in the comparison of WPPSI Performance IQ Score at four years and the remaining comparisons were consistent with this single significant finding.

What light do these findings throw on the development of conduct and neurotic disorder and the difference in rates found in boys and girls in this respect? The factors relating to outcome showed a certain consistency which it is convenient to summarize at this point.

In both boys and girls, both antisocial and neurotic disorders at eight years are related to the presence of a depressed mother at three years. Further, severe and moderate behaviour disorders at three years are likely to terminate in an unfavourable behavioural outcome at eight years, and the outcome is more likely to be an antisocial problem than a neurotic problem. An adverse emotional environment at eight years was also related to poor

Table 11.4. *Characteristics at 3, 4 and 8 years associated with antisocial disorder at 8 years of age in boys and the behaviour problem group (N = 52)*

| Characteristics | Percentage of boys in the group showing characteristics at 3, 4 and 8 years or mean score for the group — Clinical rating at 8 years — Boys | | |
	Antisocial disorder (N = 27)	No disorder (N = 14)	P^a
At 3 years			
Difficult to control	63%	29%	0·08
Overactive, restless	78%	29%	0·006
Poor relations with siblings	52%	8%	0·03
Clinical rating of marked problem	71%	29%	0·04
Mean score on BSQ	12·4	11·1	0·06
Mother depressed	37%	21%	N.S.
Mean score on Griffiths scale D	100	114	0·02
Mean score on Griffiths scale E	98	112	0·01
At 4 years			
Mother depressed	82%	50%	0·08
Mean score on EPVT	99	109	0·01
Mean WPPSI Verbal IQ	91	101	0·05
Mean WPPSI Performance IQ	89	105	0·001
Mean WPPSI Full Scale IQ	89	103	0·002
At 8 years			
Mean WISC Verbal IQ	108	119	0·01
Mean WISC Performance IQ	103	116	0·009
Mean WISC Full Scale IQ	105	115	0·014
Adverse emotional environment Index of 3 or more	50%	21%	N.S.

^{a}Significance level of chi-square test, d.f. = 1, for percentages and of *t*-test for means

Table 11.5. *Characteristics at 3, 4 and 8 years associated with antisocial disorder at 8 years of age in girls in the behaviour problem group (N = 42)*

Characteristics	Percentage of girls in the group showing characteristics at 3, 4 and 8 years or mean score for the group — Clinical rating at 8 years — Girls		
	Antisocial disorder (N = 8)	No disorder (N = 22)	P^a
At 3 years			
Difficult to control	63%	50%	N.S.
Overactive, restless	75%	55%	N.S.
Poor relations with siblings	29%	44%	N.S.
Clinical rating of marked problem	63%	100%	0·02
Mean score on BSQ	13	13	N.S.
Mother depressed	25%	36%	N.S.
Mean score on Griffiths scale D	113	107	N.S.
Mean score on Griffiths scale E	106	109	N.S.
At 4 years			
Mother depressed	67%	59%	N.S.
Mean score on EPVT	102	101	N.S.
Mean WPPSI Verbal IQ	102	97	N.S.
Mean WPPSI Performance IQ	102	93	N.S.
Mean WPPSI Full Scale IQ	102	95	N.S.
At 8 years			
Mean WISC Verbal IQ	113	107	N.S.
Mean WISC Performance IQ	105	106	N.S.
Mean WISC Full Scale IQ	108	106	N.S.
Adverse emotional environment Index score of 3+	60%	18%	N.S.

[a]Significance level of chi-square test, d.f. = 1, for percentages and of *t*-test for means

Table 11.6. *Characteristics at 3, 4 and 8 years associated with neurotic disorder at 8 years of age in the behaviour problem group (N = 52)*

Characteristics	Percentage of boys in the group showing characteristics at 3, 4 or 8 years or mean score for the group — Clinical rating at 8 years — Boys		
	Neurotic disorder (N = 10)	No disorder (N = 14)	P^a
At 3 years			
Fears	50%	21%	N.S.
Night waking	40%	21%	N.S.
Poor relations with peers	38%	15%	N.S.
Poor concentration	10%	29%	N.S.
Overactive, restless	40%	29%	N.S.
Night wetting	70%	50%	N.S.
Mean Griffiths scale D	91	113	0·006
Mean Griffiths scale E	98	112	0·08
Mean score on EPVT	99	102	N.S.
Mother depressed	70%	21%	0.05
At 4 years			
Mother depressed	50%	36%	N.S.
Mean WPPSI Verbal IQ	91	101	N.S.
Mean WPPSI Performance IQ	83	105	0·001
Mean WPPSI Full Scale IQ	86	103	0·01
At 8 years			
Mean Neale accuracy CArelated reading age	−9·8	+1·2	0·06
Mean Neale comprehension CA related reading age	−9·9	+5·7	0·02
Mean Schonell spelling age	76	92	0·03
Mean WISC verbal IQ	101	119	0·02
Mean WISC performance IQ	103	116	0·08
Mean WISC full scale IQ	102	115	0·02
Adverse emotional environment Index score of 3+	50%	21%	N.S.

[a]Significance level of chi-square test, d.f. = 1, for percentages and of *t*-test for means

Table 11.7. *Characteristics at 3, 4 and 8 years associated with neurotic disorder at 8 years of age in girls in the behaviour problem group (N = 42)*

| Characteristics | Percentage of girls in the group showing characteristics at 3, 4 or 8 years or mean score for the group — Clinical rating at 8 years — Girls | | |
	Neurotic disorder (N = 11)	No disorder (N = 22)	P^a
At 3 years			
Fears	46%	18%	N.S.
Night waking	46%	27%	N.S.
Poor relations with peers	36%	14%	N.S.
Poor concentration	9%	36%	N.S.
Overactive, restless	36%	55%	N.S.
Night wetting	64%	32%	N.S.
Mean score on Griffiths scale D	113	107	N.S.
Mean score on Griffiths scale E	119	110	N.S.
Mean score on EPVT	105	98	0·09
Mother depressed	55%	36%	N.S.
At 4 years			
Mother depressed	82%	59%	N.S.
Mean WPPSI Verbal IQ	103	97	N.S.
Mean WPPSI Performance IQ	105	93	0·05
Mean WPPSI Full Scale IQ	104	95	N.S.
At 8 years			
Mother depressed	73%	41%	0·05
Mean Neale accuracy CA related reading age	+15·0	+7·0	N.S.
Mean Neale comprehension CA related reading age	+5·5	+2·9	N.S.
Mean Schonell spelling age	105	97	N.S.
Mean WISC Verbal IQ	112	107	N.S.
Mean WISC Performance IQ	108	106	N.S.
Mean WISC Full Scale IQ	108	106	N.S.
Adverse emotional environment Index score of 3+	60%	18%	0·09

[a]Signficance level of chi-square test, d.f. = 1, for percentages and of *t*-test for means

outcome in both boys and girls regardless of the type of disorder developed. Further, and perhaps this is the most striking finding, in both boys and girls, symptomatology at three years is related specifically to outcome with undue restlessness terminating in conduct disorder and undue fearfulness resulting in neurotic problems. Boys and girls differed in the association between intelligence or developmental level and outcome. In general, boys who developed disorders were less bright in all spheres than those who did not, whereas the reverse was the case with girls. Brighter girls had a greater tendency to develop neurotic disorders than average or below-average girls.

Clearly, the presence of overactivity and fearfulness at three years appears to have an important influence on outcome. It therefore seems appropriate to consider what these types of behaviour involved at this age. In our questioning on overactivity at three years we asked whether the child was able to sit still at mealtimes, or to play a game or listen to a story for a long as five minutes. Because of confusion over the term "overactivity" and as there is no evidence from our study that the children rated positively on this question were indeed showing excessive motor activity, we would prefer to refer to them as "restless". In fact two boys in the sample did show a high level of overactivity and because this was combined with distractability and impulsivity, we would find it reasonable to describe them as hyperactive or hyper-kinetic. One of these was later found to have *petit mal* and both of them remained very restless and showed poor concentration at eight years. The remainder however would in our view be better described as restless or having difficulty in settling than as overactive. As far as boys are concerned, such restlessness, linked as it is with developmental problems and language delays seems to be at least to some degree physiologically determined. Evidence for genetic effects probably mediated in part by hormonal influences has emerged from a variety of sources, including the study of intersex conditions (Ehrhardt and Baker, 1974). However, it is likely that such constitutionally determined tendencies need strong social reinforcement for their manifestation. Certainly both at home and at school boys are exposed to male models showing higher levels of aggression than females. The frustration to which their developmental lags may expose boys in school work could also result in disruptive behaviour. It would certainly be of interest to carry out further in-depth investigations of children diagnosed as "restless". For example, the fact that the outcome of "restlessness" in girls is more favourable than it is in boys might be due to differential social experiences or to qualitative or quantitative differences in the type of restlessness which boys and girls show.

The question on fears in the behaviour screening questionnaire required information on whether the child was afraid of a number of specific items, and the final rating of fearfulness was based on the total number and severity of fears the child showed.

It is usual to consider fears also in a developmental context with the causes of fear changing with age (Bauer, 1976), and the phenomenon of fear itself becoming less common by school age. Whether fearfulness arises from particular temperamental characteristics and/or family interactions promoting anxiety as well as maturational influences requires further investigation. In either event it would be understandable if the fearful child later developed neurotic problems.

Our findings suggest that the course of fearfulness and neurotic behaviour might differ between the sexes. In boys neurotic disorder is associated with maturational delay and could be a response both to over-protective parents and to social difficulties encountered with peers and learning difficulties. In girls neurotic disorder is associated with high test scores. As in boys there is also a tendency for associations to occur with maternal depression and a high emotional and environmental adversity index at eight years. It could be postulated that in girls neurotic behaviour more often arises from problems which become "internalized", perhaps involving an increased sense of responsibility for a stressful family situation, and identification with a depressed mother.* Such mechanisms might explain why the rates of neurotic disorder in girls begin to increase as they get older, whereas in boys neurotic disorder improves as they mature. Again, more detailed studies of fearful children would clarify these hypotheses.

We are now in a somewhat better position to explain why more boys develop antisocial disorders than do girls. In both boys and girls as we have seen, undue activity or restlessness are related to the development of conduct problems, but (see Chapter 3), boys significantly more commonly show restlessness in their pre-school years. This early tendency to restlessness is therefore one reason why boys show a higher rate of antisocial difficulties. In addition, in boys but not in girls, early cognitive difficulties or developmental delays are also associated with a poor outcome of both antisocial and neurotic type. It seems therefore that in boys, not girls, developmental delay may reflect a general vulnerability to stress which also shows up by a general tendency to develop behavioural problems. Alternatively, boys with developmental delays, once they are exposed to the academic demands of school, become disturbed in a way that girls with such delays do not. It is interesting that pre-school boys, at least in the USA, are not more achievement-motivated than girls (Crandall and Rabson, 1960) but, despite a lack of well-documented evidence on this point, there is anecdotal evi-

---

*Girls who are more intelligent or with a greater sensitivity to inter-personal tensions might be more likely to internalize in this way.

dence that, once children enter school, both parents and teachers put greater pressure on boys to achieve academic success and it is at this point that differences in rates of conduct disorder emerge. It seems not unlikely that all these three mechanisms are involved in the production of the differentially high rate of conduct disorder in boys.

Summary

By eight years of age, reasonably well differentiated neurotic and antisocial problems are common, and the latter are present much more frequently in boys than in girls. In both sexes restlessness in the pre-school period predicts antisocial outcome, and fearfulness predicts a neurotic outcome. An adverse emotional environment in the pre-school period is of some predictive significance, and in particular, early maternal depression is strongly related to the later development of both common types of disorder. In boys, but not in girls, a slower rate of cognitive development predisposes to both types of problem at eight years. Various mechanisms are proposed to explain these findings and, in the next chapter, consideration is given to the persistence of adverse family factors and the way these may influence behavioural outcome.

12 Family and Social Factors: Continuities and Influences on Outcome

In previous chapters we have shown how, although the quality of family relationships does not help predict outcome in children with problems, it does help in determining which non-disturbed children will become disturbed over the next five years. We have also demonstrated a high level of continuity in problem behaviour in the child from three to eight years.

However, there are also separate questions to consider regarding continuity in family problems. Do families with a poor quality of family relationships when the child is three years old tend to change or do they remain stable? Do attitudes towards the children change over time? If a mother is depressed when her child is young, does she tend to remain depressed after her child has entered school? Is the continuity in child problems that we have found a reflection of continuity in family relationships? These questions are of relevance not only to children and families themselves, but also to professionals such as social workers, psychologists, adult psychiatrists and marriage guidance counsellors whose primary focus of work is not children, and yet who deal with members of families in whom children are present.

Our data enable us to examine these questions in some detail, and our methodology gave us confidence that our findings were likely to be valid. One problem in longitudinal studies relates to the fact that different criteria are sometimes used at different stages of the study so that results obtained are not truly comparable. We were careful to ensure that the same criteria were used at all stages to assess variables such as maternal depression, maternal attitudes and the quality of family relationships. If interviewers are aware of previously obtained information this may bias their findings, but we were able to arrange that in nearly all cases different interviewers were used at different stages of the study, and in all cases interviewers carried out their interviews in ignorance of ratings previously made.

It might reasonably be asked why families might be expected to change as time goes on. Certainly in our cohort it was unlikely that provision of help by social or other agencies had much influence on outcome. The number of families in receipt of such help was low, and these were naturally the families with the greatest social problems. One might however expect families to change because their economic situation improves. As fathers get older their income tends to rise, though this is less true for those in manual occupations than for men in white-collar jobs. Previous studies have shown that a high proportion of women go out to work when children have entered school, and the increase in family income, together with the widening of social contacts for the mother this entails, might lead to a general improvement in the quality of family life. Further, as their experience of child-rearing increases, parents might learn to support each other and co-operate more effectively, and thus cope more easily with their parental responsibilities. It is often said that of all the phases of family life, that period in which the children are infants and toddlers is the most stressful because it is at this period that children make greatest demands both on the physical and on the emotional resources of their parents. Again, for this reason, one might expect improvement as time goes on.

By contrast, other factors might tend to operate in the reverse direction. As time goes on inevitably the rate of divorce and marital separation increases, and obviously strain on marital relationships may increase for a variety of reasons without actually leading to marital breakdown. The birth of new sibs may bring previously inexperienced emotions of jealousy and possessiveness to the fore, thus creating new problems for parents. Secular changes may be important. When, for example, our study began in 1971 the UK was going through a period of relative prosperity, whereas by 1978 financial recession and rising levels of unemployment were already marked features of the economic situation.

In order to clarify some of these issues we have examined how families did in fact change over the five years we studied them. We thought that the most appropriate group to use for this purpose would be our representative group, as this is hopefully equivalent to a sample drawn randomly from the general population. In addition, however, we thought it would be of interest to present information on the change in family relationships in our "problem group" — families in which a disturbed child was present when aged three years.

Social changes over time

The social circumstances of the families in the representative and problem groups changed rather little over the five years we studied them except in the proportions of the numbers of women who went out to work (see Tables 12.1 and 12.2). The proportion of fathers whose occupational social class changed over the years was small (four had changed from three to four years, and 13 from three to eight years), and there was no particular tendency for upward or downward mobility. Change of housing tenure was also limited, few families having moved from Council to owner-occupied accommodation, and most families in high-rise flats continuing to live in the same or similar circumstances throughout the period of study. However, as stated, there was a marked increase in the number of women in at least part-time paid employment. In the representative group the percentage employed when their children were three years old was 26%, with 57% employed when the children were eight years old. The corresponding figures in the problem group were 20% and 53%.

Change in family relationships over time

As we have indicated, our general expectation was that there would be a general improvement in the quality of family relationships over the five years in question. This expectation was not confirmed, as can readily be seen from Tables 12.1 and 12.2. The rate of marital disharmony remained virtually unchanged. If anything this reflects an increase in the rates of disharmony, because the rating was only made when the two parents were still living together, and, in the representative group, by four years four

Table 12.1. *Prevalence of various social and family factors at 3, 4 and 8 years in the representative group (N = 98)*

| | Percentage of representative group | | |
| | AGE OF CHILD | | |
	3 years	4 years	8 years
Marital disharmony	22	28	24
High maternal criticism of child	17	15	23
Low maternal warmth to child	20	18	17
Maternal depression	30	36	37
Mother working	26	36	57
Family with 3 or more stresses in past year	29	22	28
Manual social class	72	74	75

Table 12.2. *Prevalence of various social and family factors at 3, 4 and 8 years in the behaviour problem group (N = 94)*

| | Percentage of the behaviour problem group | | |
| | AGE OF CHILD | | |
	3 years	4 years	8 years
Marital disharmony	40	44	42
High maternal criticism of child	19	12	27
Low maternal warmth to child	37	29	24
Maternal depression	39	52	46
Mother working	20	35	53
Family with 3 or more stresses in past year	35	31	33
Manual social class	76	74	74

parents had separated, while by eight years, seven further parents had separated. The rate of maternal depression was uninfluenced by the fact that a much higher proportion of women was working. Similarly, as far as maternal attitudes to the children were concerned, there was very little change in the proportions of mothers lacking demonstrated warmth or high in criticism of the child over the five years in question. Finally, the number of families suffering multiple stress defined in ways we have discussed earlier, did not change much over the years.

From Tables 12.3 and 12.4 we can see to what extent this high degree of continuity involved the same and different families. It would, for example, have been possible for the rates of maternal depression to have been the same at different ages but for different mothers to have been involved at each age. The data presented in Tables 12.3 and 12.4 show that this is, in general, not the case. For example, at four years, 76% of the marriages which had been rated as poor in quality at three years still involved parents not getting on together, whereas only 14% of those who had satisfactory marriages at three years were showing marital disharmony when their children were four years old. The corresponding figures for the marriages when the children were eight years old were 60% and 14%. Clearly therefore if a parental marriage is "good" when the child is three years old, it has a high chance of remaining satisfactory over the next five years, and there is equally high continuity in "poor" marriages. This is confirmed when rates of marital breakdown are examined. In the representative group only 6·8% of marriages rated "good" at three years had ended in separation by eight

Table 12.3. *Stability in individual family factors between ages 3 and 4 years and 3 and 8 years in the representative sample (N = 98)*

	Percentage of cases where family factor present at age 4 or 8 years		P^a
	Maternal depression at 3 years		
	Absent (N = 69)	*Present* (N = 29)	
Maternal depression at 4 years	23	69	<0·0001
Maternal depression at 8 years	28	53	<0·05
	Marital disharmony at 3 years		
	Absent (N = 73)	*Present* (N = 21)	
Marital disharmony at 4 years	14	76	<0·0001
Marital disharmony at 8 years	14	60	<0·0001
	High stress score (2 or more) at 3 years		
	Absent (N = 47)	*Present* (N = 51)	
High stress score at 4 years	30	45	N.S.
High stress score at 8 years	41	43	N.S.
	High maternal criticism at 3 years		
	Absent (N = 81)	*Present* (N = 16)	
High maternal criticism at 4 years	11	38	<0·05
High maternal criticism at 8 years	16	56	<0·01
	Low maternal warmth at 3 years		
	Absent (N = 78)	*Present* (N = 19)	
Low maternal warmth at 4 years	11	47	<0·01
Low maternal warmth at 8 years	12	37	<0·05

[a]Significance level of chi-square test, d.f. = 1

Table 12.4. *Stability in individual family factors between ages 3 and 4 years and 3 and 8 years in the behaviour problem group (N = 94)*

	Percentage of cases where family factor present at age 4 or 8 years		P^a
	Maternal depression at 3 years		
	Absent (N = 67)	*Present* (N = 24)	
Maternal depression at 4 years	23	67	<0·0001
Maternal depression at 8 years	22	50	<·05
	Marital disharmony at 3 years		
	Absent (N = 71)	*Present* (N = 22)	
Marital disharmony at 4 years	10	81	<0·0001
Marital disharmony at 8 years	13	44	<0·01
	High stress score (2 or more) at 3 years		
	Absent (N = 44)	*Present* (N = 47)	
High stress score at 4 years	27	43	N.S.
High stress score at 8 years	39	45	N.S.
	High maternal criticism at 3 years		
	Absent (N = 62)	*Present* (N = 32)	
High maternal criticism at 4 years	27	67	<0·01
High maternal criticism at 8 years	43	47	N.S.
	Low maternal warmth at 3 years		
	Absent (N = 59)	*Present* (N = 35)	
Low maternal warmth at 4 years	19	46	<0·01
Low maternal warmth at 8 years	21	29	N.S.

[a]Significance level of chi-square test, d.f. = 1.

years, whereas 25% of those marriages rated "poor" had ended in separation — nearly a fourfold difference ($P < 0.05$). The same trend was
apparent to roughly the same degree in the problem group. The same trend
occurs when maternal depression, maternal criticism and maternal warmth
are examined in the same way. By contrast, it can be seen that although
roughly the same level of stress was operating on the families at three, four
and eight years, different families were under stress at different times. There
was no significant tendency for the same families to be stressed when the
children were studied at three separate ages. From Table 12.4 it can be seen
that the trends were very similar in the problem group with, if anything, as in
the case of marital disharmony, an even stronger tendency towards
continuity over time.

Maternal depression

In view of the interest in the phenomenon of maternal depression raised
particularly by the work of George Brown (Brown and Harris, 1978), we
decided to examine the factors associated with this factor in more detail. We
were particularly interested to note that, in our sample, there was no
significant fall in the rate of maternal depression, since it has been suggested
by Brown and others that women with pre-school children are particularly
vulnerable to develop depression. From our findings it seems that mothering
an eight-year-old is equally likely to be related to a maternal depressive
state. It must be emphasized that, unlike the population studied by Brown,
our cohort is not a representative sample of women in the general population, but is representative of women with children at different ages, and
this may account for some of the differences in findings.

We examined various factors which might be associated with maternal
depression in our representative sample (see Table 12.5). Dunn and Kendrick (1980) have suggested that the birth of a younger child alters family
relationships significantly, and we thought that perhaps this might be
reflected in a higher rate of maternal depression, but this was not the case.
Brown and Harris (1978) found that the presence of three or more children
under the age of 14 years contributed significantly to the likelihood of a
mother becoming depressed when stressed by a life event, and we wondered
whether the number of children of pre-school age might relate to the
presence of depression in the mother. Perhaps surprisingly, this was not the
case. There was no relationship between the mother's mental state and the
number of pre-school children in the home when the index child was three,
four, or eight years old (see Table 12.6). Finally we wondered if older
mothers would have a greater tendency to develop depression bearing in

Table 12.5. *Relation between social/family factors and maternal depression at ages 3, 4 and 8 years in the representative group (N = 98)*

| Social/family factor | Relationship between social/family factors and maternal depression at ages 3, 4 and 8 years expressed as the significance level of chi-square (d.f. = 1) AGE OF CHILD | | |
	3 years	4 years	8 years
Social class	N.S.	N.S.	0·04
Financial stress	0·01	0·01	N.S.
High stress score	N.S.	N.S.	0·03
Type of dwelling (council v. owner-occupied)	0·05	0·05	N.S.
Living on 4th floor or above	0·01	N.S.	N.S.
Marital disharmony	0·01	0·01	0·01

mind that their physical stamina was likely to be more stretched by the presence of demanding young children at home. Again the findings were negative.

By contrast, the type of dwelling, whether owner-occupied or Council-rented, was related to the mother's mental state when the child was three and four years old, with Council tenants being more at risk. Living on the fourth floor or above in a high-rise building was also positively significantly associated with the presence of depression when the child was three years old, but not when the child was four or eight years old. This suggests that, not unnaturally, high-rise flat and estate life is more constraining when children are younger.

Women from families where the father was a manual worker had higher rates of depression (40%) than those where the father had a white-collar occupation (14%) at the time the child was eight years old (see Table 12.6), but social class differences were not found when the children were three and four years old. The reasons for this are unclear. In view of the fact that council tenants and those living in high-rise accommodation and on council estates are predominantly working-class, one would expect working-class mothers also to have higher rates of depression. The reasons that they do not might lie in the fact that those working-class women living in better accommodation have a particularly low risk of developing depression,

Table 12.6. *Social/family factors expected to be associated with maternal
depression and their actual association with maternal depression
at age 8 years in the representative group (N = 98)*

Social/family factor at age 8 years	N	Percentage where mother is depressed (Numbers in brackets)	P^a
New baby born since 4 years:			
Yes	23	48 (11)	N.S.
No	70	33 (24)	
Size of family:			
3 children or less	89	37 (33)	N.S.
4 children or more	7	28 (2)	
Social class:			
Non-manual	22	14 (3)	<0·05
Manual	67	40 (27)	
Mother working:			
No	47	45 (21)	N.S.
Yes	49	29 (14)	

[a]Significance level of chi-square test, d.f. = 1

whereas those few middle-class women living in council high-rise accommodation might have a particularly high rate. Differing social class expectations concerned accommodation may be a potent source of satisfaction and
dissatisfaction. The numbers involved are too small to make it worthwhile to
test this suggestion for statistical significance, but some explanation along
these lines seems plausible. Interestingly, financial stress but not, as stated,
social class was also related to the presence of maternal depression when the
children were three and four years old. Our measure of financial stress did
not take into account the economic level of the family, but concentrated
more on whether the family was having difficulty meeting mortgage or rent
repayments, was behind-hand in hire purchase payments, or was otherwise
in debt. It seems that there were no large social class differences in these
respects and that middle-class families were as financially pressed on these
criteria as working-class, even though the material level at which they were
living was distinctly higher.

There was, as already stated, a considerable rise in the proportion of
women working between the time the children were three and eight years
old, although the rates of depression remained the same. It could nevertheless have been the case that non-working mothers of eight-year-olds were

more depressed than those working and indeed (see Table 12.6), although the difference is not significant, there was quite a definite tendency for this to be the case. Whereas at three and four years there was very little difference in the rates of depression among working and non-working women, at eight years, 45% of non-working women were depressed compared to 29% of working women. The general lack of significant findings in the relationship between maternal depression and employment could be due to a variety of mechanisms, but it seems possible that counter-balancing effects could be at work. At worst, work can mean long or antisocial hours in a low-paid job in addition to a heavy load of housework. Moss (1980) has shown how women's employment is indeed generally poorly paid. At best however a woman's job can provide her with high status, good working conditions, an alternative source of satisfaction and social relationships, flexible hours to match family needs, as well as sufficient pay to get help in the home. These advantages and disadvantages for individuals may well cancel out when a total population is studied.

Changes in the family and changes in the child

We have already seen in Chapter 9 how, when we looked at our group of three-year-old children with problems, we found that the quality of family relationships at the time we studied the children did not predict the outcome. When, however, we looked at our control group of non-disturbed children we found that those in whom family relationships were disharmonious did have a higher chance of becoming disturbed over the next five years than those in whom family relationships were less tension-ridden. We now consider how *changes* in the quality of family relationships affected outcome.

In this case the results are presented separately for the problem and control groups. In Tables 12.8 and 12.9 we have presented the findings for the relationship of changes from three to four years and from three to eight years in five family variables to changes in the child's behavioural state. In order to clarify how these figures have been arrived at, we have provided details in Table 12.7 for one of these variables, maternal criticism. Thus it can be seen from Table 12.7 that, when one considers change in the problem group from three to four years, all children (100%) whose mothers were critical of them at three and four years were still disturbed at four years. Nearly all children (94%) of those whose mothers were critical at four years but not at three years were disturbed at four years. Quite a high proportion (53%) of those whose mothers were not critical either at three or four years, remained problematic at four years and about the same proportion (50%) of those whose mothers were critical at three years but not at four years

Table 12.7. *Relationship between high maternal criticism of the child at 3, 4 and 8 years and the persistence and development of behaviour problems between 3 and 4 years and 3 and 8 years in the behaviour problem group (N = 94) and control group (N = 91)*

	At neither 3 nor 4 years	At 3 years only	At 4 years only	At 3 and 4 years	P^a
Behaviour problem group					
Percentage with problems persisting from 3 to 4 years	N = 45 53%	N = 12 50%	N = 17 94%	N = 20 100%	<0·0001
Control group					
Percentage with problems developing between 3 and 4 years	N = 73 8%	N = 6 0%	N = 9 56%	N = 2 100%	<0·0001

	At neither 3 nor 8 years	At 3 years only	At 8 years only	At 3 and 8 years	P^a
Behaviour problem group					
Percentage with problems persisting from 3 to 8 years	N = 35 46%	N = 17 35%	N = 26 81%	N = 15 93%	<0·0003
Control group					
Percentage with problems developing between 3 and 8 years	N = 69 12%	N = 3 0%	N = 11 64%	N = 5 80%	<0·0001

[a] Significance level of chi-square test, d.f. = 3.

remained disturbed. One may conclude that, in a group of children whose behaviour is problematic at three years, there is a very strong probability indeed that, if they are disturbed at four years, their mothers will be critical of them more generally. On the other hand, quite a high proportion (about half) will remain disturbed even if their mothers are not critical of them, regardless of whether their mothers were critical at three years. In the control group, (all children who were not disturbed at three years) the findings are slightly different. Though the numbers are small, in one case very small, there seems to be a clear tendency for those children who became disturbed to have critical mothers. There is, however, also a very low rate of maternal criticism for children not disturbed either at three or four years. One may conclude from these data that disturbed three-year-olds have a pretty high chance of remaining disturbed over one year (and the remaining data in Table 12.7 reveal that this is still the case over five years), whether or not their mothers are critical of them. However, their chances of remaining disturbed are much higher if their mothers are critical of them at the time the follow-up interview is carried out, whenever this may happen to be, regardless of whether the mother was critical at the earlier age. Clearly the causal

Table 12.8. *Summary of the relationships between behaviour problems at 4 years and adverse family factors at 3 and 4 years in the behaviour problem (N = 94) and control groups (N = 91)*

| | Percentage of children with behaviour problems | | | | |
| | ADVERSE FAMILY FACTOR PRESENT | | | | |
	At neither 3 nor 4 years	At 3 years only	At 4 years only	At 3 and 4 years	P^a
Behaviour problem group					
High maternal criticism	53	50	94	100	<0·0001
Low maternal warmth	60	68	82	94	<0·06
Maternal depression	59	62	70	84	<0·08
Marital disharmony	58	89	82	78	N.S.
High stress score	68	65	62	78	N.S.
Control group					
High maternal criticism	8	0	56	100	<0·0001
Low maternal warmth	7	0	40	80	<0·0001
Maternal depression	9	0	21	31	<0·08
Marital disharmony	10	33	22	31	N.S.
High stress score	9	15	17	20	N.S.

[a]Significance level of chi-square test, d.f. = 3.

direction of this relationship — do disturbed children elicit critical behaviour from their mothers or do critical mothers produce disturbed children? — is difficult to interpret and we shall discuss this problem later in the chapter.

Table 12.9. *Summary of the relationships between behaviour problems at 8 years and adverse family factors at 3 and 8 years in the behaviour problem (N = 94) and control groups (N = 91)*

| | Percentage of children with behaviour problems | | | | |
| | ADVERSE FAMILY FACTOR PRESENT | | | | |
	At neither 3 nor 4 years	At 3 years only	At 8 years only	At 3 and 8 years	P^a
Behaviour problem group					
High maternal criticism	46	35	81	93	<0·0003
Low maternal warmth	59	40	100	80	<0·003
Maternal depression	49	67	67	73	N.S.
Marital disharmony	59	60	57	57	N.S.
High stress score	47	68	58	68	N.S.
Control group					
High maternal criticism	12	0	64	80	<0·0001
Low maternal warmth	18	40	29	50	N.S.
Maternal depression	12	8	36	58	<0·001
Marital disharmony	15	33	29	57	<0·04
High stress score	8	19	24	38	<0·09

[a]Significance level of chi-square test, d.f. = 3

In Table 12.8 results are presented in outline for the rate of persistence in disturbance in relation to four family relationship factors (maternal criticism and warmth, maternal depression and marital disharmony), as well as to the level of external stress operating on the family over the one-year period from when the child was three to four years old. In Table 12.9 the same data are presented in relation to the five-year period from when the child was three to when the child was eight years old. It can be seen that the same pattern that has been described in relation to maternal criticism holds in relation to maternal warmth. With regard to maternal depression and marital dishar- mony the trend is the same, but the findings are much less clear-cut. Most disturbed children remain disturbed over five years and the levels of mater- nal depression or marital disharmony make a slight, but only a slight differ- ence to outcome. Most non-disturbed three-year-old children do not become disturbed and, between three and eight years, persistence of adverse family relationships is associated with adverse outcome to quite a marked degree. Finally, from Tables 12.8 and 12.9 it can readily be seen that changes in the level of external stress acting on the family are hardly related at all to the tendency of disturbed children to remain disturbed, though there is a slightly increased tendency for non-disturbed children to become disturbed if the level of external stress between three and eight years remains high.

Stability in family relationships — implications

It seems clear from the findings presented earlier in this chapter that maternal attitudes, maternal depression, and the quality of the marital relationship changed relatively little over the period of time we studied our families. Although the overall impression was one of continuity and stability as far as these factors were concerned, this should not obscure the fact that in a sizeable number of families significant changes did occur. Thus, for example, although the rate of marital disharmony at the three phases of the study was 22%, 28% and 24%, and although, for example, 60% of the parents whose marriages were poor at three years still had poor marriages when the children were eight years old (compared to only 14% of those whose marriages had been "good" at three years), this still means that 40% (two out of five) poor marriages improved significantly over the five years. That is not an insignificant proportion.

Why, however, should the quality of family relationships change so little? We suspect a number of factors may be at work. Firstly, the personality structure of the parents we interviewed seemed relatively set by the time of our first interview and subsequently changed rather little. The presence of young children was a constraining influence on the degree to which external events could alter the pattern particularly of the mothers' lives and, although a number did start to go out to work, the development of career ambitions and real commitment to work was often inhibited by the demands of family life. Consequently shy women, for example, who had difficulty in initiating relationships remained inhibited, the apathetic remained lacking in energy and initiative, while, to look at the positive side, those women who were already competent in their dealings with the outside world continued to demonstrate their competence by, for example, participating in play-groups or getting themselves more interesting part-time work.

A further reason for stability probably lies in the rigidity of the interpersonal relationships within the family system. Wives whose depression elicited a feeling of despair in their husbands who themselves then turned to alternative sources of gratification in their work, in leisure pursuits, or in other relationships would naturally have a tendency to remain depressed and consequently to continue to elicit the same behaviour in their husbands.

An impatient father who repeatedly shouts at his son who then becomes irritable and demanding will not shout at his son less when the boy's behaviour becomes even more difficult. Stability in family relationships may therefore be seen as evidence of a rigid circular system on which, in our society as it is at present constituted, few external events are likely to be able to exert any significant sort of influence. The wider implications of this state of affairs are discussed in Chapter 14.

Family factors and change in the child

We have indicated how strong are the positive relationships between the presence of disturbance in the child and maternal criticism and lack of warmth. The interpretation of this high correlation is problematic and is made more so by doubts regarding the validity of the association. If an interviewer asks questions relating to disturbed behaviour, and a mother describes numerous troublesome problems, it is almost certain that she will sound colder and more critical than another whose child is not showing such problems. We made various attempts to deal with this problem by insisting, for example, that a factually given account of negative behaviour should not, in itself, constitute a positive reason for rating a mother as cold or critical, but that there should be additional evidence from the mother's behaviour or tone of voice. The problem of rating contamination is of less importance in the assessment of marital disharmony and maternal depression and, as we have indicated, the same trends are apparent as far as these factors are concerned. Further, the fact that similar trends as we identified in the problem group were also identified in the control group in whom, at the outset at least, there can have been no question of rating contamination because none of the children were significantly disturbed, is further powerful evidence in favour of a real association and indeed, of an association in which the causal process can be seen to flow from family disharmony to childhood disturbance. All the same, it is clear that the family factors we assessed cannot be the only factors of importance in determining which children became disturbed. It is, of course, certainly possible that family processes of a type we chose not to study were of importance. We made no attempt, for example, to examine the degree to which the maintenance of inter-generational boundaries was important or to study the possible effects of parental over-protection. Another possibility which we have already discussed in other chapters is that factors not involving family relationships, such as the temperamental characteristics of the child, make important contributions to the development and persistence of problematic behaviour.

Summary

The family and social factors we studied were present at much the same level at the three points in the investigation — when the children were three years, four years and eight years old. The only social factor to change significantly was the level of part-time maternal employment which rose sharply between the time the children were four and eight years old.

In general the same families showed the same sorts of problem over the three points in time. Depressed mothers tended to remain depressed, parents whose marriages were unsatisfactory continued to have difficulties in their relationships with each other. A significant number of families did improve their situation in these respects, but a roughly equal number deteriorated. Although in general it was difficult to establish a process of causation, there was a clear tendency for adverse family factors to contribute to the likelihood that non-disturbed children would become disturbed, but only a slight suggestion that they contributed to disturbed children remaining disturbed. These findings were discussed and it was concluded that, in all probability, the relationships we have identified represent a real association and are not just due to biases in interviewing or rating contamination.

In the next chapter we consider our findings in disturbed and non-disturbed children in relation to intellectual development and educational progress.

13 Intelligence and Educational Attainment — The Outcome

In previous chapters we have referred to intellectual development and educational attainment merely in terms of their relationsip to other variables. In this chapter we focus attention specifically on cognitive development, but it may be helpful first to summarize the relevant findings we have already reported in this book.

In Chapter 4 we demonstrated that three-year-old children with behaviour problems had lower developmental scores than controls in most areas of their functioning. Further, children with specific delays in development such as specific language delay had higher rates of behavioural difficulties. In Chapter 8 we reported that this trend was maintained when the children were four and eight years old with, at eight years, behaviour problem children scoring significantly less well on the verbal scale and full-scale WISC, and more often reading and spelling backward at eight years. In Chapter 10 we noted that this trend for disturbed children to score less well on intelligence and attainment tests at eight years was especially marked for boys, and was not detectable at all for girls. Further, psychological test results at three years did, to some degree, help predict outcome in behaviourally disturbed boys, with dull boys tending to persist more with their problems. In Chapter 11 we noted that three-year-old boys who later showed other anti-social or neurotic problems were duller than those who did not, and that there was, if anything, an opposite trend in girls with brighter three-year-old girls having a tendency to show more neurotic types of problems later on.

In this chapter we shall first examine the continuity of development and intelligence from three to eight years as well as the degree to which different aspects of language development (oral comprehension and expression, reading and spelling ability) relate to each other over this period of time. We shall then go on to consider the outcome of children with definite, early general developmental and language delay. Finally, we shall look at the early familial and other social factors which are related to the presence both of low mean scores in reading and to the presence of a definite delay in acquisition of some aspect of reading skill.

Stability of individual differences in development and intelligence

There was a moderately high level of agreement between developmental quotients (DQ) at three and four years and intelligence quotients (IQ) at four and eight years for the representative sample.

Table 13.1. *Correlations between DQ and IQ at ages 3, 4 and 8 years in the representative group (N = 98)*

	1	2	3	4
1. Griffiths scale EDQ at age 3 years	1·00	0·52	0·45	0·44
2. Griffiths scale EDQ at age 4 years		1·00	0·67	0·39
3. WPPSI full scale IQ at age 4 years			1·00	0·59
4. WISC full scale IQ at age 8 years				1·00

All product moment correlations significant at $P < 0.001$.

It can be seen from Table 13.1 that all the correlations are highly significant despite the fact that inevitably somewhat different functions are being measured at different ages. For example, the DQs presented are for the performance (non-verbal) scale of the Griffiths Test whereas the WPPSI and WISC full-scale scores represent both non-verbal and verbal skills. A more global assessment of ability at three years would be expected to show somewhat higher correlations with later IQ. The pattern of correlations in general shows lower levels of agreement the longer the period of time over which the two measures have been taken, and this is in general agreement with the findings of other workers. Probably the most comparable data are provided by Hindley and Owen (1978) who found a correlation of 0·78 between test results administered at three and four years, and 0·65 between three and eight years once account had been taken of regression. The tests used at different ages in that investigation were probably more comparable and this may account for the higher correlations found.

Madge and Tizard (1980) have pointed to the fact that apparently high stability of scores over time may mask considerable changes in individuals. They suggest that a test–retest correlation as high as 0·9 may be quite compatible with IQ changes of 12 points in two-fifths of a group on a retest. But real change in intellectual functioning may be smaller than this as Vernon (1976) has pointed out. Amongst other factors, the use of tests with different norms and measuring different functions at different ages, and low test reliability may exaggerate differences and give an impression of lower stability of functioning than is really the case.

Table 13.2. *Correlations between language development measures at 3, 4 and 8 years, and reading and spelling measures at 8 years in the representative group (N = 98)*

	1	2	3	4	5	6	7
1. EPVT standard score at age 3 years	1·00	0·54	0·64	0·43	0·41	0·17[b]	0·40
2. EPVT standard score at age 4 years		1·00	0·73	0·56	0·47	0·16[a]	0·44
3. WPPSI verbal IQ at age 4 years			1·00	0·64	0·51	0·17[a]	0·46
4. WISC verbal IQ at age 8 years				1·00	0·68	0·13[a]	0·62
5. Neale accuracy CA-related reading age at age 8 years					1·00	0·77	0·89
6. Neale accuracy IQ-related reading age at age 8 years						1·00	0·68
7. Schonell CA-related spelling age at age 8 years							1·00

All product moment correlations significant at $P < 0.001$, except [a] N.S., [b] $P < 0.05$.

We next examined correlations in language-related disabilities for measures taken at three, four and eight years (see Table 13.2). Again the same patterns emerged whereby the longer the time period separating the tests the lower the correlations. It is particularly interesting that all the correlations are significantly positive apart from those between language measures at three and four years and IQ-related reading age (reading age once IQ has been taken into account) at eight years. By contrast, early language measures did relate significantly to reading age at eight years where no correction for IQ was made. It seems therefore that the association between language measures and later reading ability across the range of reading skill, is mediated solely by the early relationship between early language levels and later IQ. Clinical experience suggests that in individual children, slow language development in a background of good general (non-verbal) ability may be a precursor to specific reading retardation (dyslexia). These findings show, however, that this is not a general phenomenon when the whole range of reading ability is examined.

It perhaps needs to be explained that these moderately high correlations between abilities measured at three, four and eight years do not, in themselves, carry any implications for the identification of factors producing variation in IQ or reading ability. The correlations are quite compatible with both genetic and environmental explanations. We know that there is likely to be stability of genetic influences over time, but, as we have seen in the previous chapter in which we examined the stability of family factors, the same holds true for many pertinent aspects of the environment.

Continuities in delayed development

As well as investigating the relation between early and later development in terms of the stability of individual differences across the entire range of ability, we also examined the extent to which children with delays in their development at a younger age are the same children who showed poor performance on various aspects of ability and behaviour at a later age. By analogy to the situation with intelligence, it is possible that a very different pattern of continuity will be shown by such children from that found in children with more normal early development. With IQ it is well established that the factors that produce very low scores (i.e. below 50) are different from both the polygenic and environmental influences on variation within the normal range. It is therefore possible to obtain relatively high stability in correlations of language ability as was reported in Table 13.2 and to find either a much greater or a much lower degree of continuity in children with definitely delayed development.

To test for these possibilities we have studied longitudinally a group of children showing delayed language development at age three years. These children were found in our original randomly selected sample of non-immigrant children (N = 705). A screening measure was developed which identifies those children whose expressive language ages were six months or more below their chronological age. Their expressive language ages were ascertained using the Reynell Developmental Language Scales (Reynell, 1969). We found, however, that in our randomly selected three-year-old children their performance on this test was some six months ahead of the published norms. Therefore those children we identified as language delayed were in fact some 9-12 months behind the sample mean language age. Full details of the screening procedure can be found in Stevenson and Richman (1976).

The 22 children in this language delayed group show a variety of additional characteristics that distinguish them from other children at age three years. Most importantly for assessing their outcome, as indicated in Chapter 4, children with "delayed language" showed a high incidence of behaviour problems (Stevenson and Richman, 1978). Boys were over-represented as well as children with a variety of disadvantageous social and family characteristics. In particular, children with significantly delayed language development tended to come from large families and their mothers had a high incidence of depression (Richman and Stevenson, 1977). Accordingly it was necessary to control for these associated characteristics when assessing outcome in order to establish whether any later difficulties stemmed from

Table 13.3. *Language, intelligence and behavioural outcomes at 4 and 8 years for the language delayed children and matched controls, in percentages*

	Language delay group (N = 22)	Matched controls (N = 22)	P^a
At age 4 years			
Reynell language age ≤ 40 months	65	15	0·002
WPPSI full scale IQ < 85	77	26	0·006
Behaviour score ≥ 10	57	50	N.S.
At age 8 years			
WISC full scale IQ < 85	36	4	0·01
Verbal IQ < 85	59	23	0·015
Performance IQ < 85	27	4	0·046
Full scale IQ < 70	9	0	N.S.
Neale accuracy reading age < 80 months	41	14	0·04
Neale comprehension reading age < 80 months	45	14	0·02
Schonell spelling age < 80 months	50	23	0·06

[a]Significance level of chi-square test, d.f. = 1.

the language delay rather than as a consequence of these other disadvantages. To achieve this control a group of children were selected from the behaviour problem and control groups to match individually with children from the language delay group on the following measures at three years: sex, BSQ scores, social class and mother's mental state. It is important to note that the controls were not matched for IQ. All but three children with language delay also showed general retardation and, as all children with general retardation also showed language delay, there were insufficient children available with low IQ to allow for IQ matching. The outcome at age four and at age eight for the language delayed group was compared to this matched control group to establish whether language delay *per se* was related to later difficulties.

From Table 13.3 it can be seen that language delayed children who are also, in general, globally delayed, have a poor outcome both at four and eight years when compared with same sex children with similar levels of behaviour and family disturbance. At four years, nearly four out of five (77%) of the language delayed children have a WPPSI full-scale IQ of less than 85 compared to 26% of the control. At eight years there still remains a considerable difference between the groups. However, it is important not to overestimate their significance. Thus, although 36% of the children language delayed at three years now had a WISC full-scale IQ less than 85 — a figure nine times that in the control group — it nevertheless remains true that nearly two-thirds of the children had IQs well within the normal range. Further, only two of the children in the language delayed group had IQs below 70 at eight years, so the great majority did not show a really significant degree of mental handicap. As might be expected from the fact that the original group was not really *specifically* language delayed, continuity in reading and spelling ability was at about the same level as continuity in general ability.

There was a tendency at eight years for language delayed children to show poorer behaviour than the controls as judged by parents, with 48% compared to 24% deviant on the parent behaviour questionnaire — a nonsignificant difference. However, this trend was not apparent when results on the teacher behaviour questionnaire were compared: in this case the rates of behavioural deviance were very similar (45% versus 48% in the controls). Nevertheless, the overall impression of the language delayed group is that their outlook one way or another was very poor. When we examined their outcome comprehensively we found that there were only three of the group of 22 children who, at age eight years, were not deviant on any of the following criteria: deviance on parent behaviour questionnaire, deviance on teacher behaviour questionnaire, reading age less than 80 months, WISC full-scale IQ less than 85. By contrast, nine, or 41%, of the controls were normal on all these measures ($P < 0.04$), and one should not forget that the controls were selected to include an unusually large number of children with behaviour problems and social disadvantage.

Educational problems at age eight

The demonstration of relatively high stabilities in IQ and language abilities and the poor outcome for children with early language delays might lead us to suppose that we could predict educational difficulties at age eight from characteristics of the child and his family during the pre-school period. We will examine this possibility by analysing data available on children with difficulties in their reading at age eight. Our study was not ideally designed for such an analysis in that conditions with a low prevalence at the ages subsequent to three years were not separately screened. This means that conditions such as specific reading retardation and reading backwardness with prevalence rates of roughly 6% and 5% respectively are represented by relatively few children in our representative longitudinally studied sample (N = 98). It has been necessary therefore to draw upon all the children on whom we have longitudinal data for this analysis. Tables are presented which contrast children with and without reading difficulties in the merged behaviour problem and control groups. Where the findings from this necessarily biased sample differ from the trends discernible in the smaller representative group this will be indicated in the text.

At age eight years the most relevant measure of educational progress is reading ability. As described in Chapter 8, we have distinguished two types of reading difficulty, specific reading retardation and reading backwardness. In the merged behaviour problem and control groups there were sixteen children whose reading age was more than 18 months below that predicted from their IQ and chronological age (specific reading retardation) on either the accuracy or comprehension measures of the Neale analysis of reading ability. Reading backwardness was determined by either an accuracy or comprehension reading age 18 months or more below chronological age, and was present in 17 children in this merged sample.

Table 13.4 shows the relationship between adverse social and family factors and reading problems at age eight years. It should be emphasized that the percentages of children with adverse factors in both the reading problem and the contrast groups are greater than in the representative sample because such a high proportion of the children in the merged groups have behaviour problems. However, it was thought to be more appropriate to test for significant differences between the groups showing reading problems and the residual group within the merged behaviour problem and control groups, since a comparison with the representative sample of children without reading problems would be biased towards the identification of significant differences.

In general there is a tendency for both specific reading retardation and reading backwardness to be associated with greater social and familial adversity. This reaches significance in only one comparison — 75% of children with specific reading retardation had mothers who were depressed when the children were three years of age compared to 28% of the children without this reading difficulty. Reading retardation at eight years is more closely associated with adverse family factors at age three years than it is with concurrently measured family factors. Reading backwardness shows a similar but less marked trend.

When we turn to factors in the child's developmental history that are associated with reading difficulties a clearer picture emerges. It can be seen

Table 13.4. *Percentage of children with reading problems at age 8 years with adverse social/family factors present at age 3, 4 and 8 years in the combined behaviour problem and control groups (N = 185)*

| | Type of reading problem at age 8 years | | | | | |
	Severe specific reading retardation (N = 16)	No specific reading retardation (N = 169)	P^a	Severe reading backward (N = 17)	Not reading backward (N = 168)	P^a
At age 3 years						
Mother depressed	75	28	<0·001	53	31	N.S.
High stress	63	53	N.S.	59	53	N.S.
Poor marriage	31	30	N.S.	44	29	N.S.
Clinical rating of behaviour problem	69	50	N.S.	77	49	<0·06
At age 4 years						
Mother depressed	63	41	N.S.	53	41	N.S.
High stress	50	45	N.S.	65	43	N.S.
Poor marriage	40	34	N.S.	36	34	N.S.
Clinical rating of behaviour problem	56	41	N.S.	65	40	N.S.
At age 8 years						
Mother depressed	50	36	N.S.	41	37	N.S.
High stress	50	53	N.S.	59	52	N.S.
Poor marriage	44	28	N.S.	47	27	N.S.
Clinical rating of behaviour problem	56	41	N.S.	65	40	N.S.

[a]Significance level of chi-square test, d.f. = 1

Table 13.5. *Percentage of children with specific reading retardation and reading backwardness at age 8 years showing developmental delays at age 3 or 4 years in the combined behaviour problem and control groups (N = 185)*

	Percentage of children with reading problems at 8 years with delay at 3 or 4 years					
	Type of reading problem at 8 years					
Type of delay at 3 and 4 years	Severe specific reading retardation (N = 16)	No specific reading retardation (N = 168)	P^a	Severe reading backward (N = 17)	Not reading backward (N = 167)	P^a
Mild specific language delay at 3 years	31	40	N.S.	59	37	N.S.
Severe specific language delay at 3 years	13	17	N.S.	29	15	N.S.
Mild specific language delay at 4 years	38	29	N.S.	59	27	<0·02
Severe specific language delay at 4 years	13	23	N.S.	41	20	N.S.
Mild general language delay at 3 years	31	43	N.S.	71	39	<0·03
Severe general language delay at 3 years	13	26	N.S.	53	22	<0·02
Mild general language delay at 4 years	31	32	N.S.	71	28	<0·01
Severe general language delay at 4 years	25	24	N.S.	59	21	<0·01

[a]Significance level of chi-square test, d.f. = 1

in Table 13.5 that only reading backwardness is consistently related to developmental delays. Rutter and Yule (1975) suggest that specific reading retardation is associated only with early language difficulties, whereas the history of children with reading backwardness reveals a wide range of developmental delays. The data in Table 13.5 show that, in our study, specific language delays are not associated with reading retardation, but that children with reading backwardness do show earlier delays both generally and in language development.

One of the most significant findings concerning child characteristics associated with reading difficulties is that between specific reading retardation and anti-social behaviour. Consistent findings in ten and eleven year olds (Rutter *et al.*, 1970; Berger *et al.*, 1975) suggest that reading backwardness is associated with behavioural deviance, but that this association is not specific to any particular type of deviance. However, specific reading retardation, which has a ratio of 3 to 1 of boys to girls, shows a specific association especially in boys with anti-social or conduct disorders. By comparison between children with specific reading retardation combined with anti-social deviance and children with these conditions in isolation, Rutter and Yule (1975) have shown that children with the combined condition are more like children with pure specific reading retardation than those with pure conduct disorders. This, they suggest, indicates that, for some children at least, difficulties with reading can lead to anti-social behaviour at age ten and eleven years. As they indicate, this plausible causal sequence has direct implications for preventive measures to reduce the prevalence of conduct disorders and delinquency in later childhood and adolescence. If educational failure commonly leads to anti-social behaviour, greater emphasis on early remediation could result in a reduction in delinquency rates.

The data from our study can potentially clarify the situation with regard to this proposed causal sequence since children were studied before reading skills developed. Specifically, if failure in learning to read does commonly lead to anti-social behaviour, there should be a less strong association at age eight between specific reading retardation and anti-social behaviour than has been found in older children. Children at this age have a briefer history of educational failure and the processes thought to underlie this association, lowering of self-esteem and alienation from the school setting, will have been operating over a shorter period. In addition, children with symptoms at three years that are precursors of later anti-social deviance should show no increased rate of reading difficulties. We should ideally have carried out this analysis on the representative sample but, as indicated earlier, insufficient children within this group demonstrated these conditions. As before the bulk of this analysis therefore concerns the merged behaviour problem and control groups.

A key issue in the link between specific reading retardation and reading backwardness is the sex of the child. Within our representative sample (N = 98), four boys and two girls showed specific reading retardation and two boys and two girls are reading backward — in both cases using an eighteen-month delay as criterion. In the merged sample only two girls were reading retarded and five girls reading backward, compared to 14 and 12 boys respectively. It is only possible therefore to investigate with any meaning the links between behaviour disturbance and reading difficulties in boys though some data are presented for the very small number of girls for completeness.

The association between reading difficulties and behaviour disturbance is shown in Table 13.6. It can be seen that in the total sample there was no significant association between either specific reading retardation or reading

Table 13.6. *The association between clinical rating of type of disorder at 8 years and specific reading retardation and reading backwardness for boys and girls in the merged behaviour problem and control groups (N = 185)*

Clinical rating of type of disorder at 8 years	Total Sample		Boys		Girls	
	% Specific reading retarded	% Reading backward	% Specific reading retarded	% Reading backward	% Specific reading retarded	% Reading backward
No disorder	7% (7/106)	6% (6/106)	12% (6/51)	4% (2/51)	2% (1/55)	7% (4/55)
Anti-social	13% (6/48)	13% (6/48)	16% (6/38)	13% (5/38)	0% (0/10)	10% (1/10)
Neurotic	11% (3/28)	14% (4/28)	17% (2/12)	33% (4/12)	6% (1/16)	0% (0/16)
P^a	N.S.	N.S.	N.S.	<0·02	—	—

Significance level of chi square test, d.f. = 2.

backwardness and either the presence of behavioural deviance or any specific type of deviance. Thus, of the 106 children without any behavioural deviance 7% showed specific reading retardation, compared to 13% of children with anti-social deviance and 11% with neurotic deviance (small and non-significant differences). In boys, though specific reading retardation is not associated with the presence or type of deviant behaviour, reading backwardness is associated with neurotic deviance (the numbers are small but the association is statistically significant). This finding of a lack of association between anti-social deviance and specific reading retardation at eight years, an association present at ten and eleven years, is consistent with the hypothesis that failure in educational achievement leads to antisocial disorder in a significant number of children.

Ideally we should also have been able to test the same hypothesis by seeing whether antisocial or related difficulties at three years predicted the development of reading problems. If this hypothesis were to be supported one would expect no such trend. Unfortunately our cluster analysis did not reveal a clearly antisocial group at three years, so this hypothesis could not be tested. We did examine rates of both types of reading difficulty in the five different clusters of symptons we have described in Chapter 7. The numbers were very small and few conclusions could be drawn, but it is of interest that the highest rate of children later showing specific reading retardation (22%) was in the children in the so-called "normal" cluster, i.e. those with fewest symptoms. There was no suggestion that highly symptomatic three-year-olds later developed reading problems, and this again provides modest support for the notion that more commonly it is educational failure which leads to behaviour disturbance, rather than the other way round. To complete this analysis of the relation between educational problems and type of deviance, we will examine data relevant to a second conclusion drawn from the Isle of Wight and London studies. Findings from these studies indicated that for some children, common family factors might be jointly responsible for producing both specific reading retardation and behaviour disturbance.

We have earlier established the consistent association between family and social factors and behaviour problems in our study. In Chapter 11 we introduced the summary measures of the quality of the emotional environment experienced by the children. This measure is based on the mother's mental state, quality of the marriage, stress experienced by the family over the past year, the mother's criticism of and warmth to the child. At each age a close association has been demonstrated between this composite measure and behavioural disturbance. We will use this score to explore the possibility of a set of common family characteristics causing both behaviour deviance and reading difficulties.

We first inspected the data to see whether the rates of reading problems in children with and without different types of behavioural deviance at eight years varied according to both the early emotional environment (at three years) and the current emotional environment (at eight years). For example, did the presence of an adverse emotional environment make it more likely that the child would develop a reading problem, and, if this was the case, was the effect more marked in children who later also developed some form of behavioural deviance? The numbers we had available in the different groups were small, but it seemed that in children with antisocial deviance at eight years, an adverse early emotional environment did specifically appear to be related to a lower than average ability to read in relation to IQ. By contrast, in children who did not show behavioural deviance at eight years, the presence of a currently adverse emotional environment seemed more important. When we inspected the data further to examine which aspect of the early emotional environment appeared most important, it seemed that the mother's mental state (anxiety and depression) was of greatest significance.

In order to explore this unexpected result further we looked at the variation in IQ adjusted reading age across the whole range of ability. The IQ adjusted reading age is the continuous measure of reading achievement relative to intelligence and provides a measure of the degree of specific reading advancement or retardation. We examined this variable in the representative sample to see whether our finding of an association between the emotional environment and IQ adjusted reading age might be a result arising from the use of the biased sample formed by merging the behaviour problem and control groups.

In Table 13.7 the representative sample is divided into groups by scores on the emotional environment measure at three years and eight years. The mean scores are presented for the children at three years (EPVT and Griffiths Performance DQ) and eight years (WISC IQ and Neale Accuracy IQ adjusted reading age). When the sample is divided by their emotional environments at age three, there are significant differences in the mean test scores at age three years and, most interestingly, in the IQ adjusted reading age at age eight years. Those children who were in the least favourable emotional environment at three years do least well in reading at eight years and those in the most favourable environment do best. The parallel comparison for the sample divided by emotional environment at eight years reveals no such significant differences in test scores at three or eight years. This result confirms our earlier impression that reading at age eight is most closely related to family factors at the earlier age and moreover that the result is specific to reading and is not found for general intelligence.

This result is unexpected in that almost invariably relationships between child development measures and environmental influences are most marked

Table 13.7. *Mean test scores at 3 and 8 years for groups defined by emotional environment scores at age 3 and at age 8 years for the representative group (N = 98)*

Emotional environment	N	AT 3 YEARS EPVT Standard Score Mean	AT 3 YEARS Griffiths Performance DQ Mean	AT 8 YEARS Neale accuracy IQ-adjusted reading age Mean	AT 8 YEARS WISC IQ Mean
At 3 years					
0 (good)	25	106·9	113·2	+5·07	110·3
1	38	104·1	107·1	−0·74	111·1
2	15	97·9	100·1	−0·19	109·2
3+ (poor)	17	92·2	103·1	−6·25	107·5
Analysis of variance F, P		3·54, <0·02	3·17, <0·05	3·47, <0·02	0·44, N.S.
Duncan's multiple range test[a]		0 1 2 3+	0 1 2 3+	0 1 2 3+	0 1 2 3+
At 8 years					
0 (good)	27	104·4	111·5	−0·48	112·2
1	30	103·1	102·8	+1·31	109·8
2	18	100·4	101·4	+0·43	108·0
3+ (poor)	15	98·7	103·6	−5·50	109·2
Analysis of variance F, P		1·11, N.S.	1·42, N.S.	1·21, N.S.	0·59, N.S.
Duncan's multiple range test[a]		0 1 2 3+	0 1 2 3+	0 1 2 3+	0 1 2 3+

[a] Means *not* significantly different from one another are underlined

when the variables are measured contemporaneously and the strength of
relationships diminishes the further apart in time measurements are made.
We wondered whether the result arose because poor emotional environment was associated with an adverse factor that was itself more directly
impairing reading acquisition, e.g. parental attitudes to education.

To explore this possibility of the effect of other aspects of the home
environment at age eight having an effect, we tested a variety of variables for
a significant association with the IQ related reading age. This analysis also
offered an opportunity to examine the influence of other factors on reading
ability. There were four variables (see Table 13.8) most closely associated to
IQ adjusted reading age: family size (a sizeable but non-significant difference), attendance at pre-school facility (playgroup, nursery school, kindergarten, etc.) at four years, mother working at eight years, and whether
the child read at home at eight years. Children had higher mean IQ adjusted
reading ages if their families were small, they had attended pre-school
facilities, their mothers worked when they were of school age, or the
child read at home at eight years. Whether the child read with his parents did
not relate to the measure of reading age. There were relatively few families
in the sample with four or more children and it is therefore unlikely that
family size was the mediating variable. In fact the relationship between the
emotional environment at three years and IQ adjusted reading age is just as
strong if only small families are considered.

It is incidentally of interest to note that our findings on the influence of
children and parents reading together might appear not to support the strong
association noted by Hewison and Tizard (1980). However, we did not
separately identify those occasions when the parents were reading to the
child and the children were reading to their parents, and in the Hewison and
Tizard study it was only families where the latter was frequently occurring
that children showed advanced reading ability. Our findings cannot therefore be taken to disconfirm this previous work.

The finding that children who often read at home were advanced in
reading is of dubious significance. It is equally likely that advanced reading
ability encourages children to read at home rather than reading at home
improves reading ability, and more likely still that both effects occur. In any
event the child reading at home is an unlikely candidate as a possible
mediating variable, as this factor is not significantly related to the emotional
environment at three years.

To test for the possible mediating effect of mothers working and pre-
school group attendance, a two-way analysis of variance was calculated with
the emotional environment at three years as one factor and these two
variables in turn as the other factor. Were these factors associated with early
emotional environment, and could this explain the link between early

Table 13.8. *Mean IQ-adjusted reading age and WISC full-scale IQ for groups defined by various social characteristics at 4 and 8 years for the representative group (N = 98)*

	N	Neale accuracy IQ-adjusted reading age			WISC Full-Scale IQ		
		Mean	Standard deviation	P^a	Mean	Standard deviation	P^a
Social class:							
non-manual	23	−0·67	10·84	N.S.	117·0	12·9	<0·001
manual	67	−0·55	12·02		107·9	9·5	
Family size:							
less than 4 children	90	0·41	11·85	N.S.	110·2	11·4	N.S.
4 or more children	7	−5·28	6·91		105·3	5·6	
Attended pre-school group:							
Yes	55	2·99	12·24	<0·01	111·1	10·4	N.S.
No	42	−3·90	9·59		108·1	11·9	
Mother helps with school work:							
Yes	50	0·91	13·11		110·5	10·9	
Sometimes	17	1·17	12·21	N.S.	111·6	11·6	N.S.
No	28	−2·19	8·52		107·9	11·0	
Father helps with school work							
Yes	34	0·94	12·10		112·5	10·4	
Sometimes	10	−3·28	7·94	N.S.	111·6	12·0	N.S.
No	46	−1·30	12·00		108·4	10·9	
Child reads at home:							
Yes	77	1·60	12·16		111·2	10·9	
No	19	−5·85	6·51	<0·02	105·4	10·4	<0·05
Child reads with parents:							
Yes	28	0·03	12·42		110·0	8·2	
Occasionally	27	−2·13	11·13	N.S.	110·5	13·8	N.S.
No	41	1·67	11·44		109·7	10·9	
Mother works per week (child 8 years)							
No	46	−0·85	11·20		109·9	11·5	
less than 10 hours	14	−7·84	6·99	<0·01	109·8	9·7	N.S.
more than 10 hours	35	4·37	12·29		110·0	11·2	
Mother works per week (child 4 years)							
No	61	−0·52	12·36		111·2	11·6	
less than 10 hours	9	3·95	13·59	N.S.	108·8	7·9	N.S.
more than 10 hours	26	−0·49	9·14		107·5	11·0	

[a]Significance level of one way ANOVA.

emotional environment and later reading ability? In fact there remained a marked effect of the early emotional environment IQ adjusted reading age after each of these factors had been taken into account. With pre-school group attendance it remained significant (F = 2·87, $P < 0·05$) but with mothers working the effect of the early emotional environment, though remaining sizeable, fell below the 5% level of significance (F = 2·11, $P < 0·10$). It can be seen from Table 13.8 that the relation between mothers working and IQ adjusted reading age is a complex one. It is mothers who are working less than ten hours a week whose children show the poorest reading age. In addition, the numbers in each cell for this two-way analysis of variance were small and the results must be treated with circumspection.

One possible explanation of the relation between the quality of the early emotional environment and later reading ability is that some aspects of the child's development are affected by the early family circumstances and that this aspect of development is in turn influencing reading acquisition. In some sense, if the association is not a spurious one produced by a common link with another environmental factor, some such explanation must be valid. It remains to be seen, however, if any of the child variables we investigated could be identified as responsible for the association. In Table 13.7 it was seen that the emotional environment at three years was related to language development at three years. We have also previously demonstrated (in Chapter 4) that our measure of emotional environment was related to behaviour problems at age three. An analysis of co-variance was therefore calculated with the emotional environment as the factor and EPVT scores and behaviour symptom scores as co-variables. Once these early language and behaviour problems have been taken into account in this manner the effect of the early emotional environment on IQ adjusted reading age was no longer statistically significant (F = 2·27, $P = 0·086$) but nevertheless remained sizeable and, if not due to chance, of possibly considerable educational significance. Thus, after controlling for language at three years (EPVT score) and behaviour at eight years, there is still a nine months difference in the mean IQ adjusted reading age between those children with no adverse emotional environmental factors and those with three or more present at three years. It seemed therefore that adverse early emotional environment was possibly important even after its early effect on language and behaviour had been taken into account.

To summarize, we have demonstrated that specific reading retardation is more closely related to family factors, especially maternal depression, present at three years than to such factors when they are present at eight years. The same finding emerged when individual differences in IQ adjusted reading ages were considered. The relationship between the emotional environment at three years and later reading ability could only be partly explained by a common association with either social factors, such as mothers working and attendance at pre-school groups, or with aspects of the children's development that we assessed, i.e. early language development or later behavioural disturbance.

Further analysis of our data revealed that the relationship between the emotional environment at three years and later reading is significant for both the manual and non-manual social classes; social class itself is not significantly related to IQ adjusted reading age (see Table 13.8). In addition, when the effect of early emotional environment was investigated alongside the effect of sex, the sex of the child and the quality of the early emotional environment were both found to be significant, and there was a significant interaction between the two factors ($F = 4.18$, $P = 0.008$). The interaction resulted from the fact that the relationship between early environment and reading was more marked in boys than it was in girls, for whom the effect was restricted to those living in the most adverse emotional circumstances at three years.

Conclusions

These findings on the relationships between early behaviour, language and family relationships, and later intellectual development, general reading ability, and reading skill in relation to IQ are complex and it might be helpful at this point to draw them together. It seems first of all as though there is quite a considerable degree of continuity and stability over time in different aspects of both oral and written language skill. Verbal IQ and reading ability at age eight years are related to early language development. However, the IQ adjusted reading age is not related to early language development in this way. Three-year-old children with a marked degree of language delay are usually in addition showing some degree of more general retardation. Their progress is, in general, disappointing and they have a high chance of showing later cognitive and educational deficits. Only a small proportion will show evidence of neither educational retardation or behavioural deviance later on.

Earlier suggestions that links found between specific reading retardation (delay in reading after IQ has been taken into account) and antisocial behaviour might be produced largely by children frustrated by educational failure becoming aggressive, are to some degree supported by our findings. The lack of an association between antisocial behaviour and specific educational retardation at eight years when it is known to be present at ten and eleven years suggests that a long experience of educational failure may be necessary to produce signs of aggression. Further, there was no suggestion from our findings that children showing particular behavioural difficulties at three years become educationally retarded as a result.

By contrast, when we examined the degree to which early emotional environment affected later IQ adjusted reading age across the whole spectrum of reading ability (and not just in those children showing specific reading retardation) there was a strong suggestion that an adverse early emotional environment was related to a low IQ adjusted reading age. Children from large families, children whose mothers did not work, those who did not attend pre-school playgroups, and those who did not read at home also had lower than expected IQ adjusted reading ages. When these had been taken into account, it remained the case that early emotional environment was related to later specific reading ability.

One can only conjecture on the reasons for this association. It is quite possible that a generally tense home atmosphere, a depressed mother, quarrelsome parents, all affect the child's capacity to concentrate on the task of learning to read.

It would not be surprising if tension in the home affected a child's capacity to absorb written material. It is also possible that parents preoccupied with their own emotional problems are less adequate in assisting their child in acquiring reading skills and, as Hewison and Tizard (1980) have suggested, parental involvement in listening to a child reading may make a massive contribution to the acquisition of reading skills.

It is of interest that the range of early occurrences to the child and family, such as the mother going out to work and attendance at pre-school facilities, are all linked to later levels of reading ability and that the importance of early emotional environment persists even after these have been taken into account. By contrast, definite severe delay in reading, whether IQ related or not, is unassociated with these early family factors. It could well be that definite delays are more likely to be produced by genetic or environmental effects of a comparatively simple kind, whereas, across the range of ability, a variety of factors, sometimes interacting together and sometimes more or less independently, may operate. This situation would be similar to that thought to pertain in general intellectual development in which severe retardation is thought more commonly to arise from single gene effects whereas mild and moderate retardation are produced by more complex genetic/environmental interaction.

14 Implications

In Chapter 5 we summarized the findings of the cross-sectional study carried out when the children in our investigation were three years of age. We pointed to the high rates of behaviour problems amongst the children, and summarized the way in which these related to the social setting in which they lived, their family lives, and the characteristics of the children themselves. We suggested that, in our view, the most appropriate way of considering the behaviour problems we had identified was as a product of the interaction initially between mother and child, and later between the child and the complete family. In this chapter we shall consider how the findings of the follow-up study described in Chapters 6 to 13 elaborated our views in this respect, and have enabled us to extend our thinking on the nature and course of behaviour problems in young children. We shall then consider the implications of our findings for health, education and social policy.

Nature and course of problem behaviour in the young child

(a) Persistence

Our findings firstly seem to us to contradict the view that behaviour problems in pre-school children are usually transient reactions to stress and of little significance in later personality development. This view, though rarely explicit in textbooks, is implicitly held by general practitioners and health visitors who reassure parents that their children will grow out of their problems. With 61% of problematic three-year-olds still showing significant difficulties on a clinical rating five years later, this is not a tenable view. A proportion of problematic young children will, of course, gradually become less difficult as time goes on, but the number who do so is not great enough to warrant complacency or reassurance. It seems from our findings that, once a child's behaviour is established in a maladaptive pattern, it does not readily change. Further, young children who show even slight signs of difficult behaviour are at increased risk for developing behaviour and emotional problems in school life. We do not wish to suggest that parents of children who show minor problems should be unnecessarily alarmed, for the chances of their children developing serious difficulties later on are in fact rather small, but it is of interest that even minor disturbance in young children predisposes to later difficulties in some degree. Finally, whatever the outcome, the severity of the child and family problems at three years suggests that they are a serious cause for concern in their own right.

(b) Types of problem

The fact that there is a similarity between types of problem shown by children when they are three and eight years old establishes that there is an important connection between the phenomena occurring at the two ages. Fearful pre-school children are likely, if they have disorders later on, to show neurotic deviance, whereas restless pre-schoolers are more likely to show anti-social behaviour. However, despite consistency in the type of problems shown within the limits of our methods we were unable to detect any features of the family background determining which type of problem later developed. Nor did it seem as though any one particular type of problem was especially likely to arise out of family or other stress.

Factors associated with persistence and development of problems

In Chapter 5 we considered the reasons why behaviour problems seemed to occur commonly in young pre-school children. We shall now go on to summarize the information we have obtained, which points to the reasons why some of these problems persisted to eight years and others did not, and why a number of non-disturbed young children developed problems between three and eight years.

(a) The sex of the child

Boys were more likely to continue to persist with problematic behaviour than were girls. Further, just as duller boys were more likely to develop problems than dull girls, so problems tended to persist to a greater degree in a boy of low intelligence than in a girl of similar ability. With girls, if anything, the tendency was in the reverse direction — that is, it tended to be the brighter girls who remained disturbed.

There is a number of possible reasons for these sex differences. Boys are more subject than girls to show developmental immaturity. They have, for example, higher rates of language delay and they gain control of their bladder and bowel function more slowly. Some of the behaviour problems we have described could be regarded as evidence of developmental immaturity rather than of developmental deviation. It might therefore be that, for physiological or constitutional reasons, dull boys are particularly likely both to develop and to persist in problematic behaviour. Different mechanisms may be at work in raising rates of problems in brighter girls. If, as has been suggested, girls have a strong tendency to identify with their mothers, it could well be that identificatory processes tend to be more advanced in brighter girls, and that consequently it is these who, when living with and cared for by a depressed, anxious mother, are more likely to show similar problems themselves.

Other reasons for these sex differences may, amongst other factors, lie in the different ways in which both parents and teachers interact with boys and girls. Parents tend to be stricter in their disciplinary procedure with boys (Maccoby and Jacklin, 1980), and teachers are more likely to show nurturant behaviour and encourage closeness of contact with girls (Serbin *et al.*, 1973). It could be, therefore, that in our society boys are generally subjected to more rejecting experiences and react accordingly.

(b) Family factors

We have found that the presence of currently disturbed family relationships is a very strong predictor of the persistence of behaviour problems. Thus marital disharmony between the parents, maternal depression, high maternal criticism and low maternal warmth, are all strongly associated with childhood disturbance. We have already discussed our concern as to how much reliance can be placed on the measures of maternal attitudes (warmth and criticism) to the child as independent variables, because clearly a mother of a child with problems may well *sound* colder and more critical at interview, even though this is not the case in everyday life. However, a considerable degree of confidence can be placed in the independence of the other measures of family life and the measures of maternal attitude can, at the very least, be seen as supportive evidence for the importance of the quality of family relationships in the maintenance of behavioural problems. Other studies, reviewed by Rutter (1976) have pointed to the significant role of family factors of this type, and indeed there is such a general view that young children respond to the atmosphere of the family, that it would have been surprising if we had not found such an association. Some of the possible mechanisms whereby such factors produce emotional disturbance in children in the first place have been discussed in Chapter 5, and it may be assumed that similar mechanisms are at work in the maintenance of disturbance. Although the quality of *current* family relationships is closely linked to the presence of behaviour and emotional problems, it is of interest that the presence of disturbed family relationships at three years does not provide any indication of the outcome of behavioural difficulties. A problem child from a disturbed family did not have a worse outlook than a problem child from a family in which the relationships appeared good. There are two possible reasons for this finding. It could be that in those families in which relationships *appeared* good, there were in fact subtle distortions which evaded notice at interview. This seems unlikely because the quality of the parental marriage, as assessed by us when the child was three years old, was in fact a good predictor of marriage outcome. If there were such subtle factors present they did not seem to produce conspicuous marital difficulties. A second possibility is that the non-familial factors producing disturbance are just as continuous in their influence as family problems. For example, temperamental or constitutional factors may be of predominant importance in the development of some problems and their influence may well be as unremitting as the presence of adverse family factors.

It is of interest that, as is clear from our findings presented in Chapter 12, many problem children whose family relationships improved did not by any means automatically shed their behavioural difficulties. This phenomenon can be explained in either psychodynamic or learning theory terms. It could be that some children under family stress "internalize" their problems, so even when the stress is removed from them, their emotional life continues to suffer. Alternatively, stress can be seen as inducing a maladaptive learned pattern of behaviour in the family which persists even when reinforcement or reward is absent. Which of these ways of looking at the problem is most useful is uncertain, but in view of the persisting nature of behaviour problems even when external circumstances improve, it seems particularly important to attempt early prevention or treatment.

A further reason for focusing on family relationships in considering early intervention emerges from our findings in relation to the development of disorders. The majority of non-disturbed children whose family relationships were tension-ridden when they were three-years-old had become disturbed by the time they had reached the age of eight years. This is perhaps the strongest evidence we have of the powerful effect of family disharmony in the generation of behaviour and emotional problem as, when the parents were interviewed at the time the child was three years of age, there was no possibility that their poor family relationships had been produced by a disturbed young child. The need for early intervention in disharmonious families before the children become disturbed hardly needs stressing in this situation. The need for early intervention is also indicated by the striking finding, described in Chapter 13, that the quality of family relationships at three years is linked to the presence of below average reading ability even when the child's IQ has been taken into account at eight years of age. It will be recollected that one of the original aims of our study was to clarify the mechanism whereby reading retardation and antisocial behaviour came to be associated by the age of ten or eleven years. Our findings are not as clear-cut as we might have wished, but they do suggest that the association between antisocial behaviour and specific reading retardation which has been identified at ten and eleven years may arise for complex reasons. Behaviourally disturbed children, and especially disturbed boys, do have higher rates of intellectual retardation and reading difficulties than do the non-disturbed. By contrast, children with specific reading problems do not have high rates of either neurotic or antisocial problems at eight years, although there is a tendency for boys with reading backwardness to show more neurotic problems. By the age of ten and eleven years not only do antisocial boys show more specific reading difficulties but children with reading difficulties show more antisocial behaviour. This, as we have indic- ated, suggests that the reason why antisocial boys show reading problems may lie in the fact that those same adverse early emotional relationships in the pre-school period which are associated with later reading problems are also responsible for the development of behaviour disorders, but that language delay also predisposes to both types of problem — behavioural and educational. Perhaps although these two causative influences can and do act independently when present in severe form, they also potentiate each other's influence when present to a less marked degree. One can well imagine how a child whose concentration is poor because he is distracted by anxiety about family relationships, might find it difficult to perceive the differences between, and absorb the meaning of, complex visual symbols. Similarly, a child affected by inconsistent discipline and rejection at home might well be more predisposed to develop behaviour problems later on if his efforts to learn to read at school go unrewarded because of a deficit in language development. Our finding that eight-year-old children with read- ing problems do not show high rates of antisocial behaviour suggests that the period from eight to eleven years may be crucial in the production of antisocial behaviour arising out of frustration at educational failure.

It is of interest that reading backwardness in boys is associated with neurotic or emotional disorder at eight years whereas this is not the case by ten and eleven years. We know that in some circumstances anxiety can promote learning and that emotional difficulties have a more favourable course than antisocial problems. Perhaps anxious eight-year-olds with read- ing problems despite their double handicap in the long run have a better outlook than less tense children with reading difficulties, so that by ten and eleven years old their educational retardation is more likely to have improved.

Our interpretation of our findings in this area must, however, be incomplete. It turned out that, even by three years of age, there was a strong association between language delay and behaviour problems. Clearly, therefore, the reasons for the link must lie in processes operating at an earlier age than we had the opportunity to examine. The reasons for the very early links at three years can, for us, only be a matter of speculation, but it seems possible that both behaviour and language development are influenced by similar factors as in those early parent–child interactional processes we have outlined in Chapter 5.

(c) Social factors

In agreement with other studies, we have not found any striking association between social class and either the development or persistence of behaviour and emotional problems. Nevertheless, there were a number of pointers, particularly when the children were three years old, to suggest that social factors are of some general importance. Three-year-old girls from working-class families were more likely to show disturbance than middle-class girls. Housing and financial stresses were also linked to the presence of behaviour problems. Finally, and perhaps most significantly, as described in Chapter 4, the effect on children of a poor quality of family relationships was most marked when they were living in socially disadvantaged working-class families with a high stress score and relatively less satisfactory housing. By contrast, social factors seemed of less importance in whether behaviour problems persisted or whether new problems developed between the ages of three and eight years. The social class of the family, as judged by the occupation of the father, is of no importance in this respect, and the presence of significant external stress at the age of three years did not aid prediction of outcome. Policy implications for these findings will be discussed later in this chapter.

(d) Maternal employment and attendance at pre-school facilities

Although, as already stated, many of the children who attended pre-school facilities, especially those who attended playgroups part-time, did not do so because their mothers went out to work, but for other reasons, it is nevertheless convenient to consider these two factors together. They have closely linked policy implications, and it happens that our findings were similar in relation to both of them.

To summarize our findings in these respects briefly, there was really very little evidence that either maternal employment or attendance at pre-school facilities had any strong general influence for good or ill on the behaviour of the child. The rates of depressive disorder in women whose children attended a pre-school facility, or went out to work, were virtually no different from those who did not. Apart from a slight tendency for non-disturbed three-year-olds to develop problems over the next five years less frequently if they attended a pre-school facility, the rates of behaviour disturbances were virtually unaffected by maternal employment or pre-school attendance. A child's tendency to persist in a problem over this period of five years was also similarly unaffected, and the chances of developing a definite reading problem were unchanged. By contrast, however, data presented in Chapter 13 suggests that children who attend pre-school facilities do have a significantly higher mean IQ-adjusted reading age. Does this mean that it is immaterial in the individual child's behavioural development whether he goes to a nursery school or whether his mother goes out to work? Our data, limited as they are by numbers too small to allow for very detailed analyses, do not allow us to draw firm conclusions on this point. But our impression from the interviews and from reading the relevant available literature is that the answer to this question is a complex one. Firstly, for a number of reasons, maternal employment and pre-school facility attendance may well not make too much difference provided the child comes from an adequate home and a reasonably good pre-school facility is available. However, in a proportion of children (and we have no way of knowing how many), there may well be powerful advantages or disadvantages which, when a large group is considered, roughly balance each other out. A depressed mother and her attention-demanding child who is crying out for stimulation and company may both benefit enormously from attendance at even a rather indifferent playgroup. (It is important to remember, and this is sometimes forgotten that playgroups as well as homes vary in quality and that different types of facility are likely to vary in their sensitivity to parental needs.) By contrast, a rather immature child with a mother who is only just beginning to find separation from her child tolerable and is providing good quality stimulation herself, might suffer disadvantage from attendance at the same facility. A seriously problematic child with, for example, faecal soiling and numerous tantrums might suffer rejection in one type of day-nursery and acceptance and understanding in another. The outcome might be expected to be different in each case. Similar considerations are likely to apply with regard to maternal employment. If a mother is lonely and finds the task of bringing up a child provides inadequate satisfaction, her chances of developing depression if no job is available must surely be considerable. If, however, the woman would rather stay at home, but is driven to work by economic necessity and is unable to find satisfactory substitute care for her child, there may be little advantage, other than financial, for either mother or child in her working. If children from some types of home benefit from maternal employment and attendance at pre-school facilities while those from other types of homes suffer, and if the quality of pre-school facility is another important variable affecting outcome, it is not surprising that the figures balance out and that no effects of mothers going out to work or children attending facilities are demonstrable. From other evidence we know that severely deprived children do benefit considerably from attendance at highly-structured, very well staffed facilities (Garber and Heber, 1977), and that, although some high quality programmes may have both immediate and long-term impact on children's intelligence and school attainment (Brown, 1978), children do not seem to benefit from the sort of relatively brief pre-school experiences which were generally provided under the Headstart programme run in the United States in the 1960s.

Our findings do not provide a basis for supporting views, either that there should not be an expansion of the present type of pre-school provision, or that employment opportunities for women should remain limited and that mothers should be encouraged to stay at home and look after their under-fives. They do suggest strongly that the present situation needs changes dictated by other considerations. We shall discuss the nature of changes we recommend in the next section.

Implications for policy

(a) General, social and economic measures

In the randomly selected illustrative examples of childhood behaviour disturbance, maternal depression, and marital disharmony which we have provided, we have tried to give a flavour of the unsatisfactory quality of life which many families with young children suffer at the present time. Further, it would be wrong to assume, because their rates of depression were lower, that the situation was significantly better for fathers. Men are less expressive regarding their feelings, but their reaction to stress may be manifested in other ways. The high rates of alcoholism amongst men and the high prevalence of diseases thought to be related to stressful situations, such as heart disorders, suggests that the health of men may well be at risk from family tensions to the same degree though not in the same way, as is the case with women. The focus tends to be on women because they are generally better at articulating emotional dissatisfaction, and also because they are more likely to be available to provide information in surveys such as ours, but it is more appropriate when considering the needs of families with young children to concentrate on the needs of the family as a unit, rather than to consider separately the needs of mothers and children.

As we have indicated in Chapter 4, there was a definite tendency for the adverse family relationships and parental mental health factors (poor parental marriage, maternal depression, etc.) to have a more marked effect on the child's behaviour in the presence of poor social circumstances. This suggests that policies directed towards the alleviation of social disadvantage would have some effect on the rate of childhood disturbances. The case for better housing, the reduction of financial strain on young families and improved employment opportunities rests mainly on the need to relieve injustice, inequality and financial disadvantage in the society in which we live. The fact that the quality of family life and of the personal development of children is clearly affected by the presence of social disadvantage provides an additional reason for political and social action in these respects.

(1) There are many social measures which, if taken, could be seen to be helpful to families with young children. Our own view is that the setting of child benefit at a more generous level, accompanied by simultaneous index-linking of this benefit, would be the single measure most likely to result in improved circumstances for families living in social adversity. Children, like the elderly, whose pensions are index-linked, constitute a group of dependents for whom society needs to take greater responsibility. The notion that it is the family which must take responsibility for children is not in opposition to this view. Indeed, improved child benefit can and should be seen as the most effective means to allow the family to discharge its responsibilities more effectively.

(2) A further series of social and economic measures which need more active consideration are those which govern the relationship between work and the family. Moss and Fonda (1980) have pointed to the strains which are increasingly experienced by both men and women who attempt to combine work and family life. Women are disadvantaged in their career and work aspirations by the fact that they have to work part-time, or cease work completely for some years while their children are young. Men are often under strain and deprived of much of the enjoyment which family life can bring because, so often, their energy is sapped by the demands of their work. Children, and especially young children, are not infrequently disadvantaged

because of the inadequate substitute child care arrangements which are made for them when both their parents are out at work. Kamerman (1980), after reviewing the various ways in which governments have tackled this problem in different countries, suggests that the preferable solution would be along the lines of that implemented in Sweden where legislation has introduced a "benefit-service package", making it possible for either the father or the mother to take time off work when the child is very young, or, later on, when the child is sick. It is our view that it would be advantageous to all members of young families if a similar system of family benefit was introduced in the UK. Such measures would seem to provide the best framework within which a couple could plan for the care of their children as well as for their own work and careers in the most flexible manner possible. Such a framework seems desirable if men and women are to support each other more effectively both in work and family life than seems to be the case for many parents in our study.

Linked closely to the question of maternal employment is the issue of nursery provision. The arguments in favour of an expansion of facilities for pre-school children have recently been forcibly argued by Hughes *et al.* (1980). Our own data suggest that, at the present time, most mothers of pre-school children still do not wish to work, though there is a sizeable proportion that do. We also have some slender evidence to suggest that attendance at a pre-school facility is linked to a reduced likelihood to develop behaviour problems over the next five years, as well as a higher score in reading at eight years. The evidence further suggests that the persistence of a behaviour problem in a child is unaffected by the child's attendance at a playgroup. There is, therefore, at least no evidence at all that children are affected adversely by playgroup and nursery school experience, and slight evidence to suggest they subsequently benefit.

The case for an expanded nursery school sector cannot, in our view, be based on possible emotional benefits to the child. It might, however, be very reasonably argued that, if mothers wished to work and if there is no evidence that the child's behavioural or cognitive development is impaired, it should be easier than it is to make satisfactory substitute arrangements. In the meantime there is a need to look more closely at the functioning of the pre-school facilities which exist. It was our impression that many of these were not at all tolerant of children with behaviour problems, and that there was a tendency for parents to be told the child was "not ready" to attend if behavioural difficulties arose in the playgroup or nursery setting. The mother then often experienced a feeling of rejection on behalf of herself and her child, and was left to cope with her difficult child without help in the privacy and isolation of her own home. A more positive approach to the way in which playgroup and nursery school staff could tackle problem behaviour seems indicated. This suggestion has implications for training, which we shall discuss further below.

(3) Finally, in our list of general social measures which might be taken to improve the situation, we should like to stress ways in which the environment might be altered to make the world a friendlier and more suitable place for children to grow up in. Pringle (1980) has pointed to numerous ways in which this could be achieved. Quite apart from the question of an increase in the availability of pre-school facilities, she has suggested an improvement in the amount of both public and private playspace for pre-school children. At the present time playgrounds are often inaccessible and, even when reachable, lack equipment suitable for the younger child. The increased rate of disorder amongst the children in our study living in tower blocks, particularly if they were on the fourth floor or above, suggests that high-rise flat-dwelling is inimical to healthy child development, and that those concerned with housing policy need to bear this in mind when planning accommodation for families with young children. If flat-living is inevitable for some, then at least adequate public play space should be available within easy walking distance of every mother and child not lucky enough to have a sufficiently-sized garden. Better design of roads and pavements for pram-pushers and those walking toddlers by the hand, entitlement of families with young children to a telephone for emergency calls — these and many other measures would be practical and useful aids for child-rearing which could incidentally, improve the currently very low status accorded to the task of bringing up children.

(b) Education for parenthood

Throughout our interviewing we were struck by the unpreparedness of parents for the problems and difficulties, both cognitive and behavioural, which their children showed. It will be apparent from some of the case histories that we have provided that many of the problem children tyrannized their parents, who had little clue how to control their offspring and, at the same time, maintain respect for their individuality and encourage their autonomy. Now there is a real question whether information exists that could be helpful to parents in this respect and, if it does, whether we have the skills to transmit it. Fashions in the provision of advice to parents are notoriously ephemeral, especially in the area of permissiveness and control. Is there any good evidence to suggest that one way of bringing up children is better than another, or that, for example, parents with strong beliefs transmitted by their own parents, are likely to be influenced to the slightest degree by what any "expert" may say? Nevertheless, though health education programmes do remain largely unevaluated, there is a small number of encouraging pointers. Nearly 20 years ago. Brazelton (1962) demonstrated that counselling mothers on what he regarded as a sensible approach to toilet training when their children were nine months old, appeared to reduce the rate of later bedwetting and soiling in his practice to a very low level. The study was uncontrolled, but the results were nevertheless impressive. Cullen (1976) carried out a controlled study in which he gave 12 20-to 30-minute interviews to mothers at three- to six-monthly intervals over the first five years of their children's lives. The interviews involved discussion of appropriate child-rearing practices in a number of different areas of potential difficulty. At six years, the experimental children had fewer fears, sleep disorders, eating problems, and showed less aggressive behaviour than a control group. The parent–child relationships were also reported to be more positive in the experimental group. Chamberlin and Szumowski (1980) showed that, although the differences were not marked, the more time and effort doctors put into counselling of mothers in the first month of their children's lives, the more knowledgeable were the mothers likely to be of normal child development. The results are sufficiently encouraging to make it worthwhile to extend efforts in health education and education for parenthood well beyond the scale on which these are currently attempted.

When should such education be attempted? In a Royal College of General Practitioners report (1981) on prevention in psychiatry, it is suggested that individuals and families are most susceptible to change when going through a period of psychosocial transition — a phase in which a person's internal view of himself and of other around him must inevitably change because of changing circumstances. From the point of view of education for parenthood, mid-adolescence, and the antenatal and postnatal periods would seem to present ideal opportunities. At these times young people inevitably come to see themselves in new roles, and it is at just such times that the potential for change is greatest. Dominian (1979) has pointed out how the nature of the marriage relationship undergoes most rapid change at the time of the birth of the first child.

What type of information most needs transmitting? It is our impression that mothers and fathers today are reasonably well informed on many aspects of normal child development — when young children might be expected to walk and talk, etc. — and, in general, their basic health knowledge is also adequate. They tend to know when children should be vaccinated and immunized and they are capable of maintaining satisfactory hygiene in the home. Of course this is by no means the case for all parents, and, in particular, amongst deprived mothers and especially young deprived mothers, ignorance of even these matters can be striking. But in other areas ignorance is much more widespread. There is often absence of appropriate expectation concerning the demanding nature of young children and the time, physical and emotional energy, needed to care for them properly. There is a lack of awareness of individual differences between children and the need to behave differently to the child according to its personality characteristics and at different developmental stages. There is commonly a deficiency in the understanding of issues of discipline and control and the way in which effective control can be combined with a respect for the child's autonomy and need for acceptance and affection. It is unlikely that knowledge on these matters could be transmitted to most people through written material or formal lectures. Health education curricula for teenagers already exist in abundance, and one can only assume that the reasons for the lack of impact they have had so far on the quality of child care must lie either in the irrelevance of their content, in the teaching methods employed, or in the fact that caring for children naturally arouses deep, irrational feelings not readily amenable to change. Our own view is that there is a need for a more practical element to such courses (e.g. personal contact with preschool children and their parents) and that unless courses are "skill-orientated" (e.g. they teach how to deal with a temper tantrum, sleep problem, etc.) they are unlikely to be effective. Certainly, however, there continues to be a need to develop and evaluate health education measures for teenage girls and boys in their last years of schooling, and for men and women who have embarked on parenthood. Health Visitors can be seen to have a particular role in continuing health education after a child is born.

(c) Enhancement of local community supports

The fathers in the families we studied were less depressed than the mothers, though their lives were nevertheless often very stressful. It was our impression from interviews with fathers that the better mental health apparently enjoyed by them sometimes arose at least partly from the fact that they enjoyed a sense of participation and community involvement in their work. This sense of belonging to a common enterprise shared with other people was markedly lacking in the lives of most of the mothers. If, as we have suggested, work and family life were structured so that both fathers and mothers could participate on a more equal basis, this would go some way to meet the problem, but there is a need also for measures which can be applied to mothers in the present situation.

There are various ways in which this might occur. Our suggestions in this respect are based on initiatives which have already been undertaken in some areas of the country but are not widespread. The most rewarding approach which seems so far to have been undertaken is in those developments which involve cooperative activity undertaken towards a common end. The pre-school Playgroups Association and its numerous local groups is the best example we have available. All over the country parents have joined together to produce flexible arrangements for the education and stimulation of their children. The limitation of the Association's work lies in its inability to involve women in deprived circumstances and in deprived areas, and in the fact that the women involved are naturally those with older pre-school children (three- to five-year-olds) so that women with children in the first three years of life are much less commonly involved. It is in these two deficiencies that we see most scope for active intervention on the part of health visitors and voluntary workers. Groups run by the National Childbirth Trust have succeeded in bringing women with very young children together to share experiences and assist each other practically. The focus of such groups need not, however, necessarily focus exclusively on motherhood. Many women's groups have emerged which are more concerned with raising the consciousness of women regarding their position in society, but which have, incidentally, provided strong social and emotional support for the mothers with young children who have participated.

In so far as they have assisted in the more effective articulation of women's needs, membership of such groups has strengthened family life by making it easier for women to voice their dissatisfaction and find their own means of overcoming it. Finally supportive voluntary groups of parents of children with special needs such as Twin Clubs and associations linking parents of children with similar disabilities need more active encouragement and publicity.

(d) The role of professionals

Our findings make it clear that the rate of behaviour and emotional problems in children is so high that it is in no way feasible to think of professional health and social services taking the major role in prevention and treatment. Instead the task must be seen to fall firmly on parents themselves, hopefully aided in their task by professionals who should see themselves as partners with parents in a common endeavour, rather than an experts who always know more and can do better (Department of Education and Science 1978, Children's Committee 1981). This important partnership role of professionals who work with families with young children can be defined in various ways:

(1) The early identification of difficult children and families with young children at risk for developing problems. We have demonstrated how it would be possible, using our simple screening procedures, to identify be-

haviour and language problems, for health visitors to assist parents in developing greater awareness of the existence of such difficulties in their children. The argument might be put forward that this will result in the "labelling" of children as deviant who would otherwise be regarded by their families within the normal range. We are not, however, suggesting that parents should be encouraged to regard their children as "deviant", rather that, where appropriate, parents should be more aware that their children are showing delays or difficulties which, unless modified, stand a high chance of affecting their child's subsequent personality development in an adverse manner. It is no kindness to children to avoid alerting parents to aspects of child behaviour which may, if unresolved, call for special education or psychiatric treatment later on.

(2) Early treatment. There is uncertainty and disagreement over the most effective means of helping parents to deal with behaviour and emotional problems in their young children. Some emphasize a non-directive approach with the main emphasis on the offer of a supportive relationship. Others prefer a more active role for the professional, with frequent advice on practical management. The problem lies in the fact that neither approach has been properly evaluated. Our own preference is to attempt to provide a supportive relationship for those families who are isolated, but, in addition, to foster more supportive relationships with non-professionals (relatives, friends, volunteers, etc.) in the community in which the family lives. In such families, however, and in many others in whom the problem is not primarily one of social isolation or family disharmony but where the child has nevertheless significant difficulties, we prefer a more practical approach in which parents are more actively involved in modifying the behaviour of their young children (McAuley and McAuley, 1977). In our experience parents want to be given practical ideas how to cope, and it should become increasingly possible for health visitors and family doctors to provide this. One of us (N.R.) is, for example, currently collaborating in developing methods of dealing with sleep problems in young children. Peine and Howarth (1975) have many practical ideas how parents can deal with behaviour problems.

Early treatment need not, however, necessarily be provided on an individual basis. In some areas it has been possible to set up therapeutic playgroups for children at risk (Rose, 1973), and in others mental health professionals have advised teachers in nursery schools and day nurseries on the management of difficult children. Such group methods do not usually provide much advice and support for parents. Day centres for difficult pre-school children and their parents (Bentovim and Landsdown, 1973) have now been established for many years, but our attempt to evaluate the efficacy of one of these has not been encouraging (Woollacott *et al.*, 1978).

There is probably a need for the development and evaluation of more focused methods than we have so far been able to evolve.

(3) Implications for training of professionals. At the present time the content of training programmes for nursery teachers, playgroup leaders, nursery nurses, health visitors and family doctors, often puts little emphasis on the identification and management of behaviour difficulties in young children. Yet, as we have demonstrated, these are very common, constitute a considerable load on family life, and frequently come to the attention of all these groups of professionals. As a result of their lack of training, professionals are regrettably prone to provide reassurance where this is unjustified or, alternatively, to deal with a problem as if it were hopeless and unhelpable when in fact effective treatment might well be undertaken.

Participation in partnership with parents of young children can be a rewarding task for professionals. When such children have emotional difficulties or delays in development, the task is more challenging but, in our experience, can be equally rewarding. We hope we have been able to provide information which will allow professionals engaged in this work to undertake it with greater awareness of the frequency with which such problems occur and with a better idea of their usual outcome.

References

Bates J. E. (1980). The concept of difficult temperament. *Merrill–Palmer Quart.* **26**, 299–319.

Bauer D. H. (1976). An exploratory study of developmental changes in children's fears. *J. Child Psychol. Psychiat.* **17**, 69–74.

Behar L. and Stringfield (1974). A behaviour rating scale for the pre-school child. *Dev. Psychol.* **10**, 601–610.

Bentovim A. and Lansdown R. (1973). Day hospitals and centres for disturbed children in the London area. *Brit. Med. J.* **4**, 536–8.

Berger M., Yule W. and Rutter M. (1975). Attainment and adjustment in two geographical areas. The prevalence of specific reading retardation. *Brit. J. Psychiat.* **126**, 510–19.

Blennow-Persson I. and McNeil T. F. (1979). A questionnaire for measurement of temperament in six month old infants: development and standardization. *J. Child Psychol. Psychiat.* **20**, 1–13.

Bone M. (1977). Pre-school Children and the need for Day-care. London, H.M.S.O.

Brazelton T. B. (1962). A child-orientated approach to toilet training. *Pediatrics* **29**, 121–8.

Brazelton T. B., Koslowski B. and Main M. (1974). The origins of reciprocity: the early mother-infant interaction. *In* (M. Lewis and L. A. Rosenblum, eds) The Effect of the Infant on its Caregiver. New York, John Wiley.

Brimer M. and Dunn L. (1962). Manual for the English Picture Vocabulary Test. Bristol, Education Evaluation Enterprises.

Brown B. (1978). Found: long-term gains from early intervention. Boulder, Colorado, Westview Press.

Brown G. and Harris T. (1978). Social Origins of Depression. London, Tavistock Publications.

Brown G. and Rutter M. (1966). The measurement of family activities and relationships: a methodological study. *Hum. Rel.* **19**, 241–263.

Brown R. and Hanlon C. (1970). Derivational complicity and order of acquisition in child speech. *In* (J. R. Hayes, ed.) Cognition and the Development of Language. New York, John Wiley.

Cantwell D. (1976). Hyperkinetic syndrome. *In* (M. Rutter and L. A. Hersov, eds) Child Psychiatry: Modern Approaches. Oxford, Blackwells.

Cantwell D. P., Baker L. and Mattison R. E. (1980). Psychiatric disorders in children with speech and language retardation. *Arch. Gen. Psychiat.* **37**, 423–5.

Carey W. B. and McDevitt S. C. (1978). Stability and change in individual temperament. Diagnosis from infancy to early childhood. *J. Amer. Acad. Child Psychiat.* **17**, 331–7.

Cazden C. (1966). Sub-cultural differences in child language: an interdisciplinary review. *Merrill-Palmer Quart. 12*, 185–219.

Chamberlin R. W. and Szumowski E. K. (1980). A follow-up study of parent education in pediatric office practices: impact at age two and a half. *Am. J. Pub. Health* **70**, 1180–0.

Children's Committee (1981). The needs of the under fives in the family. Mary Ward House, Tavistock Place, London.

Clarke R. V. G. (1978). Tackling Vandalism. Home Office Research Study No. 47. London, H.M.S.O.

Coleman J., Wolkind S. and Ashley L. (1977). Symptoms and behaviour disturbance and adjustment to school. *J. Child Psychol. Psychiat.* **18**, 201–9.

Condon W. S. and Sander L. (1974). Neonate movement is synchronised with adult speech: interactional participation and language acquisition. *Science* **183**, 99–101.

Cox A. D., Rutter M., Yule B. A. and Quinton D. (1977). Bias resulting from missing information: some epidemiological findings. *Brit. J. Prev. Soc. Med.* **31**, 131–136.

Crandall V. and Rabson A. (1960). Children's repetition choices in an intellectual achievement situation following success and failure. *J. Genet. Psychol.* **92**, 161–8.

Cromwell R. E., Olsen D. H. L. and Fournier D. G. (1976). Tools and techniques for diagnosis and evaluation in marital and family therapy. *Family Process.* **15**, 1–49.

Cullen K. J. (1976). A six year controlled trial of prevention of children's behaviour disorders. *J. Pediat.* **88**, 662–6.

Department of Education and Science (1978). Special Educational Needs. London, H.M.S.O.

Department of Health and Social Security (1976). Fit for the Future. Report of the Child Health Services Committee. London, H.M.S.O.

Dominian J. (1979). Second phase of marriage. *Brit. Med. J.* **2**, 720–2.

Douglas J. W. B. (1973). Early disturbing events and later enuresis. *In* (I. Kolvin, R. MacKeith and S. R. Meadow, eds) Bladder Control and Enuresis. Clinics in Developmental Medicine Nos. 48/49. SIMP. London, Heinemann.

Dunn J. and Kendrick C. (1980). The arrival of a sibling: changes in patterns of interaction between mother and first-born child. *J. Child. Psychol. Psychiat.* **21**, 119–132.

Earls F. (1980). Prevalence of behaviour problems in three year old children. *Arch. Gen. Psychiat.* **37**, 1153–7.

Earls F. E. and Richman N. (1980a). The prevalence of behaviour problems in the three year old children of West-Indies born parents. *J. Child. Psychol. Psychiat.* **21**, 99–106.

Earls F. E. and Richman N. (1980b). Behaviour problems in pre-school children of West-Indies born parents: a re-examination of family and social factors. *J. Child. Psychol. Psychiat.* **21**, 107–17.

Erhardt A. and Baker S. (1974). Fetal androgen, human central nervous system differentiation and behaviour sex differences. *In* (R. C. Friedman, R. M. Richert and R. L. Van der Wiele, eds) Sex Differences in Behaviour. New York, Wiley.

Everitt B. S. (1974). Cluster Analysis. London, Heinemann.

Everitt B. S. (1977). The Analysis of Contingency Tables. London, Chapman and Hall.

Freud A. (1973). Normality and Pathology in Childhood. Harmondsworth, Penguin.

Garber H. and Heber R. (1977). The Milwaukee Project: indications of the effectiveness of early intervention in preventing mental retardation. *In* (P. Mittler, ed.) Research into Practices in Mental Retardation. Vol. 1. Baltimore, University Park Press.

Gath D., Cooper B., Gattoni F. and Rockett D. (1977). Child Guidance and Delinquency in a London borough. London, Oxford University Press.

Gersten J. C., Langner T. S., Eisenberg J. G., Simcha-Fagan O. and McCarthy E. D. (1976). Stability and change in types of behavioral disturbances of children and adolescents. *J. Abn. Child Psychol.* **4**, 111–127.

Glick I. D., Kessler D. R. (1980). Marital and Family Therapy. 2nd Edition. New York, Grune and Stratton.

Goodenough F. L. (1931). Anger in Young Children. Minneapolis, University of Minnesota.

Graham P. and Rutter M. (1968). The reliability and validity of the psychiatry assessment of the child, II Interview with the parent. *Brit. J. Psychiat.* **114**, 581–592.

Graham P., Rutter M. and George S. (1973). Temperamental characteristics as predictors of behaviour disorders in children. *Am. J. Orthopsychiat.* **43**, 328–339.

Group for the Advancement of Psychiatry (1966). Psychopathological disorders in childhood. Theoretical considerations and a proposed classification. New York, Group for the Advancement of Psychiatry.

Harrell J. C. and Ridley C. A. (1975). Substitute child care, maternal employment and the quality of mother-child interaction. *J. Marr. and the Family.* **37**, 556–64.

Hetherington E. M., Cox M., and Cox R. (1977). The aftermath of divorce. *In* (J. Stevens and M. Matthews, eds). Mother-child, father-child behaviors. Washington D.C., NAFYC.

Hewison J. and Tizard J. (1980). Parental involvement and reading attainment. *Brit. J. Educ. Psychol.* **50**, 209–15.

Hindley, C. B. and Owen, C. F. (1978). The extent of individual changes in IQ for ages between six months and 17 years in a British longitudinal sample. *J. Child Psychol. Psychiat.* **19**, 329–350.

Hughes M. Mayall B., Moss I., Perry J., Petrie P. and Pinkerton G. (1980). Nurseries Now. Harmondsworth, Penguin Books.

Jephcott P. (1971). Home in High Flats: some of the human problems involved in multi-storey housing. Edinburgh, Oliver and Boyd.

Kamerman S. (1980). Managing work and family life: a comparative policy review. *In* (P. Moss and N. Fonda, eds) Work and the Family. London, Temple Smith.

Kohn M. and Rosman B. L. (1972). A social competence scale and symptom check-list for the pre-school child: factor dimensions, their cross-instrumental generality and longitudinal persistance. *Dev. Psychol.* **6**, 430–444.

Kohn M. and Rosman B. L. (1973). A two factor model of emotional disturbances in the young child: validity and screening efficiency. *J. Child Psychol. Psychiat.* **14**, 31–56.

Kolvin I., Fundudis T., George G. S., Wrate L. and Scarth L. (1979). Predictive importance-behaviour. *In* (T. Fundudis, I. Kolvin and R. Garside, eds) Speech Retarded and Deaf Children. London and New York, Academic Press.

Kolvin I., Fundudis T. and Scanlon E. (1979). Early development, types and prevalence. *In* (T. Fundudis, I. Kolvin and R. Garside, eds) Speech Retarded and Deaf Children. London and New York, Academic Press.

Kushlick A. (1968). Social problems in mental subnormality. *In* (E. Miller, ed.) Foundations of Child Psychiatry. Oxford, Pergamon.

Lapouse R. and Monk M. (1959). Fears and worries in a representative sample of children. *Amer. J. Orthopsychiat.* **29**, 803–818.

Lewis M. (ed.) (1976). Origins of Intelligence. London, John Wiley.

Little A. and Smith G. (1971). Strategies of compensation: a review of educational projects for the disadvantaged in the United States. Paris, OECD Publications.

MacFarlane J. W., Allen L. and Honzik P. (1954). A developmental study of behaviour problems of normal children between 21 months and 14 years. Berkeley and Los Angeles, University of California Press.

Madge, N. and Tizard, J. (1980). Intelligence. *In* (M. Rutter, ed.) Scientific Foundations of Developmental Psychiatry. London, Heinemann.

McAuley R. and McAuley P. (1977). Child Behaviour Problems. London, Macmillan.

Maccoby E. and Jacklin C. (1980). Psychological sex differences. *In* (M. Rutter, ed.) Scientific Foundations of Developmental Psychiatry. London, Heinemann.

Miller F., Court S. D. M., Knox E. G. and Brandon S. (1974). The School Years in Newcastle-upon-Tyne. London, Oxford University Press.

Minde K., Lewin D., Weiss G., Lavigubun H., Douglas V. and Sykes E. (1972). The hyperactive child in elementary school: a five year controlled follow-up. *Except. child.* **38**, 215–221.

Minde R. and Minde K. (1977). Behavioural screening of pre-school children: a new approach to mental health. *In* (P. J. Graham, ed.) Epidemiological Approaches in Child Psychiatry. London and New York: Academic Press.

Moss P. (1980). Parents at work. *In* (P. Moss and N. Fonda, eds). Work and the Family. London, Temple Smith.

Moss P. and Fonda N. (eds) (1980). Work and the Family. London, Temple Smith.

Mussen P. H. and Bouterline-Young H. (1964). Relationships between rates of physical maturing and personality among boys of Italian descent. *Vita Humana* **I**, 186–200

Newson J. and Newson E. (1965). Patterns of Infant Care. Harmondsworth, Penguin Books.

O'Donnell J. P. and Tuinan M. V. (1979). Behaviour patterns of pre-school children: dimensions and congenital correlates. *J. Abnormal Child Psychol.* **7**, 61–65.

Oppel W. C., Harper P. A. and Rider R. V. (1968). Social, psychological and neurological factors associated with nocturnal enuresis. *Paediatrics* **42**, 627–641.

Peine H. and Howarth R. (1975). Children and Parents. Harmondsworth, Penguin Books.

Pringle M. K. (1980). A Fairer Future for Children. London, National Children's Bureau.

Quinton D., Rutter M. and Rowlands O. (1976). An evaluation of an interview assessment of marriage. *Psychol. Med.* **6**, 577–86.

Randall D., Reynell J. and Curwen M. (1974). A study of language development in a sample of three year old children. *Brit. J. Dis. Comm.* **9**, 3.

Registrar General (1971) Classification of Occupations. London, H.M.S.O.

Reynell J. (1969). Reynell Developmental Language Scales. Experimental Editions, Windsor, N.F.E.R.

Richman N. (1974). The effect of housing on pre-school children and their mothers. *Dev. Med. and Child Neurol.* **16**, 53–58.

Richman N. (1977). Behaviour problems in pre-school children: family and social factors. *Brit. J. Psychiat.* **131**, 523–7.

Richman N. (1977). Is a behaviour check-list for pre-school children useful? *In* (P. J. Graham, ed.) Epidemiological Approaches in Child Psychiatry. London and New York, Academic Press.

Richman N. and Graham P. (1971). A behavioural screening questionnaire for use with three year old children. *J. Child Psychol. Psychiat.* **12**, 5–33.

Richman N. and Stevenson J. (1977). Language delay in three year olds: family and social factors. *Acta Paediat. Belg.* **30**, 213

Richman N., Stevenson J. and Graham P. (1975). Prevalence of behaviour problems in three year old children: an epidemiological study in a London borough. *J. Child Psychol. Psychiat.* **16**, 222–287.

Richman N. and Tupling H. (1974). A computerised register of families with children under five in a London borough. *Health Trends* **6**, 19–21.

Roberts K. and Schoellkopf J. (1951). Eating, sleeping and elimination practices in a group of 2½ year old children. *Amer. J. Dis. Childh.* **82**, 121–52.

Rose N. (1973). Ten Therapeutic Playgroups. London, N.S.P.C.C.

Royal College of General Practitioners (1981). Prevention of psychiatric disorders. London, Royal College of General Practitioners.

Rutter M. (1965). Classification and categorisation in child psychiatry. *J. Child Psychol. Psychiat.* **6**, 71–83.

Rutter M. (1967). A children's behaviour questionnaire for completion by teachers. *J. Child Psychol. Psychiat.* **8**, 1–11.

Rutter M. (1970). Sex differences in children's responses to family stress. *In* (E. J. Anthony and C. M. Koupernik, eds), The Child and his Family. New York, John Wiley.

Rutter M. (1976). Separation, loss and family relationships. **In** (M. Rutter and L. Hersov, eds) Child Psychiatry: Modern Approaches. Oxford, Blackwells.

Rutter M. (1980). Maternal deprivation 1972–1978. New findings: new concepts: new approaches. *Child Dev.* **50**, 283–305.

Rutter M. and Brown G. (1966). The reliability and validity of measures of family life and relationships in families containing a psychiatric patient. *Soc. Psychiat.* **1**, 38–53.

Rutter M., Cox A., Tupling C., Berger M. and Yule W. (1975). Attainment and adjustment in two geographical areas. *Brit. J. Psychiat.* **126**, 493–509.

Rutter M., Graham P., Chadwick O. and Yule W. (1976). Adolescent turmoil, fact or fiction? *J. Child Psychol. Psychiat.* **17**, 35–36.

Rutter M., Tizard J., Whitmore K. (1970). Education, Health and Behaviour. London, Longmans.

Rutter M. and Yule W. (1975). The concept of specific reading retardation. *J. Child Psychol. Psychiat.* **16**, 181–97.

Serbin L., O'Leary K., Kent R. and Tonick I. (1973). A comparison of teacher response to the pre-academic and problem behaviour of boys and girls. *Child. Dev.* **44**, 796–804.

Schaffer R. (1977). Mothering. London, Open Books.

Schaffer D., Meyer-Bahlburg F. L. and Stokman C. L. J. (1980). The Development of Aggression. *In* (M. Rutter, ed.) Scientific Foundations of Developmental Psychiatry. London, Heinemann.

Shepherd M., Oppenheim A. N. and Mitchell S. (1971). Childhood Behaviour and Mental Health. London, University of London Press.

Starte G. A. (1975). The poorly communicating two year old and his family. *J. Roy. Coll. Gen. Pract.* **25**, 800.

Stern D. N. (1974). Mother and infant at play: the dyadic interaction involving facial, vocal and gaze behaviour. *In* (M. Lewis and M. A. Rosenblum, eds) The Effect of the Infant on its Caregiver. New York, John Wiley.

Stevenson J. and Ellis C. (1975). Which three year olds attend pre-school facilities? *Child: Health, Care and Development* **1**, 397–411.

Stevenson J. and Richman N. (1976). The prevalence of language delay in a population of three year old children and its association with general retardation. *Dev. Med. and Child Neurol.* **18**, 431–441.

Stevenson J. and Richman N. (1978). Behaviour, language and development in three year old children. *J. Aut. and Childh. Schiz.* **8**, 299.

Steward W. F. R. (1970). Children in Flats: a family study. London, N.S.P.C.C.

Thomas A. and Chess S. (1977). Temperament and Development. New York, Brunner/Mazel.

Thomas A., Chess S. and Birch H. G. (1968). Temperament and Behaviour Disorders in Children. New York, New York University Press.

Thomas A., Chess S., Birch H. G., Hertzig M. E. and Korn S. (1963). Behavioural Individuality in Early Childhood. New York, New York University Press.

Tittler B. I., Friedman S. and Klopper E. J. (1977). A system of tailoring change measures to the individual family. *Family Process* **16**, 119–121.

Ullman L. P. and Krasner L. (1969). A Psychological Approach to Abnormal Behaviour. Englewood Cliff, New Jersey, Prentice Hall.

Vaughn B., Deinard A. and Egeland B. (1980). Measuring temperament in paediatric practice. *J. Paediat.* **96**, 510–4.

Vernon, P. E. (1976). Development of intelligence. *In* (V. Hamilton and M. D. Vernon, eds) the Development of Cognitive Processes. London and New York, Academic Press.

Walker D. K. (1973). Socio-emotional Measures for Pre-school and Kindergarten Children. San Francisco, Jossey-Bass.

Wallston B. (1973). The effects of maternal employment on children. *J. Child Psychol. Psychiat.* **14**, 81–96.

Weissman M. M., Paykel E. S., Siegel R. and Klerman G. L. (1971). The social role of performances of depressed women: comparisons with a normal group. *Amer. J. Orthopsychiat.* **41**, 390–405.

Wender P. (1971). Minimal Brain Dysfunction in Children. New York, John Wiley.

Woollacott S., Graham P. and Stevenson J. (1978). A controlled evaluation of the therapeutic effectiveness of a psychiatric day-centre for pre-school children. *Brit. J. Psychiat.* **132**, 349.

Wolkind S. and Everitt B. S. (1974). A cluster analysis of the behavioural items in the pre-school child. *Psychol. Med.* **4**, 422–7.

Yancey W. L. (1971). Architecture, interaction and social control. *Environment and Behaviour* **3**, 3–21.

Yudkin S. and Holme A. (1963). Working Mothers and their Children. London, Michael Joseph.

Appendix 1

BEHAVIOURAL SCREENING QUESTIONNAIRE
(BSQ)

1. How about eating?....Is X going through the faddy
   stage?....How has his/her eating been in the
   past 4 weeks? Does X eat everything or is he/she fussy?....
   How often do you feel X isn't eating enough, or isn't
   getting the right food? What do you do about the eating....
   do you have to make special meals? Is this a problem?

   No eating problems (include here
   the occasional missed meal or fad)   0
                                                a) Poor appetite   ☐
   Some eating difficulties (has a
   few fads, or has a poor appetite
   for one meal a day or less)   1
                                                b) Faddy eater   ☐
   Marked difficulties (appetite
   poor for at least ½ the meals:
   diet mainly milk &/or baby foods
   or sweets and biscuits, or eats
   only a few articles of food or
   refuses practically all meat and/
   or vegetables

2. How often has X had an accident - soiled - in the past 4
   weeks?

   None   0
   Twice a week or less   1   Soiling   ☐
   Three times a week or more   2

3. A lot of children don't like going to bed....What about X?
   How long does it take to settle him/her? What about going
   to sleep? Does X sleep right through the night? (What
   happens?....How long does it last?....How often is this?).

   No problem or problems less than
   once a week   0

   Problem occurs 1-2 a week only   1   a) Going to bed/   ☐
                                               going to sleep
   Problem occurs 3 times a week or
   more and either takes more than
   1 hour to get to sleep, or wakes   b) Waking at night   ☐
   at night for more than a few
   minutes, or goes into parents'
   room or bed   2

3c. How often do you take X into your bed, or sleep in
    X's bed because X is upset?

    Never sleep with the child   0

    Occasionally: all night once a
    week or less, or for a couple   ☐
    of hours only, more often   1

    Frequently: all or most of the
    night twice a week or more   2

4. How active is X? Is he/she the sort of child who doesn't
    like sitting still even for meals? How many minutes will
    he/she sit at meal times usually? What about for a story....
    TV?

    Not markedly active   0

    Very active   1

    Hyperactive: sits still for meals
    or on other occasions usually
    less than 5 minutes   2

    Underactive: spends most of the
    time stationary and unoccupied
    (apart from habits)   3

5. What does he/she like playing indoors? What's the longest
    time X will <u>usually</u> stick at one thing indoors if interested?

    Concentrates <u>usually</u> for 15 minutes or more 0

    Concentrates <u>usually</u> for 5-14 minutes or
    <u>very variable</u>   1

    Concentrates <u>usually</u> never more than
    a few minutes   2

6. How has X got on with brothers/sisters in the past 4 weeks?
    Do they squabble much? How much is playing together affected?
    Is he/she jealous at all? What about with other children? Are
    there any around for X to play with? How do they get on?

    Trivial or no difficulties   0

    Some difficulties, play disrupted
    or prevented most times but only   a) Sibs
    for short periods   1

    Marked difficulties: play
    disrupted or prevented most of   b) Peers
    the time   2

    No sibs/no opportunity to play
    with others   3

7a. Does X keep asking for attention, ask to have things done
    which could do for self, e.g. feeding....dressing....Will
    X play on his/her own or....does she/he want you to play with
    her/him all the time? Is this a problem? How is she/he with
    others?

    Rarely demands undue attention   0

    Sometimes demands undue attention   1   Attention seeking

    Continually asking for attention   2

7b. Is X independent or does (s)he cling a lot? Can X be left with
    people (s)he knows....who do you leave him/her with? At
    home does (s)he follow you around all day....even into the
    bathroom? Will X allow people (s)he knows to do things
    for him/her....even if you are around?

Reasonably independent for age   0

Some dependency; upset if left,   Dependency
takes some time to get over it   1

Marked dependency; cannot be left
at all, continually demands to be
with mother   2

8. Most children are difficult to manage at times.... how do
   you find X? Can you take X shopping....visiting without
   trouble? Is (s)he ever destructive? Do you ever feel X is
   out of control or difficult to discipline? How long has
   this been going on? Is (s)he easier with other people?

   Easy to manage and discipline   0

   Sometimes difficult or out of
   control or hard to discipline for
   short periods   1

   Long or very frequent periods,
   nearly every day, when difficult to
   manage or discipline   2

9. Does X have temper tantrums? What happens? Is it a real
   tantrum with shouting....screaming....banging....kicking?
   How often in past 4 weeks? How long do they last? When
   did they start? What about with other people?

   No tantrums   0

   Brief tantrums lasting a few
   minutes one or two a day   1

   Frequent tantrums, three a day or
   more, or tantrums lasting more than
   15 mins.   2

10. Does (s)he have moods of being miserable or irritable.
    Is (s)he usually happy? How has X been in the past 4 weeks?
    How often does this happen? When did it start? How long do the
    moods last?

    Usually happy except for brief
    periods   0

    Sometimes miserable/irritable/
    discontented for periods less
    than 1 hour on most days and/or
    for longer periods once or twice
    a week   1

    Frequently miserable/irritable on
    most days and/or for long periods
    3 times a week or more   2

11. Is X a worrier....gets anxious about something that might
    happen....about plans or changes? What about if X loses
    something? Does (s)he brood over things....like accidents....
    falls....illnesses....monsters? Does (s)he ever keep
    repeating questions about something....like being left....
    being loved....death?

(A worry is apprehension about something that may happen; a fear is apprehension about something thought to be present or actually present all the time).

Never or rarely worries   0

Some worries for brief periods   1

Many different worries, or worries
over certain things for long
periods   2

12. Most children have some fears. What is X afraid of?
    What about....

Dogs	▢	Scale A for individual fears
Cats	▢	Not afraid 0
Other animals/insects	▢	Somewhat afraid: uncertain about approaching, requires
Thunder/loud noises	▢	reassurance 1
The dark	▢	Marked fear: runs away or avoids, clings to adult,
Strangers	▢	cries, has to be comforted 2
Going out	▢	
Car, bus, train, tube	▢	Scale B for overall rating of fears
Life, escalators	▢	
Water, the bath	▢	Is somewhat afraid of 1 or 2 things or has no fears 0
Haircut	▢	Has 1 or 2 marked fears or 3-5 fears altogether 1
Doctors	▢	
Stories	▢	Has 3 or more marked fears or 6 or more fears
TV programmes	▢	altogether 2
Hoover	▢	
Other	▢	

Anything else? What does X do?

Appendix 2

BEHAVIOUR CHECK LIST

Below is a list of behaviours which are often seen in children. Opposite each behaviour please put a cross (X) in the columns which you think applies best to your child <u>at the present time</u>.

Name of the child ....

1.   Usually has a good appetite   ☐

        Sometimes has a poor appetite   ☐

        Nearly always has a poor appetite   ☐

2.   Not faddy about eating   ☐

        Has a few fads, won't eat certain things   ☐

        Very faddy, won't eat many different foods   ☐

3.   Never wets at night   ☐

        Wets the bed up to once or twice a week   ☐

        Wets the bed 3 or more times a week   ☐

4.   Never wets during the day   ☐

        Wets during the day up to once or twice a week   ☐

        Wets during the day 3 or more times a week   ☐

5.   Completely bowel trained. Never dirties pants   ☐

        Occasionally soils, up to once or twice a week   ☐

        Soils pants 3 or more times a week   ☐

6.   Easy to get to bed and to sleep   ☐

        Some difficulties in settling at bedtime   ☐

        Often takes over an hour to settle at bedtime   ☐

7.   Hardly ever wakes at night

      Sometimes wakes at night

      Frequently wakes at night and
      difficult to settle

8.   Never sleeps with parent

      Occasionally sleeps with parent because
      upset or doesn't want to sleep alone

      Frequently sleeps with parent because
      upset or doesn't want to sleep alone

9.   Not active enough

      Not markedly active

      Very active

      Too active, won't sit still for meals
      or at other times for more than 5 mins

10.   Concentrates on play indoors for
      15 mins or more

      Concentration 5-15 mins or very variable

      Hardly ever concentrates for more than
      5 mins on play indoors

11.   Not clinging, can easily be left with
      people he/she knows

      Gets upset if away from mother but gets
      over it

      Very clinging; can't be left with others

12.   Independent; doesn't ask for a lot of
      attention

      Sometimes asks for a lot of attention,
      follows mother around all day

      Demands too much attention, follows
      mother around all day

13. Easy to manage and control ▢

    Sometimes difficult to manage or control ▢

    Frequently very difficult to manage or control ▢

14. Doesn't have temper tantrums ▢

    Sometimes has tantrums (lasting a few minutes) ▢

    Has frequent or long temper tantrums ▢

15. Usually happy except for brief periods, when tired for instance ▢

    Sometimes miserable or irritable ▢

    Frequently miserable or irritable ▢

16. Not a worrier ▢

    Sometimes worried for short periods ▢

    Has many different worries, broods over things, e.g. illness, accident, monsters, changes ▢

17. Few or no fears ▢

    Has some fears ▢

    Very fearful, has a lot of different fears ▢

18. Gets on well with all brothers and sisters ▢

    Some difficulties with brothers or sisters ▢

    Gets on badly with brothers or sisters ▢

19. Gets on well with other children ▢

    Some difficulties playing with other children ▢

    Finds it very difficult to play with other children ▢

20. Speaks sentences of 3 or more words ▢

    Uses single words ▢

    No recognisable words ▢

21. Clear speech

   Sometimes speech not clear

   Speech can't be understood by people
   outside the family

Thank you very much.

Signature ....

Subject Index